Shawn Reynaldo

First Floor
Reflections
on   **Volume I**
Electronic
    Music
Culture

Velocity Press

First published 2023

velocitypress.uk
firstfloor.substack.com

Printed and bound
in Great Britain by
Clays Ltd, Elcograf S.p.A.

Cover design
Joe Gilmore
qubik.com

Typesetting
Theo Inglis
theoinglis.co.uk

ISBN: 9781913231347

For Dania, who makes me laugh every day, definitely has better taste than I do and didn't balk when I told her, "I'm starting a newsletter."

CONTENTS

Foreword
by Martyn

—

Throughout our careers in music, Shawn and I have run into each other in various capacities. He organized one of the earliest regular "bass music" manifestations in San Francisco, a series of events called Icee Hot, at which I DJed in the late '00s. He also interviewed me for XLR8R magazine and we met again a few years after that at a conference in Montreal where we spoke as part of a Red Bull Music Academy event. I remember this well, because during this conversation Shawn asked, "I've noticed you have been quite feisty on Twitter lately, why is that?" I was taken aback by that question, as it was the first time I was asked about my social media presence as an artist—something that was usually not discussed in an "offline" interview. URL and IRL were two separate worlds then, but perhaps that question signaled a future in which those existences gradually merged into one. Funnily enough, a few friends of mine were in the audience that day and turned that question into kind of a running gag, asking me why I was so feisty on Twitter at the most inconvenient of moments (during dinners, in the middle of DJ sets, etc.) for a number of years!

After being active in the electronic music world for 20+ years both Shawn and I are now slightly uncomfortable "veterans" and consider it both a blessing and a curse. In his piece "Who's in charge of the Culture?," Shawn addresses how the moment a music fan enters a new scene defines a ground zero-like frame of reference for their personal experience of the music. In other words, the artists and music that you discover in those early moments become the standard to which you weigh anything that comes after that. The longer you are involved in music, the harder it can be to imagine how that initial, enthusiastic, exciting moment of discovery would translate to a different set of circumstances, a few decades removed. Whether in the mid '90s you spent hours digging through stacks of vinyl, trying to find that one record that looked intriguing and exciting enough to spend your hard-earned 19 euros on (Autechre on Warp), or whether your best friend on Discord DMs you a Bandcamp link of some complete unknown producer from Brazil with the message "this track made me think of you," the moments are just as special; one is never better than the other. However long you are involved in music, if you thrive on that energy, you will understand the similarities across generations, even when they manifest themselves in a different form. Instead of getting bitter about how things have changed, you can use your "veteran" experience to provide insight and thrive in a scene for as long as you want. I do a jazz radio show on NTS, and while I am by no means an "authority" on the genre, every month I try to make listeners part of my own journey of discovery in the music; that specific energy, more than the actual music I play, is the key to the show. My favorite pieces in this book are the ones like "The Latin Music Gold Rush," where you can almost feel that you're discovering new things about the music (or the industry surrounding it) along with the author. In a good opinion piece, compelling stream-of-consciousness writing demonstrates the process of knowledge gaining and shares that journey with the reader. Even if you don't agree with the general point of the piece, you still enjoy that journey.

Pretty much any First Floor reader would acknowledge that the power of the newsletter is not in its lyrical waxing, but in its strong opinion writing. And just as I'm sure Shawn doesn't love all of the music I've put out, his pieces have led to some interesting back-and-forths between us. More than once they have given me a different perspective, or provided the opportunity to define my own opinions about the subject more clearly, purely based on how staunchly I opposed Shawn's view. I think that's how good music/culture criticism should serve the reader; not by doubling down on ideas you already agree with, but by providing well-articulated jump-off points for deeper understanding and better consideration. Almost all of the pieces collected in this book have been sources for contentious discussion on the state of electronic music and the industry that supports it. A good example of that, specifically for artists such as myself, is "That Album You Made Might Have Been a Giant Waste of Time." Shawn's argument is not against albums per se, but to be more considerate about the decision whether you should or shouldn't write one and how the current reshaping of the music industry is affecting that decision. Seasoned musicians often forget to question the things they have been doing for years.

Several pieces in this collection deal with music media itself. In "The Crumbling Palaces of Electronic Music Media," Shawn laments the gradual decline of traditional music journalism, which, over the last few years, has suffered from strained budgets, declining ad revenue and a severe shrinking of its workforce. But good opinion writing hasn't left the music world altogether, and (almost ironically) First Floor is an example of that. It's a fact that music writing is heavily in flux; an increasing amount of quality writing has moved from the traditional outlets to independent, subscription-based Web 2.0 platforms. It is more direct, less edited and less constrained perhaps by format and word count, and most importantly it leans on direct support from readers instead of ad clicks or sponsored content. Writers decide their own scope, can be hyper focused on niche subject matter, or take a comparative view on cultural movements across different disciplines of art. I think Shawn's work in that realm is a great example of a reshaping of the music writing ecosystem. Within the electronic music media industry, First Floor is one of the most successful outlets, and so while Shawn signals there's a problem with media, he himself is helping to shape the solution.

Introduction

First Floor started small.

Truth be told, it actually started as a weekly radio show, and ran for more than three years while I was working with the Red Bull Music Academy. But when that gig suddenly evaporated in 2019, I wasn't quite sure what I wanted to do next. By that point, I'd already been working as a music journalist for more than a decade (and had logged nearly another decade in radio before that), and was all too aware of how quickly circumstances could change (often for the worse) at more traditional media outlets, yet the freelance grind of constantly pitching to editors didn't sound particularly appealing either. I wanted a project that I could control, and eventually settled on a newsletter, figuring it was something manageable that I could take on—at least until my next proper job came along.

A weekly digest that included a round-up of electronic music news, some track recommendations and a little bit of my own commentary, First Floor wasn't launched with any real expectations. The first edition only went out to 89 people. Within a few months, however, those numbers had climbed significantly, and I gradually came to a realization: people were actually reading this thing. Moreover, they seemed to really like it. Friends and colleagues who'd seen my work for years suddenly started saying things like, "I can hear your voice when I read the newsletter." I'd spent my entire career striving to keep myself out of my writing, literally avoiding the use of the first person whenever possible, but First Floor was something different. Though it was still rooted in journalism, it was also a personal endeavor, and little by little, I began to take down artificial barriers. I was still writing about the various goings-on of electronic music and its associated industry, but for the first time, I was openly filtering those topics through the prism of my own thoughts, opinions and experiences—and, much to my surprise, that was what people responded to.

At some point, First Floor basically became my full-time job, and has continued to grow, despite being published in an era when long-form writing is said to be on the decline and music journalism on the whole is routinely whittled down to whatever works best in a social media post. Admittedly, many of the articles and essays I've put together have been critical—a fact that isn't always appreciated, especially by folks working in the music industry—but even at their harshest, my words are driven by one thing: a genuine passion for electronic music. Having spent more than half my life immersed in various facets of independent music culture, I've seen a lot of artists, trends, scenes, hype cycles and operating practices come and go. Electronic music—and dance music in particular—has always been a highly transient space, and there's something undeniably exciting about that, but when even the most engaged participants tend to drop out of the scene after a few years, it does frequently feel like historical perspective and institutional knowledge are in short supply.

With First Floor, I do my best to counter that, diving deep into not just electronic music, but the culture and industry that surround it. There's practical stuff in there too (e.g. news, reviews, links to things I find interesting), but on a larger scale, the newsletter is an ongoing attempt to reckon with electronic music as it moves through a period of intense economic, cultural, stylistic and generational change. Though the genre has never been static, its recent evolution has repeatedly unfolded in ways few would have anticipated, and sometimes seems to run entirely counter to the norms and values the culture was founded upon. That's not always a bad thing, but such a profound transformation does at least merit a bit of consideration and conversation—something that today's electronic music press, weakened by years of structural decay, is increasingly ill-equipped to provide.

As a longtime writer and editor, I've worked within that press machinery for much of my career, and very much sympathize with the struggles faced by music publications both big and small. (For those interested in specifics, I've previously been on staff at

XLR8R and RBMA, and have also contributed to Pitchfork, NPR, Resident Advisor, SPIN, DJ Mag, Beatportal and Bandcamp Daily; I list those outlets here to avoid having to include a disclosure every time one is mentioned in the pages of this book.) First Floor may not be the antidote to those struggles, but it is a blank canvas, one in which opinions can be expressed and ideas can be explored without worry of turning off advertisers or potential brand partners.

That, at its essence, is what this book is all about. Though it's ostensibly a collection of my most thought-provoking pieces, those pieces together form what I hope is a nuanced, wide-ranging exploration of contemporary electronic music. To make things easier, I've grouped the selected essays by topic into four separate sections, and while the individual pieces appear largely unchanged from when they were first published in the newsletter, I've written a brand-new introduction for each one. Some of these reach into the past, providing additional context about what I was thinking at the time or how the piece was initially received, while others break down how my thoughts on the given subject matter have changed since I first wrote the essay. The book also contains one wholly new piece, an afterword that casts an eye toward the future of electronic music culture—and may surprise readers with its assessment of where things stand.

Like any culture and industry, electronic music has its problems and challenges, and admittedly I don't have all the answers. First Floor is meant to foster discussion, not agreement, and regardless of whether I'm dissecting the inequities of the streaming economy or examining the changing nature of fandom and artistry, the pieces I write and perspectives I provide are rarely designed to be a definitive final word. In my experience, asking thoughtful questions can often be just as important as providing actionable solutions, and if my words stimulate further dialogue on a topic that's generally been ignored—or has simply been superficially talked about the exact same way for years on end—then I feel like I've made a positive contribution.

During the past few years, I've often self-deprecatingly said that First Floor is "just a newsletter," but as I've pored through the thousands of words I've written, I've started to realize that it's something more. This book is a testament to that, and I'm immensely thankful to everyone who's ever taken the time to read what I have to say.

I.
Things
Have
Changed

Electronic Music Is Getting Old
a.k.a. What does futurism mean in the context of a genre that just turned 40?

October 19, 2021

—

Electronic music and I are roughly the same age.

The veracity of that claim of course depends on what one considers to be the origin point of modern electronic music, but with all due respect to Kraftwerk, disco and the various synth explorers of the '60s and '70s, I tend to point to the early 1980s, when techno was first created in Detroit. That moment, at the very least, laid down a template for not just how the music sounded, but what it was meant to represent, projecting futuristic visions of joy, liberation and world-altering innovation that eventually became a defining part of the genre's character.

It took a while for those visions to find their way to me—although I was born in 1979, it wasn't until the latter half of the '90s that I took a proper interest in electronic music—and while I can't deny their ageless appeal, in recent years I have found myself pondering whether or not they truly represent the reality (or even the aims) of electronic music as it exists today.

Admittedly, much of this pondering has taken place during a time when I've increasingly found myself away from the dancefloor. The pandemic obviously had something to do with that, but even as things have reopened during the past year or so, my appetite for late-night revelry remains diminished. Nightlife has always been—and probably should always be—fueled by youth, and I, strictly speaking, am no longer young.

That said, neither is electronic music, and in many ways, the genre is starting to show its age, settling into comfortable patterns and increasingly adopting practices that don't quite square with the revolutionary vigor of its youthful rhetoric. A gap exists between electronic music's stated priorities and its contemporary practices, and it's only widened in the time since the following essay was first published.

What happens when an innovative cultural movement stops innovating? Can a genre truly represent the future when so much of its output sounds like the past? Electronic music is in the midst of wrestling with those questions, and the genre's core identity may very well be retooled in the process.

———

Techno turned 40 this year

Is that old? Maybe not, especially in comparison to other genres, but it's fair to say that techno's days of being a plucky young upstart have long since passed. Like it or not, the music has officially entered middle age, and that transition hasn't necessarily been a graceful one.

From the very beginning, the philosophy (and mythology) of techno has been tied up in ideas of futurism. Cybotron's Juan Atkins and Rik Davis were famously both fans of futurist philosopher Alvin Toffler, and the aspirational, forward-facing, technology-driven aesthetic they established with 1981's "Alleys of Your Mind"—which is widely regarded as the first techno record, alongside "Sharevari" from fellow Detroit outfit A Number of Names—remains the dominant stylistic blueprint for much of electronic music, four decades later.

As the years pass, however, it's sometimes hard to differentiate between which artists are truly pushing things forward, and which ones are merely maintaining a sort of techno pastiche. Although the future that techno artists imagined in the '80s (i.e. robots, lasers, interplanetary space travel, liberation through technology, etc.) is still largely the stuff of fantasy, sheer repetition has sapped that vision of its prior potency. After 40 years, those dreams have already been dreamed too many times.

Over time, electronic music has widely settled into a particular set of conceptual tropes, to a point where even explicitly future-oriented works often feel more like retro-futurism. The music itself has also proven to be increasingly rigid. It's difficult to make a track sound like it's from 2099 when its drum pattern is something that's been endlessly recycled since 1999 (or probably earlier), yet many of the biggest trends in electronic music over the past few years (e.g. electro, UK garage, drum & bass, trance, industrial techno) have effectively been revivals of older sounds, as opposed to something genuinely new.

Does this mean that electronic music is out of new ideas? Probably not, but even if that were true, would it definitely be a problem? Quality releases still land in my inbox every week, and although few of them are taking the music in bold new directions—in fact, many of them are actively mimicking records from decades gone by (the '90s in particular)—that doesn't necessarily make them less enjoyable. If innovation is the primary thing you're after, then yeah, a lot of contemporary electronic music might seem pretty stale, but if you're merely looking for something that'll get hearts pumping and dancefloors moving, the genre still does the trick.

That basic functionality is commendable (or at least useful), but it does come at a cost. There's no getting around the fact that something approaching a formula does exist for techno and most other branches of the electronic music family tree, and these formulas have a lot more to do with musical parameters than any sort of attitude, philosophy or worldview. The genre's revolutionary vigor has faded with time—in some cases, it's been diluted into little more than hackneyed marketing slogans—and while futurism might still be part of the music's conceptual "brand," so is nostalgia, and the latter has arguably taken up a dominant position. Even the production side of electronic music has caught the nostalgia bug, as today's artists continue to fetishize vintage gear, wildly driving up the price on machines that, ironically, were already out of date in the 1980s.

And when it comes to marketing and promotion, electronic music regularly throws the nostalgia floodgates wide open, touting countless artists and releases as "legendary" (regardless of whether they actually deserve that descriptor) and celebrating a seemingly endless stream of anniversaries. It's an inevitable part of the aging process for any genre—just look at how much time and effort rock music has spent regurgitating and mythologizing its own history in recent decades—but it now feels like electronic music is celebrating a new "milestone" anniversary nearly every week.

In 2021 alone, both Tresor and Nervous Records have celebrated their 30th anniversaries with expansive new compilations. James Ruskin's Blueprint label is doing the same thing for its 25th anniversary, while Metalheadz has spent this year honoring its 25th trip around the sun with a special series of reissues. Squarepusher's debut album *Feed Me Weird Things* also turned 25 this year, and was remastered and reissued on Warp. Dub-techno outpost Echocord and techno label EPM are both celebrating 20 years of existence with new compilations, and The Avalanches offered up a deluxe version of their landmark LP *Since I Left You* to mark its 20th birthday. Daft Punk didn't do anything to celebrate the 20th anniversary of their seminal *Discovery* album, but music journalist Ben Cardew did write a whole book (*Daft Punk's Discovery: The Future Unfurled*) about it.

That list is by no means comprehensive, and if it was expanded to include 10-year anniversaries, then I'd also need to mention the compilations offered up this year by 100% Silk, Auxiliary, Acid Test, Dome of Doom, Infinite Machine and Butter Sessions. (I'm not even going to bother with five-year anniversary releases and celebrations, but those definitely exist too.)

Now, is looking backwards (or simply stopping to take a victory lap) inherently a bad thing? Of course not. Electronic music hasn't been the best steward of its own history during the past 40 years, so there's obvious value in examining (and celebrating) the past.

On a more cynical level, nostalgia also sells. In a time when everyone is chasing clicks and even established artists and labels often struggle to garner attention, it's hard to fault anyone for playing the "remember when?" card—it's a lot more likely to get people reading, engaging or buying than any "check out this new thing" plea they might put together. (Yes, this is depressing, but it's one of the many unfortunate byproducts of an oversaturated media marketplace in which the deluge of new content basically never stops.)

Nostalgia is a tricky thing, mostly because it's so damn easy. Looking to the past (particularly when it's done with rose-colored glasses) is one of the fastest ways to get people excited and bring them together. Does it move culture forward though, or even prompt bouts of thoughtful reflection? Maybe on occasion, but not usually, and that speaks to its specific shortcomings in the world of electronic music. How can a genre that constantly wraps itself in the flag of futurism be so deeply (and increasingly) in thrall to the past? It's a glaring contradiction, and one that flies in the face of where the music came from.

Knowing this, it would be easy to crank out a jaded "electronic music sucks now and things were better before" diatribe, but even that would feel like an overly nostalgic (not to mention pointless) exercise. Plus, I still like electronic music. Lots of people do. On a global level, it's arguably more popular now than it ever has been before. The genre has undoubtedly drifted over the years, both stylistically and culturally, and not always in a positive direction, but it's still incredible that its Detroit originators (and the many artists they inspired during the '80s and '90s) created sounds and templates that continue to resonate so strongly today. That said, it's also disappointing that so many of today's electronic music producers and fans don't seem to share their predecessors' pioneering spirit.

Like many 40-year-olds, techno has gotten comfortable, and many of electronic music's other genres seem to have plunked themselves down on the couch right alongside it. Considering the impact they've had on the world, maybe they've earned it. Electronic music innovation hasn't stopped, after all—it's just that very little of it seems to be happening under the banner of techno, house, electro and all the other styles with multiple decades of partying under their belt. Newer sounds—many of which are emerging from places outside of Europe and North America—often flicker out as quickly as they appeared, but regardless of their staying power, it's hard not to appreciate their willingness to push the music into places it's never gone before.

In the meantime, electronic music is left with its own sort of generational divide, one in which the traditions and routines it's built up over the past 40 years often come into conflict with the boundary-pushing instincts of certain (usually younger) artists and fans—many of which have been relegated to the genre's fringe. What's more important: protecting the vision of the future that Cybotron and their followers dreamed up in the '80s and '90s, or maintaining a constant push into new futures in response to the ever-evolving demands of the present?

There's no definitive right answer, and that uncertainty is at the heart of many conflicts that spring up in electronic music circles today. On a more basic level, there's also the fact that many people who got into the music in the '80s and '90s are now literally approaching their 50s and 60s (if they're not already there), while newer fans tend to be millennials and Gen Z. These generations already have trouble seeing eye to eye—why would it be any different when it comes to electronic music?

What does the future of electronic music look like? I don't know, but its current attempt to simultaneously be both a constant source of innovation and a glorified (albeit highly enjoyable) nostalgia-based feedback loop likely isn't sustainable in the long run. That said, regardless of which side "wins" this conflict (or if some new "third way" emerges), the genre's future will ultimately be shaped by younger artists and fans, and what they come up with might very well look, sound and feel a whole lot different from what Cybotron imagined back in 1981.

After decades of laying claim to the future, electronic music's most experienced practitioners are getting old, just like everyone else. They've picked up plenty of wisdom over the past 40 years—and hopefully we'll all be smart enough to tap into it—but the levers of control are already slipping from their grasp. That's a tough pill to swallow, especially because there's no guarantee that whatever's coming next is going to be better—and yes, even the idea of "better" is totally subjective—but electronic music's collective ability to accept that reality will likely determine just how bumpy the transition is going to be in the years to come.

Welcome to middle age.

Maybe Local Scenes Don't Matter Anymore
a.k.a. Why support your hometown if the internet can take you anywhere?

November 19, 2019
—

Much of my writing for First Floor begins with one simple thought: "This doesn't make sense."

That was certainly the case here, and this essay—which I wrote just a couple of months after I'd started the newsletter—was one of the first instances in which I put one of my own long-held beliefs under the microscope. The veneration and prioritization of local music is something I've personally been practicing since I was a teenager, but with life now increasingly being lived online—particularly by those under the age of 30—the bleeding edge of culture feels increasingly unencumbered by the need for IRL engagement and the limitations of working with whoever happens to live nearby. That reality was already evident in 2019 when I first published the piece below, but the pandemic put the phenomenon fully into overdrive, and while I'd very much like to *believe* that local scenes are still essential, the facts on the ground—not to mention the preferences and practices of the younger generations who are now driving electronic music culture—seem to be saying something different.

————

I'm starting to think that local scenes don't matter anymore.

This is both 1) a gross generalization and 2) not something that makes me happy. Let's tackle the latter first. As someone who came of age in various indie/DIY circles, the idea of supporting my local scene is practically woven into my DNA. Local artists, local promoters, local venues, local radio, local record stores, local music… celebrating these things was something I always held up as a virtuous pursuit, an unquestionable ideal that all real music fans should aspire to. It was about community, and an unshakable belief that these local pillars ultimately served as the foundation for the entire music industry.

As passionately as I held that belief, when I look back now, I'm not sure that it was ever really true—after all, the music industry has been a grossly capitalist and largely ruthless enterprise since, well, forever—but I have little doubt that it's less true now than it was 20, 10 or even five years ago. Why? The internet.

Before the internet, participating in a music scene usually required some level of face-to-face interaction. Seeing an artist meant going to shows. Checking out an album required a trip to the local record shop. To find like-minded people, you had to actually leave the house and talk to other human beings. More importantly, geography mattered. From one city to the next, let alone one country to the next, the dynamics of a music scene—and the music it produced—could be radically different. This is why even in a relatively compact country like the UK, cities like London, Bristol and Manchester offered such unique sounds and styles during the '90s; it's not like musicians from these places never talked to each other, but these scenes were still operating in relative isolation, with each one developing its own norms and following its own distinct path.

This pattern follows across the globe and across genres. Hip-hop, funk, soul, punk, indie, jazz, electronic music... so many of the greats from these scenes were defined, at least in part, by their surroundings. Dischord Records couldn't have happened in Los Angeles any more than Wu-Tang Clan could have come out of Atlanta.

These days, however, how many local scenes truly matter? If we limit our focus to electronic music, a lot of attention is given to places like Berlin, London, Amsterdam, New York and Los Angeles, but do any of them really have a distinct sonic signature at this point? Not really. I would argue that these places are important because they host large-scale clusters of creative types; they're industry hubs, not incubators of unique local scenes or sounds.

Of course unique music scenes aren't completely extinct. Uganda's Nyege Nyege Tapes (and its annual festival) have clearly tapped into something special (and wildly different than what's happening in Europe and North America) in East Africa. Over in Portugal, the Príncipe crew and its various offshoots have spent years showcasing a distinct brand of batida/kuduro/ house hybrids that have yet to be duplicated elsewhere. There are numerous other examples, many of them based in the Global South (and/or their diasporas in Europe and North America), and while it's exciting that these places are gradually being plugged into the larger international electronic music network, their individuality may be fleeting. It's not a coincidence that many of the most innovative new electronic sounds are being created in communities that are largely isolated from the dominant music culture. Oddly enough, it's in these (often remote) places that the "local scene" dynamics I described earlier are thriving.

Where I live in Barcelona, however, supporting the local electronic music scene isn't much of a priority for most people. (For what it's worth, this isn't a Barcelona-specific problem. I think this charge could be leveled at most places these days.) And why would it be? Electronic music, like pretty much all music nowadays, has become another piece of the creeping monoculture. Thanks to the internet, fans here have access to everything. They can listen to pretty much whatever music they want on Spotify, they can watch their favorite DJ on Boiler Room and if they really want to see someone play live, they can just wait until the next giant festival happens, which will bring not only that artist but probably a whole slew of other interesting acts too. And if the local festivals don't offer exactly what someone is looking for, they can just hop on an easyJet flight to London or Berlin or wherever and engage in a bit of techno tourism.

It's easy to criticize giant festivals like Sónar and Coachella for encouraging this sort of behavior, but the tastemaker crowd—you know, the people who are supposed to genuinely care about supporting local scenes—are often just as guilty as everyone else. How many people make special weekend trips to check out De School in Amsterdam or hit up Berghain in Berlin? What percentage of Unsound attendees come from outside of Kraków? These days, music fans of all stripes are chasing premium experiences.

We're living in an age of content on demand, and many people have adjusted their fandom accordingly. Other factors contribute of course (the endless feedback loop between the internet's click-based economic model and poptimist music writing comes to mind[1]), but when the average consumer has access to countless options, it's not surprising that many shy away from the risk of "unknown" experiences (e.g. a night out at a small local show with artists they don't know, who might not be that good), especially when more familiar options (e.g. a festival with a lineup full of "known" artists they already like) are readily available.

Moreover, this phenomenon isn't limited to experiences; it extends to people too. The world is smaller than ever, and with the rise of social media and online communities, people no longer have to leave the house to find others who share their interests and worldview. Why bother going to a local show or popping into the neighborhood record shop if you can just stay home and trade zingers with strangers on Twitter about your new favorite record? If someone can find community online, that's certainly a lot easier than trying to build one wherever they live, particularly if that place isn't one of the designated major creative hubs I mentioned before.

For folks of a certain age, all of this likely sounds depressing, but that response, at least in part, is driven by sentimentality. When I think about the integral role that local scenes played in my own life, it makes me sad to think that they now don't matter, or at least matter a lot less than they used to. At the same time, the changing dynamics I've outlined haven't resulted in less, or worse, music being created. On the contrary, artists can now easily

---

1. The term "poptimism" is referenced several times throughout this book, and can essentially be boiled down to the idea that pop music is as worthy of professional critique and interest as rock. It most directly rose to prominence in the aftermath of music writer Kelefa Sanneh's October 2004 essay for *The New York Times*, "The Rap Against Rockism."

pull from a diverse array of influences from around the world, making music without worrying about whether or not it will fit in with what's happening in their particular postal code. Moreover, it's not like music scenes no longer exist; they're just no longer tied to geography, and there's something exciting about that.

The indie/DIY culture that I grew up with had this baked-in idea that genuine fandom involved work. Part of what made the music in these scenes valuable was its scarcity, the fact that it was hard to find and quite possibly even hard to enjoy. Looking back though, there was a whole lot of privilege in that sentiment. Most people are already working hard in their everyday lives; are we really supposed to expect them to work hard when it comes to listening to music too? Not everyone has the time, resources or social connections to know about the best local record store or get the details for the latest obscure warehouse party; that doesn't mean they're a bad person, or even that they don't genuinely like music. And if we factor in how overtly white, male and straight so much of indie/DIY culture was and often continues to be, it makes sense that so many music fans, particularly ones from marginalized groups, tend to find community online. Can you really blame them?

Anyways, like many things I write about in this newsletter, I don't have a definitive position here. In theory, local scenes are wonderful and I'd like to see them thrive, but I can also see the writing on the wall. And as much as I might personally lament these changes, as long as artists out there keep making quality music, I can't get too upset.

I'm getting too old to be going out all the time anyways.

Going Through the Motions
a.k.a. Dance music's enthusiasm gap.

March 29, 2022

—

First Floor has many recurring themes (the inequalities of the streaming economy, the shortcomings of the music press, intergenerational tensions within dance music, to name just a few), but there is also something much more visceral at the core of much of my writing: frustration.

The first essay in this book was called "Electronic Music Is Getting Old," and this one is in many ways a kind of addendum, zeroing in specifically on the genre's seeming lack of new ideas. Written during a time when it felt like the most spirited dance music conversations were focused on seemingly everything but the music itself—a phenomenon that continues to this day—the piece charts how much the genre has seemingly driven itself into a creative cul-de-sac, foregoing innovation in favor of rehashing old ideas. It's difficult to talk about stagnation without sounding like someone who's simply out of touch with contemporary culture, but this time around, I didn't have to go it alone: my thoughts were spurred on by like-minded comments from one of dance music's most respected artists.

———

Last week Mixmag published an interview with Joy Orbison. It's probably the most revealing "on the record" conversation that the UK artist has ever had, delving deep into his family history, his personal insecurities and his ever-evolving relationship with dance music. The whole thing is worth a read, but there's one particular passage that really grabbed me:

> *"... we're getting to a point where the spirit and innovation that was in dance music, is not in dance music any more," he reflects, suggesting the "people who would have been making dance music are now making other forms of music" such as drill, hip hop and "weird pop music – you didn't have that when I was growing up."* [1]

I think he's right.

Don't worry, I'm not about to launch into a cliché "dance music is dead" diatribe. People—usually folks struggling to come to grips with the fact that they're simply getting older—have been trotting out that argument for decades, and they almost always wind up sounding like the personification of the "old man yells at cloud" meme.

Even Joy Orbison made sure to clarify that his thoughts aren't rooted in nostalgia for the "good old days," stating:

> *"I hate the idea of being like 'it's all shit now,' because I don't think it is."*

Dance music isn't dead. Far from it. Even after weathering two years of a global pandemic, the dance music industry appears to be in decent shape. Clubs are filling up again. Summer festivals are selling out. And as for the music itself, there's certainly no shortage of new material finding its way into the world. On the contrary, it's quite possible that more dance music is being released now than at any point in the genre's history. Vinyl plants literally can't keep up with demand, and thanks to platforms like Bandcamp, artists can (and often do) sell their tunes without having to worry about things like getting signed or working with a label. Even the streaming sphere is bursting with new dance music, as producers—both new and established—continue to post their tunes on Spotify/Apple/Amazon/etc., despite the fact that doing so is unlikely to generate much in the way of income. (In such a crowded landscape, the mere possibly—no matter how

1. Hinton, Patrick. "Bigger Vision: Joy Orbison Is Ready for the Next Step." *Mixmag*, March 21, 2022, https://mixmag.net/feature/joy-orbison-dj-mix-interview-cover-feature-xl-still-slipping.

remote—of getting noticed is often enough to prompt people to engage and "play the game.")

So, if the live music industry is getting back on its feet and the veritable firehose of new dance music releases continues unabated, what exactly is the problem? What is Joy Orbison talking about? Loath as I am to speak on his behalf, I'll instead share my own opinion: dance music is very much alive, but creatively, it's suffering from an acute lack of energy and innovation.

I've written before about dance music's struggles to live up to its futurist ideals, but it bears repeating that the culture—especially when it comes to new releases—feels stuck. The sounds of the past (and the '90s in particular) have been endlessly reconstructed and rehashed, and the artists often hailed as the most innovative these days are the ones experimenting with pop music. It's not that there's a shortage of good music—I struggle to fit all of the new tracks I like into the newsletter each week—but how much of it feels truly essential? Lots of anthemic tunes are being made, but not many are becoming bona fide anthems.

Covid certainly has something to do with this—it was tough for any dancefloor-oriented tune to gain momentum while clubs were closed—but this trend pre-dates the pandemic. Looking back at Resident Advisor's Best Tracks of 2019 list, there are lots of familiar names in there (e.g. Burial, Special Request, Marie Davidson, DJ Python, Aurora Halal, Four Tet, Peggy Gou), and some truly excellent tunes, but if we're being honest, many of these songs have largely been forgotten already, and even the biggest "hits" were relatively niche successes, even by the already niche standards of "underground" dance music.[2]

Like most cultural sectors, dance music has been beset by intense fragmentation over the past decade. (Within the context of a scene/industry that's always had a tendency to endlessly divide itself into obscure subgenres, that's really saying something.) Thanks to the internet and social media, there's no longer a need for music fans of any genre to deeply engage with any sort of larger monoculture, even one that's nominally "underground."

(Hell, engaging with dance music doesn't even require leaving the house anymore.) Nowadays, people who are excited about a certain kind of music can go online and find not only the one specific thing they're looking for, but also a cluster of like-minded folks who share the exact same thoughts/opinions/perspectives about it.

These virtual communities—which are probably better described as micro-communities—offer an ease of connection that's never before been available, especially for those who struggle in real-world social situations. That's probably a good thing, and potentially opens all sorts of doors to discovery and exploration. However, it does come with a cost, in the sense that these groups also tend to be self-reinforcing, both creatively and philosophically. Real-world communities are limited by geography and require person-to-person interaction, including with people whose perspectives likely differ from your own. Online, people can simply block or mute anyone they don't see eye to eye with, and if the interests or character of a particular community fail to align with their own, it's never been easier to simply opt out and find another one altogether.

That can be great for those needing to escape/avoid toxicity (which should of course be prioritized), but it's not something that necessarily fosters an exchange of ideas. There's a fine line between communities and bubbles, and when a music culture tips too far toward the latter, it doesn't take long for creative stagnation to set in. Across dance music, artists are increasingly playing to the norms of their self-selected (and some might say insular) social and creative circles, and combined with the growth of highly specific instructional production tutorials (e.g. "how to make an X-type beat" videos), it's no wonder that so many new releases sound like the product of someone simply following a recipe. The tunes they cook up might be delicious, but their impact is limited when they're simply recreating something that was first thought up decades prior.

Perhaps that's why dance music's most spirited discussions these days often have little to do with the actual music. Looking at social media or even at what content is getting published by electronic music media outlets, what topics generate the most engagement? Mostly ones that revolve around the economics and power structures of the industry. The sale of Bandcamp to Epic Games has arguably been 2022's biggest story within the independent music world, and critical dissections of Spotify and other streaming platforms have been reliable discourse generators for a few years now. Additional discussions of how things work behind the scenes have branched out from there, and while many of these conversations were clearly long overdue, it's still somewhat bizarre to see them so frequently taking precedence over talk of artists and the music they make.

Don't believe me? Look at Resident Advisor, which has just created (and is currently hiring) a new position called the Futures Editor, who will be "responsible for investigating new technologies—beyond hardware and its intersections with electronic music culture." When the world's leading electronic music publication is bolstering its editorial team with someone whose purview will include "clubbing in the Metaverse, the future of decentralized autonomous organizations and venues, the evolution of streaming and rights, or the latest trends in the virtual world," it's clear that music alone isn't enough to keep even ardent fans engaged.

That same dynamic colors the larger conversations around crypto and Web3, which have (not very gracefully) elbowed their way into dance music discourse during the past year or so. (First Floor has admittedly been a part of that discursive push.) The ethics around crypto are definitely murky, but irrespective of that issue, the topic is generating more passion—amongst evangelists and skeptics alike—than almost anything else in dance music right now. That's not a great sign for the creative health of the genre.

To be fair, DJ and club culture aren't going anywhere. As long as there are young (and young-ish) people in the world, at least some of them will want to congregate on dancefloors and collectively lose their minds to a barrage of loud music. What that music sounds like, however, is changing, and all of the styles traditionally lumped together under the dance music umbrella—house, techno, electro, jungle, dubstep, trance, garage, etc.—are losing ground. That doesn't mean that genuine creativity isn't happening elsewhere, but for aging electronic music fans (myself included), it can be a bit sad.

For decades, the identity of dance music has been rooted in its opposition to the mainstream. Pirate radio, illegal raves, white label 12"s—none of these things were designed for mass consumption, and discovering them offered membership in a sort of secret society, one guided by its own rules, norms and values. The ideological pillars of that society have eroded over the years—and in many cases, have been co-opted by the mainstream—but for those old enough to remember how things used to be, it does feel like something has been lost. That's normal of course; times change, and so do cultural trends, but now that dance music's most celebrated new heroes are often the ones whose work impacts the pop sphere (even in a subversive way), it can feel like the genre's foundational ethos has been turned on its head.

Maybe these things are simply intergenerational growing pains. Maybe they're a byproduct of a larger cultural "flattening" brought on by streaming platforms and easy access to almost all of recorded music. Maybe it's something else, but regardless of what's happening, much of dance music—again, as it's been known for the past few decades—appears to be hitting a creative and stylistic wall, its various rhythms and forms growing increasingly calcified with each passing year. More often than not, the music feels like a known quantity, and while there's a certain comfort to that, a neverending pantomime of '90s rave culture has limited appeal, no matter how many times it's redressed and repackaged.

This is what I think Joy Orbison was talking about. True innovators might want to reference and recontextualize the past, but few of them will want to recreate it outright. I may not be enthralled with artists creating TikTok-friendly jungle jams or making reggaeton/drill/hardstyle hybrids (especially when they do so purely in the hope that a pop diva takes notice), but at least they're attempting to break the mold. Moreover, their work is generating genuine excitement, and frequently doing so without relying on overarching political/economic/social trends that are only tangentially related to the music itself.

"It should only be about the music" can be a problematic phrase, especially when it's used to avoid accountability, but there's a flipside which feels more true: when a genre gets to a point where it's almost never about the music, the artistic vitality of said genre is likely in trouble. Considering that dance music is currently in a spot where talk of NFTs and streaming economics usually generate a more impassioned response than even the biggest tunes, perhaps it's time to sound the alarm.

Wrestling with Pop Embarrassment
a.k.a. The changing role of pop in electronic music.

November 30, 2021
—

Reading over my work, I sometimes wonder what younger readers must think when they see me agonizing over things like commercial pop music. For someone who's 20 years old, it must seem completely ridiculous, but then again, they didn't come of age during a time when "selling out" was basically the worst possible thing that someone in independent music could do. That idea remains on some level hard-wired into my worldview, and as "underground" dance music—a genre that was once largely hostile to the mainstream—has increasingly flirted with commercial pop sounds and tropes in recent years, it's prompted quite a bit of soul searching on my part.

This essay was my first attempt to do that publicly, and as I was writing it, I actually surprised myself—not because I suddenly loved all these pop-sounding records, but because I found a way to appreciate what's interesting about them, even when they didn't align with my own personal tastes. (That may not sound like a big deal, but for a veteran music critic like myself, it was no easy feat.)

———

A couple of months ago, I was commissioned to write the press materials for an upcoming album. The LP in question—which hasn't been announced yet, and will have to remain anonymous for now—has a decidedly pop bent, and given its creators' extensive techno pedigrees, it's likely to surprise people, and might even rub some purists the wrong way.[1] Knowing that, my initial draft took on an almost defensive tone, taking little

---

1. The album was *Arrival*, the debut full-length from Aasthma (a.k.a. Peder Mannerfelt and Pär Grindvik), and despite my trepidations, there was ultimately no major uproar about the duo's embrace of pop sounds.

potshots at techno orthodoxy and laying out justifications for why these artists would choose to take their music in such an unexpected direction.

That was my own hangups talking.

Over the past 40 years, electronic music (i.e. house, techno, electro and the countless offshoots they've spawned) has mostly been framed as an "underground" phenomenon, its (frankly over-idealized) DIY spirit fueled by illicit raves, independent promoters, mixtapes, dubplates, limited-edition white labels, obscure record shops and an entire cultural network that tends to fly beneath the mainstream radar. Like many other musical subcultures, electronic music does have its own, largely self-sustaining ecosystem, and though its "renegade" mentality doesn't always line up with reality—things like the "electronica" boom of the late '90s, the EDM explosion of the 2010s and the towering influence of acts like Daft Punk all run counter to the culture's subversive image—there's still a feeling amongst its proponents (especially the ones over, let's say, 35 years old) that the music exists (or at the very least, ought to exist) in opposition to the mainstream.

That mindset isn't unique to electronic music, and its prevalence in genres like indie rock, punk, metal and various strains of experimental music was a big part of why the poptimism debates of the past decade were often so ferocious. For a certain strain of music fans who came of age during the '80s, '90s and 2000s (myself included), there was a clear divide between the pop mainstream and the "underground," and built into that divide was the notion that the former was inherently shallow, while the latter represented a deeper, purer form of artistic expression.

Was that an oversimplification? Of course. Was it a way for these music fans (many of them white dudes) to feel a sense of superiority over what they saw as the bland tastes of the "unenlightened" masses? Absolutely. Does that mean they were completely off base? It depends on who you ask. Some folks portray all anti-pop sentiment as an elitist vestige of the patriarchy and anti-Black sentiment. Others argue that irrespective of the social context, there's a huge difference between an artist like Taylor Swift and an artist like Grouper, and that difference—in which a select few artists are promoted with the full weight of the commercial music industry—is worthy of critique.

Who's right? Both? Neither? I don't know, and rehashing the poptimism wars for the umpteenth time isn't a particularly appealing prospect. Either way, the poptimist camp has clearly won the debate—just look at what sites like Pitchfork are mostly covering these days—and that's made things somewhat confusing for all of the "underground" music fans who were reared with an entirely different value set.

In retrospect, there was always an element of pantomime in independent music fandom. No matter how much of a purist someone claimed to be, it's not like they weren't being exposed to pop music. Growing up, I was never a fan of Mariah Carey or The Backstreet Boys, but that didn't stop me from repeatedly hearing (and even memorizing) their songs. I might have loved Sleater Kinney when I was a teenager, but the truth is that I probably know more Britney Spears songs by heart. Am I proud of that? Definitely not, but I'd also be lying if I didn't admit that all sorts of mainstream/commercial/pop music found its way into my brain during my formative years, and undoubtedly influenced me—and, more importantly, my taste.

For a long time, most "serious" independent musicians couldn't credibly make the same sort of admission. Plenty of independent and "underground" artists have experimented with pop over the years, and indie pop itself became a full-fledged genre, but even then, there was often a clear distinction made that what a band like Belle and Sebastian was doing was profoundly different (and better) than whatever was in the Top 40. Electronic music tended to follow the same line of thinking, and while lots of artists did dabble in pop tropes, it was frequently done with a knowing wink or some other ironic pretense, signaling to the audience (and to critics) that engagement with this "lower" artform was more of an experiment or academic exercise than something born out of a genuine passion for the music.

Looking back, these attitudes can seem silly and unnecessarily pretentious, and I'm guessing that for many younger music fans, they must appear to be completely ludicrous. For generations raised on YouTube and Spotify, the mental divide between pop and "underground" music doesn't really exist, and the way that they consume and experience the work of an artist like Future and an artist like Galcher Lustwerk might be exactly the same. Twenty years ago, most musical subcultures had significant barriers to entry, and finding your way in usually required knowing someone, doing a fair amount of research or both. Although I'm not idealistic enough to say that all barriers have now been removed, it's certainly true that in 2021, curious music fans can quickly sample new sounds with just a few clicks of the keyboard.

Music fandom was once an almost tribal undertaking, but how many young people these days would primarily identify themselves as being a punk, a goth or a raver? Although genre barriers had already begun to slowly disintegrate during the '90s and 2000s, they've been completely obliterated during the Spotify era, and that's given rise to a generation (or maybe even multiple generations) of musical polyglots. And now that many of them are producing music of their own, their borderless vision is creeping into even the weirdest corners of independent music.

In electronic music, DJs and producers have obviously been retooling mainstream hits for decades, but things definitely began to accelerate during the 2000s, particularly as the increased availability of music-making software gave rise to regional variants of club music all around the globe. Baltimore club (and later Jersey club), baile funk, juke, footwork and countless other styles all borrowed heavily from pop music, as did the mash-up phenomenon, blog house and the extended Hollertronix network, which spawned Diplo and a whole generation of young producers with a similar willingness to cross established genre lines.

Later on, the ascension of SOPHIE and PC Music during the mid 2010s was perhaps the point when the floodgates truly burst open, and in the years since, the lines between pop and "underground" electronic music have only become blurrier. I recently reviewed the debut full-length from Parris, a London producer who'd originally made his name on dusty beats and off-kilter bass manipulations. But when the time came to put together his first album, who did he cite as key influences? "Charli XCX, Lana Del Rey, Frank Ocean, Kewngface, Digga D, SL, Unknown T, Vince Staples, Lil Peep, Denzel Curry and Emmy the Great." Ten or twenty years ago, that kind of list might have been laughed at by dance music tastemakers. Nowadays though? It's practically a badge of honor.

Now, does Parris' LP actually sound like those artists? Not really. Perhaps it does on some granular level, but the truth is that his record is never going to sniff the Top 40. I sincerely doubt it was intended for the pop charts—and the music's carefree weirdness is undoubtedly a major reason why I enjoyed it so much—but regardless of what Parris had in mind, there's something refreshing about his willingness to not just own his influences, but openly celebrate the artists and sounds that shaped his musical vision.

Not all artists are going to spell out their influences in such a direct fashion, but that doesn't mean that pop and mainstream sounds (both past and present) aren't coloring their music. Just last week, Spanish producer JASSS released *A World of Service*, her first full-length for Ostgut Ton. Unlike her previous outings, which moved between corroded beat constructions, industrial stomp and rave-ready techno, the new LP is a vocal-driven, pop-oriented effort that mostly ignores the dancefloor. The record may have been released on one of the world's preeminent techno labels, but its eight tracks include a grinding Spanish-language lament ("Camelo"), a sultry Auto-Tune R&B lullaby ("Luis"), a gothy bit of alien-voiced trip-hop ("In Your Mouth") and a surging, alt-rock-flavored closer ("Wish") that sounds like *Celebrity Skin*-era

Courtney Love sitting in with Nine Inch Nails (or maybe even Linkin Park).

It's not an Ariana Grande record, but these are big creative swings, and they're unlikely to be appreciated by the average techno reply guy. That said, nothing about *A World of Service* feels disingenuous. (Full disclosure: I do know JASSS personally, but I haven't spoken to her about the new album at all, so all of these thoughts on the record are entirely my own.) During the late '90s and early 2000s, electronic music artists would regularly get signed to a big label and then populate their albums with half-baked genre experiments and (frequently awkward) pop-crossover attempts, but it seems unlikely that JASSS was engaging in anything that cynical. It's not like Ostgut Ton was pushing her to fill the album with marketable pop singles, and from a purely commercial standpoint, it might actually have been wiser to make an LP that hewed closer to her DJ sets and the high-energy, club-smashing sound she's generally known for. *A World of Service* is ostensibly a pop record, but it also feels like an intensely personal one, and if JASSS had any hesitations about the creative chances she was taking, she clearly ignored them.

There's a real sense of freedom in that, and regardless of whether people like *A World of Service*, its lack of encumbrance is enviable. While many electronic musicians and fans (especially the aging ones) are still hamstrung by anti-pop sentiment and an aversion to all things mainstream, more and more producers are happily letting their pop flags fly (both consciously and unconsciously), pilfering the radio hits and Top 40 anthems of the past in the same way that they do classic house, jungle and rave records.

Do I always like the results? Not really, and it's not always easy to distinguish how much of that is based on the actual quality of the music, as opposed to my own personal preferences, which naturally skew toward the electronic music templates I heard—and loved—during my 20s and 30s. I've definitely rolled my eyes when I've been sent something from a "cool" artist/label that sounds like it's taking heavy cues from *NSYNC, Slipknot or My Chemical Romance, and don't get me started about all of the throwaway R&B-inspired tunes that land in my inbox.

At the same time, there's something fascinating about what's happening right now, and while it's easy to boil it down to "electronic music producers messing around with pop," what they're doing is actually a byproduct of much larger social and cultural changes, particularly in relation to music consumption and the very nature of fandom. The gatekeepers are being vanquished, and irrespective of whether that's a good idea—I'd argue that it's definitely not the wholly positive development it's often depicted to be—it's created a void that artists are filling with their unbridled (and often unfiltered) creativity, traditional notions of taste be damned.

That's undoubtedly prompted a glut of (what sound to me like) tacky tunes in recent years, but it's important to note that not everyone who's wading into pop waters is making saccharine, radio-ready earworms. Take someone like aya, a UK producer whose *im hole* album came out on Hyperdub. Although her music owes a clear debt to pop culture—one track on the new LP literally mentions Billie Eilish—there's nothing easily digestible about it, as she careens through a myriad of high-octane club rhythms, filling out her compositions with patches of static and provocative lyrics that sometimes border on spoken-word poetry. It's not easy listening, and it's not for everyone, but it's unquestionably experimental, and aya is certainly pushing more boundaries than all of the producers still following an IDM template that was laid out approximately 25 years ago.

It seems counterintuitive to think of pop-referencing artists as the ones most actively taking electronic music forward, but that frequently does seem to be the case—at least right now. That assertion may make a lot of older heads grumpy, and understandably so; if someone got into techno in 1995 because they loved Robert Hood, or fell in love with dubstep in 2005 after hearing Loefah, expecting them to now embrace something that could double as a Top 40 pop record (or just heavily references the commercial mainstream) is a big ask, and likely goes against their ingrained notions of what electronic music is "supposed" to sound like.

That being said, music—like any form of cultural expression—is fluid, and doesn't necessarily "belong" to anyone. Recognizing origins and honoring traditions is obviously important, but time moves on, things change and not everyone is going to like it. Intergenerational conflicts are seemingly everywhere these days—and have been turbo-charged by social media—so why would electronic music be any different? So much of the current "discourse" involves 1) techno curmudgeons complaining about how the music (and the scene) has gone off the rails and 2) younger fans dunking on the older ones for their supposedly retrograde thinking. It's a play we've all seen countless times before, and in many cases, no one is technically "right" in these debates, but time is obviously on the side of the younger generations. (That is, until the next generation comes along and tells *them* why their way of thinking is now backwards.)

So what are aging electronic music fans to do? Roll over and let the culture become awash in pop tropes? That trend probably can't be stopped, but it's not the end of the world. The good news is that more electronic music is being made and released than ever before, and a whole lot of it follows the genre's more traditional templates. If you're not interested in some new record that borrows from 2000s-era boy bands and garish Europop, there are plenty of other things to choose from—and plenty of outlets that are more than happy to cater to your taste.

At the same time, when a genre gets locked into endless, nostalgia-driven loops, the music surely loses some of its vitality. Even if I often don't enjoy electronic music's more pop-oriented offerings, I can at least acknowledge that the artists making them are honest reflections of a world in which pop music is everywhere, and has affected just about everybody. The idea of a purely "underground" musical existence is essentially a fantasy, and as someone who was taught to embrace and aspire to that fantasy in my younger days, I'm admittedly a little jealous that younger generations' engagement with music is unburdened by what was ultimately a false dichotomy. (There are plenty of other things about younger generations' relationship with music that I'm not jealous of—and am even concerned about—but that's best left for another essay.)

When I hear pop music—or something that just sounds like pop music—I immediately think of major label excess, vacuous (and often disposable) artists, endless radio play, the prioritization of business over art and all of the other things that make the commercial music industry a rather gross enterprise. All these associations loom large in my brain, and the mere presence of certain songwriting approaches and production techniques activates an immediate, profoundly negative emotional response. I don't think I'm alone in that, but it's rooted in antiquated thinking. What's bothersome about pop music is the machine behind it, not the aesthetic of the music itself. An artist might vaguely sound like Justin Bieber, but if that artist is a kid singing in his bedroom over some noisy breakcore he made on a cracked version of Ableton, perhaps what he's doing isn't necessarily pop music at all.

It's a tough pill to swallow, and not all electronic music fans will be able to stomach it, but I'm hoping that the next time I have to write the press materials for some pop-influenced record, I won't feel the need to justify why the artist went down that path.

Lots of Bangers, Not Many Anthems
a.k.a. Thoughts on the current state of "big tunes" in dance music.

September 13, 2022

—

"The Bells." "Show Me Love." "Energy Flash." "Sandstorm." "One More Time." "Footcrab." "Inspector Norse." "Higher State of Consciousness." "Midnight Request Line."

Dance music has always had its anthems, and while they may prompt eye rolls from the "too cool for school" crowd, only the biggest cynics can deny that when deployed at the right time, these tunes have enormous power, unleashing waves of euphoria that can unite even the most diverse crowds on the dancefloor.

But are new anthems still being created? The supply seems to have dwindled in recent years, and coming out of the pandemic, it suddenly felt like DJs looking to drop a "big tune" were more likely to reach for a hit record from 1992 than 2022. People can argue whether that's been good or bad for dance music, but either way, it's something different, and this piece was my attempt to properly reckon with what's been going on.

———

2022 isn't over yet, but with the summer festival season more or less wrapped up (at least in the Northern Hemisphere), it feels like a good time to take stock and ask, "What does dance music sound like right now?" And more specifically, "What are the year's biggest tunes?"

The answers to those questions are highly subjective, but after conducting a(n admittedly unscientific) poll of friends and colleagues during the past few days, a couple of trends do seem clear:

1. Bangers (i.e. big, bright, fun and often somewhat goofy tunes) are both abundant and in very high demand.

2. Few of those tunes, however, seem to have much in the way of long-term staying power.

This isn't an entirely new phenomenon. Back in the early days of First Floor (November 2019 to be exact), I actually penned an essay about the dwindling supply of certifiable dance music anthems, and in the nearly three years that have passed since then, that shortage has only grown more acute. (As I said back then, "let's consider an anthem to be the kind of track that is supported by a wide range of DJs across different genres, scenes and styles, to the point where it becomes almost ubiquitous, at least within electronic music circles.")

The pandemic obviously had something to do with this, as two-plus years of lockdowns, club closures and festival postponements/cancellations deprived potential anthems of the testing grounds (i.e. dancefloors) they needed to thrive. (Those years also prompted a seemingly infinite number of ambient side projects, which varied in quality but very rarely produced anything resembling a hit song.) Things have obviously changed in 2022, but even during a year when the world's party infrastructure has by and large been up and running, only a handful of dance tracks have made what feels like a lasting dent in the culture.

What tracks exactly? Here are the songs from this year I'd definitely put into the anthems category.

• Eliza Rose's "B.O.T.A. (Baddest of Them All)," a playful, sultry, '90s-flavored cut that's become a genuine TikTok phenomenon and recently hit #1 on the UK Singles chart.

• Nick León's "Xtasis," a Latin-tinged rave-up the Miami producer made in collaboration with Venezuelan raptor house originator DJ Babatr. (It also came backed with a potent Pearson Sound remix that's become many DJs' version of choice.)

• Four Tet's "Looking at Your Pager," a wobble-bass-infused R&B flip that the UK veteran finally released under his KH moniker after caning the bootleg for more than a year. (The song was so highly anticipated that the mere announcement that he'd cleared the vocal sample—which he lifted from "No Home," a 2000 track by American girl group 3LW—prompted a wave of news stories across the dance music press.)

• Two Shell's "Home," which first emerged as a white label in 2021, is a chipmunk-voiced slice of candy-colored rave-pop that quickly caught fire when the song was officially released in January, snagging "Best New Track" honors from Pitchfork and setting off a giant wave of hype that's propelled the anonymous duo to the forefront of dance music.

Those four feel like the "no doubters," but other tracks probably deserve to be at least part of the conversation. Pariah's gurgling techno workout "Caterpillar," Rhyw's absolutely manic "Honey Badger" (which hasn't even been properly released yet but already appears to be a club/festival staple) and Joy O's bass-soaked garage shuffler "pinky ring" have all made for plenty of memorable dancefloor moments, and there was a time earlier this year when seemingly every DJ in the world (or at least on social media) was banging Bianca Oblivion's souped-up grime throwback "Selecta."

There are surely others I haven't mentioned here, and depending on who you ask, the list of 2022's biggest tunes will vary wildly, especially outside the more obvious "anthems" tier. Although the dance music industry is still finding its post-pandemic feet—and is at times visibly struggling to do so—the culture has come bursting out of lockdown with a new sense of neon-streaked energy. Restraint, nuance and "good taste" are out. Escapism, hedonism, grandiosity and (most importantly) FUN are in, as are intentionally garish Y2K aesthetics and an absolute disregard for the idea that certain musical lines are not to be crossed. The bouncy sounds of UK garage are enjoying a full-blown revival, and tempos are seemingly rising everywhere, with once reviled (at least in certain corners) sounds like trance, drum & bass and hardcore—both of the happy and classic UK variety—now becoming commonplace. (Side note: I have to give some credit here to fellow music writer Gabriel Szatan, who pointed out to me that a lot of what's big in dance music right now has a distinctly British flavor.)

Many of these trends have left older dance music fans shaking their heads in disapproval, but young ravers—lots of whom likely got into the music during lockdown via livestreams and social media—are piling onto the dancefloor, and they don't much care about what dance music's aging chin-strokers have to say about it. That attitude manifests in many different ways, but it's particularly obvious when one considers the sudden proliferation of nosebleed-inducing reworks of Britney Spears and seemingly every other pop diva from the past 25 years. When even critical darlings like Objekt and Call Super are dropping psytrance edits of Kylie Minogue on Boiler Room at Dekmantel, the vibe has definitely shifted.

This new generation lacks a certain amount of historical/institutional knowledge—numerous DJs have commented to me in recent months that once-reliable classics frequently fall flat with today's crowds—but its appetite for big (or at least big-sounding) tunes is absolutely ravenous. Raised on the blistering pace of social media and already attuned to an on-demand lifestyle where content (which includes everything from movies and television shows to TikTok videos and pop songs) is essentially disposable, these ravers expect a constant influx of dopamine-inducing material. Scores of bangers are released every week to meet that demand, but few of them—even the ones that employ EDM-level sonics—have anything more than a fleeting impact.

In a flooded market, only a few songs can realistically gain any kind of traction, and even when that does happen, the near-instantaneous burn rate on viral trends (including hot tracks) means that it's not uncommon for a popular song's momentum to have fizzled out by the time it's officially released. (Things like licensing issues and vinyl pressing delays don't help either, as production lines these days almost always move slower than the speed of culture, especially when that culture is increasingly experienced and developed online.)

Assuming that prevailing trends continue, the days of the proper anthem may be numbered. Regardless of what dance music sounds like—and to be clear, the exuberantly hyperactive, retro-rave glee that characterizes many of today's dancefloors is unlikely to remain dominant forever, or even more than a few years—it's hard to imagine even its biggest hits gaining more permanence in the wider culture. In a time when even major news stories frequently fail to keep their place in the discourse for more than a day or two, individual club and rave tracks don't stand much of a chance of keeping people's attention, especially when more and more of those tracks are appearing every year.

This isn't necessarily a bad thing, as the decline of agreed-upon anthems arguably opens up room for more diversity in dance music. DJs have to play something after all, and if there are fewer than 10 certified dancefloor smashers that seemingly everyone is playing in any given year, they're still left with a whole lot of time to potentially experiment and explore new sounds. In theory, this opens up avenues to develop more regional sounds and move away from dance music's central monoculture. Admittedly that's an optimistic take, and cynics could easily envision a future where that space is instead filled up with cornball anthems from the past that everyone immediately recognizes. (By some accounts, this is already happening to a certain degree, as multiple people have expressed surprise to me about how much they've heard DJs dropping artists like the Vengaboys and the Bee Gees into their sets this year—and at credible parties/festivals no less.)

The future is difficult to predict, but even if anthems (as they were once known) are gradually disappearing, dancefloors—at least for now—are very much filled with big, gregarious tunes, and crowds that are loving them. Those crowds might not know the name of each one, but they're demanding bangers all the same. The vibe they're cultivating isn't for everyone, but it isn't exactly new either. In truth, the idea of kids gathering en masse to dance and lose themselves while getting pummeled by loud, fast and irrepressibly ebullient tunes—tunes that they probably don't know the name of and that would likely annoy most adults—sounds a whole lot like the early days of rave culture. Considering how much those years (i.e. the late '80s and early '90s) are constantly being lionized in dance music circles, perhaps that's not the worst possible result.

Down with Techno
a.k.a. At a moment when the genre is arguably more popular than ever, many artists are actively defining themselves in opposition to it.

November 15, 2022

—

Track any genre over the course of a few decades, and the various ups and downs of its relevance and cool factor are bound to look more volatile than the stock market. Trends come and go, and something that sounds fresh today might be the butt of jokes a year from now.

As a music journalist, it's my job to know this (or at least keep it in mind), yet I have to admit that the "fuck techno" sentiment that's arisen in recent years amongst certain sectors of the dance music crowd was not something I anticipated. Although I myself have never really been a dedicated techno guy—I like it, but let's just say that I've always enjoyed Panorama Bar more than Berghain—the genre is still one of modern dance music's foundational styles, and seeing something so foundational to the culture be not just written off as uncool, but frequently held up as an object of scorn and ridicule, was a clear sign that something had shifted in the culture. That prompted me to take a closer look in this piece, and also examine why so many of techno's most vocal detractors were simultaneously so determined to gain entry to its most storied spaces.

———

Of all the clichéd images that DJs tend to post on social media, few are more recognizable than the obligatory post-gig photo in front of Berghain. How this trend began isn't exactly clear, but the "why" seems fairly obvious, as the Berlin nightspot—which is generally regarded as the top club in the world, often with reverential language describing the place as a "church" or "temple"—doesn't allow photos to be taken inside.

Given that, DJs who want to document their Berghain experience can't default to the usual parade of triumphant behind-the-booth shots and video clips of crowds going apeshit. Doing something outside the venue is the only option, and during the past decade, a new default has emerged, one in which the DJ posts up in front of the hulking former power plant and takes a photo, which is then usually shared with a gushing caption that may or may not resemble the quasi-motivational tone of a high school valedictorian's graduation speech.

It's easy to goof on this practice, but in a culture where publicly patting oneself on the back has been normalized, and in an industry where press coverage, promoters' booking decisions and even audience interest are increasingly detached from what music a DJ actually plays, many artists probably feel like they have to take part. A post-gig photo might be presented in the form of a thankful humblebrag, but at its essence, it's marketing. Playing Berghain is a measurable benchmark, and those pictures, cliché or not, send an easily identifiable message to the world that the artists in them have (supposedly) reached a certain level of acclaim and are worthy of wider attention.

Berghain has come to symbolize many things over the years, but in terms of genre, it's always been most closely associated with techno, even as Panorama Bar, its upstairs room, has consistently featured house, disco and other variants of dance music. Though the club was launched with relatively little international fanfare in 2004, as its stature grew and resident DJs like Ben Klock and Marcel Dettmann became verifiable global stars, the place effectively became the center of the techno universe, its gravitational pull affecting audiences and artists alike. (The number of DJs and producers who moved to Berlin during the 2010s and suddenly started playing/making techno is honestly too high to count, and innumerable acts have prepared for their Berghain debuts by attempting to assemble the "perfect" techno set.)

Post-pandemic, however, things feel a bit different. Berghain is still for all intents and purposes the most celebrated nightclub in the world, and artists still want to play there, but a growing slice of them—especially those who are young and/or new to the club—don't necessarily want to play techno. Although the post-gig photos continue unabated, the tenor of the accompanying captions has increasingly taken on an almost defiant tone, with some DJs boasting that they dropped reggaeton, gabber, jungle, hip-hop, footwork or something else that is absolutely not techno. Unlike their predecessors, they haven't come to Berghain to pay tribute to the techno temple; they've come to upend the soundtrack altogether.

It's not just Berghain either. Across much of dance music, techno's cultural stock seems to have dipped, and the term "business techno" has become a widely used insult. In all honesty, when was the last time that techno on the whole was perceived to be as seemingly bland and uncool as it does right now? (The early 2000s come to mind, when frustration with what felt like an endless sea of faceless techno producers helped give rise to the colorful camp and pop flirtations of electroclash.)

In fairness, techno isn't dead. Far from it. In many ways, the genre is bigger than ever. Techno might presently be the butt of jokes and snarky social media sentiment, but it's still the dominant sound at Berghain (and dozens of other respectable clubs). Plenty of old-school heads (including many of the Detroit originators) are still admirably doing their thing, and there are artists—many of them young Black DJs and producers in North America—determined to follow in their spiritual footsteps. Meanwhile, the genre's more commercial tier is economically thriving; critics may sneer about the growth of "business techno," but that music has essentially become the default sound of clubs and festivals in Europe—and increasingly around the world.

At the same time, although techno was born in Detroit and first championed by Black and queer communities, the genre has veered exceedingly far from those roots over the years, and has for many come to represent dance music at its most stale and soulless. (It certainly doesn't help that amidst the music's commercial explosion, so many of today's most prominent techno artists are straight white men of European origin; the genre is essentially Exhibit A for anyone who wants to talk about whitewashing in dance music.) On a creative level, techno often seems stuck, endlessly recycling decades-old norms and ideas, and while that's hurt its standing amongst the tastemaker set, it's the genre's mass commercialization that's arguably done the most damage to its reputation. As big-room techno increasingly nudges EDM aside in many of electronic music's tackier (and wildly profitable) corners, the music is now seen as the go-to soundtrack for clueless punters who prefer massive dancefloors and don't mind shelling out $75 at the door.

In short, techno has become something much bigger than just the music, and that's reflected in contemporary critiques of the genre. The term "business techno" technically has the word "techno" in it, and originally targeted the techno and tech-house culture of places like Ibiza and Miami, but it's now frequently hurled at pretty much anything in dance music that seems overtly commercial in nature. When viewed through a certain cultural lens, techno—or perhaps just the idea of techno—has essentially become an effective stand-in for cultural appropriation, creative stagnation, musical conservatism and the prioritization of profit over art. It's the status quo, and artists will always push against that, forming new scenes, sounds and subcultures that may or may not catch on more broadly, but nonetheless work to move things forward.

Taking potshots at a few sacred cows (e.g. the supposed "rules" of what can be played at Berghain) is part of that process. It may seem petty, but no generation likes to be told what it can or can't do, and given that the pandemic helped usher in a new crop of DJs whose values don't always line up with those of their elders, it makes sense that they'd partake in a bit of bratty rebellion. Playing reggaeton at a techno club—or any other genre that isn't traditionally associated with that kind of space—is something of an exercise in playful trolling, and if it can fire up the dancefloor while simultaneously pissing off a few purists, many young selectors would consider that a win-win.

Berghain may not be Ibiza, but as a cultural symbol, it arguably looms just as large. Moreover, it's inextricably linked to techno—and not just any techno, but the more rigid, big-room-oriented variant of the genre that's taken root around the globe. (In fairness to the club, its programming long ago expanded beyond what's generally thought of as the stereotypical "Berghain sound"—greyscale, industrial-flavored techno—but its reputation has yet to catch up to that reality.) As long as the dance music world—and the wider culture—continues to hold the place up as techno's most sacred house, it's inevitable that artists will attempt to crash through its gates and subvert its rules. Playing a gabber remix of Britney Spears may not be revolutionary in the traditional sense of the word, but when it comes to dance music, certain DJs' "fuck techno" sentiment does increasingly feel like a rallying cry for change.

Coming out of the pandemic, the dance music generating the most excitement is loud, bright, colorful and frequently filled with pop hooks—in short, there are a lot of bangers out there—and while part of that can probably be traced to audiences' desire to let loose and have fun after two years of Covid lockdowns, those kinds of tunes also slide effortlessly into the instant-gratification, short-attention-span dynamic of today's streaming and social media ecosystem. Need proof? Eliza Rose's "B.O.T.A. (Baddest of Them All)," a cheeky, retro-flavored vocal house tune which hit #1 on the UK Singles chart earlier this year, has already been featured in nearly 495,000 TikTok videos. It's hard to imagine a functional techno track gaining the same sort of traction.

Mainstream success obviously isn't on every artist's wishlist, but even for more discerning listeners, techno is a genre that, at least in its current form, often fails to line up with contemporary music consumption patterns. Think about it: in the context of a DJ set, a series of generally linear, tool-ish (and mostly instrumental) long-form cuts can be weaved together into a transcendent musical offering, but a standalone techno track? That rarely makes for a gratifying listening experience, let alone quality fodder for a streaming playlist or TikTok video. Although fans of the genre—myself included—likely see that quality as part of what makes techno (and other functional dance music sounds) special, for younger listeners reared on YouTube and Spotify, it's a major potential roadblock.

How that will affect the music in the long run is uncertain, but for now, techno is still everywhere. Its cool factor may be diminished at the moment, but even as a noisy slate of up-and-coming artists gleefully define themselves in opposition to the genre, they seem more determined to remake techno culture in their own image than cast it aside completely. They may not be shy about ruffling feathers, but in the end, they do want to participate. They'll add a caption defiantly bucking techno hegemony to their post-Berghain photo, but they still post the photo, and still accept the gig in the first place. Regardless of what the music sounds like inside, these artists—and their fans—still want the Berghain experience, or at least what they imagine that experience to be.

In some ways, the sound of techno has become almost secondary. It's the vibe and aesthetic most audiences are after, and while promises of unbridled hedonism and wild, round-the-clock partying do tend to have a wide-ranging, evergreen appeal—which has undoubtedly helped fuel the genre's commercialization and the influx of "normies" into nightlife—it's nonetheless telling that even as the music has changed, so many other aspects of the culture have not. People, fueled by the legend of places like Berghain, have clear expectations of what a night at the club is supposed to be like, and will eagerly dress up to play their part. (It's not a coincidence that so many of today's party people are still dressing up like characters from a fetish porn spoof of *The Matrix*. Berghain's influence on contemporary fashion, both inside and outside of club spaces, is immeasurable.)

Techno—and by extension Berghain—may have once been shrouded in mystery, but both have now leapt past whatever boundaries they once faced and have seeped, along with other aspects of dance music and culture, into the mainstream. That transformation hasn't always been pretty, and certain things—including a few foundational principles—have been lost along the way, but some idea of techno remains, and still seems to have a massive appeal.

What will that idea ultimately look like? Only time will tell, but there's a good chance that many of today's techno diehards aren't going to like it.

Who's in Charge of the Culture?
a.k.a. Intergenerational tensions in dance music are rarely about the music itself.

September 6, 2022
—

As a music fan, one of the hardest parts about getting older is that with each passing year, it becomes increasingly difficult to find things that sound genuinely new. After a while, everything starts to seem like a half-baked take on something that was done decades prior, and even worse, the historical sounds being rehashed by contemporary artists usually aren't even the best bits of whatever was happening in the era they're referencing.

This is frustrating! And while it's tempting to scream "these kids are doing it wrong" and serve up wholesale dismissals of today's music culture, I've managed to maintain some level of composure via the following:

1. Evaluating new music on its own merits, regardless of whether or not it's something I personally want to listen to.

2. Recognizing that music culture is cyclical, and that today's aging grumps were once the proverbial "kids" pissing off their elders.

In a media environment that rewards harsh critique and merciless takedowns, it's not always easy to take a step back and try to provide a sober piece of analysis. This essay was one of my first attempts to do that while looking at dance music's latest arrivals, and it also afforded me a chance to talk about emo and the internal politics of college radio, which I should find a way to do more often.

At some point during the late '90s, the word emo entered my vocabulary. I'm not quite sure exactly where I heard it first—although there's a good chance that a blustery, mid-concert conversation with fellow teens on the back patio of San Francisco venue Bottom of the Hill had something to do with it—but as soon as I had the most tentative of grasps on the term, I was all in. Bands like Sunny Day Real Estate, Far, At the Drive-In, Knapsack, The Get-Up Kids, The Promise Ring and countless others quickly rocketed to the top of my favorites list, and emo became one of my personal calling cards. As a kid who was barely out of high school, emo was more than just music; it was an entire subculture, and one whose mere existence seemed to validate both my budding sense of individual autonomy and corresponding desire to reject all things mainstream. (Remember that this was when the Top 40 was anything but cool and the stigma of "selling out" was arguably at its height.)

All of this is somewhat embarrassing to admit now, especially given emo's trajectory in the years that followed and the word's current status as a kind of universal shorthand for "depressed drama kids in eyeliner at the mall." Back in the late '90s and early 2000s, however, I wore the music—and my (admittedly limited) knowledge of it—like a badge of honor, loudly proclaiming its greatness to anyone within earshot. I'm eternally thankful that social media didn't exist back then, just as I'm grateful that the tape of my interview with At the Drive-In vocalist Cedric Bixler-Zavala is now nowhere to be found, as I definitely asked him something along the lines of "So... what do you think about emo?"

That interview was for my weekly radio show at KALX 90.7 FM Berkeley, a place where my emo enthusiasm didn't always go over particularly well, especially with the volunteers who were a bit older than me. Although they weren't actually old—most of the more vocal objectors were in their mid-to-late 20s—they were old enough to have lived through prior iterations of emo, and knew that the "emo" I was championing was miles away from Rites of Spring and the genre's more overtly punk/hardcore origins. (It also didn't help matters that the other style of music I was really excited about—electronic music, and specifically day-glo trance and rave music—was something most indie/punk/emo fans of that time would never listen to, and in fact tended to openly mock. For what it's worth, many of the more veteran electronic music fans at the station, who tended to gravitate toward styles like Detroit techno, jungle and IDM, didn't much appreciate my tastes either.)

Simply put, I was a brash, overconfident kid, and like many brash, overconfident kids, my enthusiasm outpaced my actual knowledge of the music I was shouting about. When it came to emo, trance or any other genre I was into, my frame of reference essentially began at the moment I "discovered" the music, and didn't go back much further. The idea of doing some research and properly learning about the roots and history of a genre? That wasn't something that fully took root in my brain until years later.

More than two decades later, I myself am no longer a young person, but the behavior of budding music fans in many ways hasn't changed all that much. By and large, young people—even those whose tastes veer away from the mainstream—are still most excited about the contemporary artists they "discover" themselves. Although streaming, social media and the general memeification of culture have arguably moderated this dynamic somewhat—the *Stranger Things*-fueled success of Kate Bush's "Running Up That Hill" and Metallica's "Master of Puppets," and the TikTok-fueled success of Fleetwood Mac's "Dreams" are things that likely couldn't have happened even five years ago—there's still no changing the fact that each generation wants to assert its own identity, and does that in part by building up and celebrating its own cohort of artists and icons. The "newness" of said artists and icons is arguably their most important feature, even when the music that they're making is little more than warmed-over versions of genres and styles that were popular in previous eras.

This is particularly true when it comes to dance music, a genre that bills itself as a bastion of futurism, but in reality has spent the bulk of the past two decades endlessly recycling sounds, styles and techniques from the '80s and '90s. New producers pop up all the time, but how many of them are genuinely breaking new musical ground? Not many, yet new tracks continue to blow up and fresh-faced artists are consistently being invited onto the international DJ circuit.

Young ravers want their own heroes, and many of them don't really care what prior generations have to say about it. This isn't something that's unique to dance music, but it is interesting that even as the genre has largely stayed the same—or at least ceased to innovate with the same gusto that drove its development and initial explosion during the '80s and '90s—old and aging dance music heads continue to criticize younger generations anyway. Those critiques might be framed as claims that kids these days are churning out "shit" trance, "cheap" old-school jungle knockoffs or inane rehashes of happy hardcore, but it doesn't take a psychiatrist to see that many of these complaints aren't about the music at all. They're about control, and the anxiety one generation feels when that control passes to those who've followed in their footsteps.

Thinking back to my emo days, those older heads I brushed up against weren't necessarily upset about the bands I was listening to. Their distaste sprung from the fact that the indie/punk/emo mantle had been taken up by a new crop of fans, one that didn't necessarily accept their authority over the genre or recognize whatever norms and values had been laid down previously. Simply put, they'd lost control of the narrative, and they were pissed about it. Was that petty? Perhaps—especially considering the extremely low stakes involved—but their frustration was also understandable.

Seemingly without warning, a new group of people was suddenly setting the agenda, and the music's preexisting fan base hadn't been consulted on the matter. Notions of tenure rarely matter much in the world of music, and accepting the inevitable onward march of culture can be a bitter pill to swallow. As a young emo convert, it sucked to be on the receiving end of that bitterness, albeit not enough to stop me from acting the exact same way just a few years later. Once emo's more blatantly commercial third wave kicked in, and the genre was increasingly defined not by the bands I loved but acts like Dashboard Confessional and My Chemical Romance, I didn't gracefully accept the transition. I got upset and quickly abandoned ship, making sure to vehemently badmouth the music's new, supposedly inauthentic direction on my way out the door.

In a society that worships youth, no one likes to be alerted to their waning relevance, which is why variants of my emo story are constantly playing out all across the musical and cultural landscape. Punk, indie, emo, hip-hop, jazz, electronic music... pretty much every modern genre has gone through these kinds of growing pains, and pretty much every dedicated music fan over the age of 25 has seen a genre they loved morph into something they no longer recognize or fully identify with. These shifts are normal and natural, and yet people's primary response to them is usually one of anger and dismissal, an endless parade of eye rolls and "these kids have no idea what they're talking about."

And to be clear, it's true that sometimes the proverbial "kids" don't have any idea what they're talking about, but that ultimately doesn't matter much—least of all to them. Contemporary dance music is a perfect example of this, especially considering the culture's current celebration of exceedingly fast tempos, cartoonishly colorful sound palettes and garish Y2K aesthetics. Very little of today's club and rave culture fits within the parameters of what older heads would consider "good taste," but young party people—many of them diving into the culture headfirst after two-plus years of Covid lockdowns—are brazenly charging ahead anyways, largely unburdened by such concerns.

Again, what they're doing isn't necessarily all that new. (Even their much-ridiculed preference for dizzyingly fast tempos is something that rave culture has experienced multiple times before.)

What's different is how the music and culture is being reshaped and presented, and the shifting parameters of what is and isn't acceptable. Someone who actually raved in the '90s probably finds a track like Benny Benassi's "Satisfaction"—which was quite literally a global pop smash when it first came out in 2002—to be a tacky bastardization of "real" dance music, but for someone who wasn't even born in the '90s, such worries are likely immaterial. For them, it's just a fun tune that's been making people dance for as long as they can remember; why wouldn't they want to hear it at a party? And if they're a DJ, why wouldn't they want to play it? Because some guy in his 40s who probably doesn't even go out anymore says it's not cool? If anything, that's probably more incentive for them to keep it in their DJ bag (or, more likely, on their USB stick).

Recycling has long been at the core of dance music culture, but every generation wants to make its own decisions about what source material they'd like to reference. Fifteen years ago, genres like trance, jungle, gabber and happy hardcore largely felt like relics, and were more likely to be held up as objects of ridicule than respected corners of the dance music ecosystem. Today, those sounds are all enjoying healthy revivals, and are arguably at the forefront of the entire culture. In an increasingly genreless world, musical boundaries—especially the ones based upon subjective tastes and stylistic taboos—often feel flimsy, and are almost always temporary.

Eliminating these boundaries doesn't always result in the best new music, and today's crop of reggaeton-gabber hybrids, Europop-meets-drill-meets-IDM concoctions and nu-metal-influenced club bangers does often feels less than inspiring—at least to me. But do I not like these sounds because they're objectively bad, or because they simply don't line up with the sounds/aesthetics that I personally identify with and associate with "good" electronic music? As much as I'd like to think it's the former, I can't honestly discount the latter, and if my peer group were to take an honest look in the mirror, I'm guessing that most of them would have to admit they feel the same way.

Without devolving into "everything is subjective" relativism —because I don't believe in that either—I can make an admission: older electronic music fans are no longer in charge of the culture. (What constitutes older? That's most likely a matter for debate and is perhaps more about a person's state of mind than the concrete number of trips they've taken around the sun, but for the purposes of generalizing, let's say mostly folks over 35. By that age, even the most dedicated fans of the music have usually dialed back their party calendar significantly.) That doesn't mean that they have nothing to contribute, or that their wisdom can't be shared with future generations. It does, however, mean that decisions about what the music is and where it's going are no longer in their hands, and that no amount of grumbling about how things used to be is going to change that.

Coming to terms with that reality isn't always easy, even within a subculture where notions of "PLUR" and "community" are supposed to serve as foundational values. (Anyone who's scrolled through Facebook comment sections about electronic music has surely noticed that some aging ravers appear to be completely incapable of accepting their new place in the pecking order.) There's an old adage that "youth is wasted on the young," and while that may or may not be true—in my opinion, it's certainly true at least some of the time—the young are still in control of the musical narrative. Older fans don't have to like that, but accepting it will likely go a long way toward reducing their stress levels.

Raving as Folk Art
a.k.a. Why post-pandemic dance music feels fundamentally different.

October 18, 2022

—

I'm not an academic, and while I've written quite a lot about electronic music over the years, it's not often that I venture into anything that might be described as cultural theory. However, based on the impassioned response this piece generated, perhaps it's something I should attempt to do more often. (It also helped that the article was originally published during the same week that rumors of Berghain's imminent closure made the rounds in the German press and on social media. That closure obviously didn't happen, but for a few days there, seemingly all of dance music was talking about "the end of an era" and questioning exactly where the culture was headed.)

I'll cop to the fact that even attempting to apply the word "folk" to contemporary electronic music was a purposefully provocative choice, but as I explain in the essay, it wasn't my idea in the first place. Moreover, the more that I looked into the broader definition of folk art and all it represents, the more it felt like a conceptual template that pulled together all the disparate dance music threads I'd been writing about in the newsletter. It's quite possibly the closest thing to a eureka moment I've ever experienced, and if someone were to ask me today to explain the current state of dance music culture, I'd likely suggest that they start with the following text.

———

For all intents and purposes, 2022 is the first year that dance music has been properly "back" after the onset of Covid. Things haven't always gone smoothly, but the industry has soldiered on, gradually finding its feet as people reintroduce themselves to the dancefloor. But even as those early logistical issues have subsided, it doesn't necessarily feel like everything is "back to normal." On the contrary, there seems to be a stubbornly persistent narrative that dance music as a whole (i.e. the music, and especially the culture and industry that surround it) is fundamentally different than it was before.

Some of this narrative—which usually surfaces in the form of complaints from dance music's older and more established corners—undoubtedly stems from the usual intergenerational tensions that rise up whenever a younger cohort of artists and fans begin to assert themselves within a musical subculture. Many of the most common gripes can be boiled down to some version of "kids these days are doing it wrong," and depending on who you talk to, dance music has supposedly become too fast, too loud, too shallow, too commercial, too colorful, too pop, too formulaic and too obsessed with social media.

Still, the idea that dance music has fundamentally changed can't be entirely chalked up to the curmudgeonly musings of semi-retired ravers who now spend more time in Facebook comment sections than they do on actual dancefloors. Things do feel different, and it's fair to wonder whether or not a defining era of club culture has come to an end.

The 2010s ushered in a global dance music boom, one in which Berlin—and, in many ways, Berghain itself—essentially functioned as the genre's creative and aesthetic center. (No offense to London and New York, which also played major roles.) The dissolution of that system wouldn't necessarily be a bad thing—the last thing anyone needs is another black-clad crew/club/promoter trying (and most likely failing) to recreate a Berghain vibe in their hometown—but there's no guarantee that whatever emerges in its place will be better or more interesting. Recent years have seen a massive influx of new, younger and more diverse voices enter dance music, yet even in today's post-pandemic landscape, where those voices are increasingly ascendant, the genre often feels creatively stagnant. Records are being made, parties are happening, production values are high and big tunes are abundant, but despite all that activity, the music itself, not to mention the ways in which it's created and presented, has largely stopped innovating.

Those most excited about contemporary dance music often cite its increasing overlap with genres like pop, hip-hop, reggaeton and dancehall, and while that's given rise to some intriguing new permutations of existing sounds, it's hard to describe much of today's offerings as something explicitly new. Though the culture has always relied heavily on recycling, that impulse seems to have gone into overdrive in recent years; dance music's most established genres (e.g. house, techno, jungle, electro, garage, dubstep, etc.) frequently sound as though they're stuck in a never-ending time loop, with sounds from the '80s, '90s and 2000s being constantly regurgitated for fresh crops of ravers. Considering that even the most dedicated club kids will usually cycle out of nightlife within a few years, this kind of creative stagnation is perhaps easier to get away with than it would be in other scenes, yet it's still something that's glaringly at odds with dance music's supposedly "futurist" ethos.

Dance music often swaddles itself in sci-fi imagery and utopian fantasy, but in many ways, it's become a deeply nostalgic realm, with a healthy fetish for formats (e.g. vinyl and cassettes), gear (e.g. vintage synths and drum machines) and general modes of operation that were once cutting edge, but are now frequently impractical, wildly expensive or both. And when it comes to presenting the music in a live setting, things might be a bit flashier these days, and the associated technology has certainly become easier to learn and manipulate, but the core concept of a night out (i.e. a lone DJ mixing tracks and holding sway over a pulsing dancefloor) is effectively the same now as it was 20, 30 or even 40 years ago.

None of this is necessarily a problem, and only the grumpiest of fans would assert that people on today's dancefloors aren't having powerful experiences and forging authentic connections with the music. Jeff Mills' "The Bells" is more than 25 years old, but a fresh-faced raver who first hears the song—or any of the hundreds (thousands?) of similarly styled tunes that have come along during the past two-plus decades—in 2022 can still have their mind blown.

At the same time, the moment has probably arrived for dance music to relinquish its claim to not just futurism, but its "underground" credentials as well. For all of the genre's history of illegal spaces, clandestine social networks, limited-edition releases and general activity outside the cultural mainstream, only the smallest remnants of those things still exist today. Dance music and DJ culture are no longer subversive, and arguably haven't been for at least a decade; they're now quite literally everywhere, to a point where they're commonly being used by aspiring celebrities, social media influencers, international fashion houses and a litany of corporate brands, all for purposes—many of them blatantly commercial—that are anything but "underground" in nature.

Like many other musical subcultures, dance music has been commodified, flattened and largely subsumed by the wider pop culture. The average person still doesn't know about the genre's origins or the finer points of its culture and history, but terms like "DJ" and "rave" have become part of the vernacular, and in many cases, now sadly conjure unflattering images of some V-neck-wearing dickhead smugly leaning into his headphones and making "wocka wocka" hand motions as a dopey crowd goes wild. That's a cartoonish stereotype of course—and one that EDM played a major role in cementing into the collective psyche—but even for those who regard the culture with a bit more nuance, the perceived parameters of dance music have by and large been set. DJs, clubs, the music itself—they're all expected to look and/or sound a certain way, and at this point, those who seek out the culture generally aren't interested in deviations from the norm.

As those expectations continue to calcify, it becomes necessary to place dance music in a different cultural framework, one that doesn't revolve around ideas of innovation, futurism and pushing the envelope. In many ways, dance music is transitioning—or perhaps has already transitioned—into a kind of folk art, and regarding it as such could potentially allow its most dedicated defenders (myself included) to stop howling about the genre's lack of new ideas, or at least make peace with its current place in the wider musical universe.

The idea of "dance music as folk art" isn't one that I came up with myself. I actually first heard it discussed by Penny Fractions' David Turner and Mat Dryhurst on the latter's *Interdependence* podcast, and while neither of them lay claim to coming up with the idea—yes, I wrote them both to inquire—they also couldn't say where they'd first heard it.[1]

Admittedly, the word "folk" initially seems like something completely counter to contemporary dance music, even when the latter is viewed through the most conservative of lenses. Maybe a song like Avicii's "Wake Me Up" could qualify as "folk" on some level, and artists like The Books (and even Four Tet) first made their names with music that was sometimes classified as "folktronica," but when I describe dance music as a kind of folk art, I'm not referring to the use of acoustic instruments and allusions to classic Americana. The classification is instead much closer to the multi-pronged definition provided by the Museum of International Folk Art, which says that folk art:

- May be decorative or utilitarian

- May be used every day or reserved for high ceremonies

- Is handmade; it may include handmade elements, as well as new, synthetic, or recycled components

- May be made for use within a community of practice or it may be produced for sale as a form of income and empowerment

---

1. A bit of subsequent research on my part has unfortunately also come up empty, but if anyone reading this has come across a similar thesis in an article/book/dissertation, please do let me know.

• May be learned formally or informally; folk art may also be self-taught

• May include intangible forms of expressive culture like dance, song, poetry, and foodways

• Is traditional; it reflects shared cultural aesthetics and social issues. It is recognized that, as traditions are dynamic, traditional folk art may change over time and may include innovations in tradition

• Is of, by, and for the people; all people, inclusive of class, status, culture, community, ethnicity, gender, and religion[2]

Do all of these descriptors square perfectly with modern-day dance music? Of course not, and it's unlikely that those who've dedicated a healthy portion of their life to dance music—especially those who first got involved during a time when it genuinely was a hub of musical and cultural innovation—will respond positively (at least initially) to the idea of the genre being categorized as some kind of museum piece. Music and dancing may date back to prehistoric times, but contemporary dance music isn't rural basket weaving. It's not a fringe or antiquated interest; it's a global enterprise, and one that's constantly evolving in response to new developments and shifting trends in both technology and the culture at large.

That said, few artforms—especially contemporary ones— would tick all of the boxes laid out in the description above, and while viewing dance music as folk art does imply a certain lack of innovation, it doesn't mean that the genre, its practices or its associated culture are wholly frozen in time. Things can—and do—continue to change within dance music, and it's telling that so much of the most impassioned discourse (or what passes for it on social media), from debates over the merits of vinyl releases or arguments about how opening DJs should approach their sets, is rooted in the tensions arising from those changes.

2. "What Is Folk Art?" *Museum of International Folk Art*, https://www.internationalfolkart.org/learn/what-is-folk-art.html.

At the same time, few of those changes would qualify as genuine paradigm shifts. When house, electro and techno first appeared during the 1980s, they represented not only a new musical universe, but an approach to music composition, production, distribution, presentation and consumption that was—with all due respect to disco and other dance music forerunners—almost entirely new. Today's changes are important, especially for those already involved in dance music, but they aren't changing the world or seriously altering people's perceptions of what the music is or could be; they're essentially fiddling at the margins of an artistic template that was laid down decades earlier.

Dance music isn't alone here, and while the term folk art is most frequently applied to genres like bluegrass and the sounds of rural Appalachia, it could credibly describe all kinds of different music, including jazz, blues, rock n' roll, hip-hop and even punk rock. Genres have something of a natural life cycle, and as an insurgent sound or style gains wider recognition and acceptance, its aesthetics and methodologies are gradually absorbed by the culture at large. Again, that doesn't mean the genre stops innovating altogether, but it does take on something of a fixed general identity that becomes increasingly difficult to shake. (That identity is also something that future generations of musicians will eventually respond to and/or rebel against, giving rise to new insurgent sounds and starting the cycle anew.)

Does that make dance music less interesting than it once was? Perhaps. The genre is without question no longer a serious driver of constant, world-changing innovation, and while it once had a certain air of mystery, its various secrets have by and large been revealed to the masses. In many ways, dance music has become just another established spoke of the broader culture, and while that's undoubtedly disappointing to some of its (mostly older) fans and participants, that doesn't mean that the genre is now without value.

In purely economic terms, dance music is arguably more valuable than ever, but even on a more spiritual/emotional level, it can also still be celebrated—and enjoyed—as a shared set of practices and traditions. (In that sense, it actually is like rural basket weaving.) Its cool factor may have faded—a development that's surely sent some diehards rushing for the exits—but the greater acceptance and understanding of what dance music is, even on a rudimentary level, has also made it easier to pass the music (and its associated heritage) down to future generations.

Did this transformation suddenly happen during the pandemic? Of course not. It's been in the works for years, maybe decades, but dance music's gradual, often imperceptible evolution was jarringly interrupted by Covid. In its aftermath, a stark "before" and "after" divide has emerged, prompting numerous people to claim that things have fundamentally changed. That much is true; dance music has changed, but its transformation goes a lot deeper than a rash of Zoomer DJs posting endless selfies and giddily blaring hardstyle remixes of teen-pop divas at 10:30pm. As odd as it sounds, dance music has become a kind of folk art, and as such, has been woven into the fabric of the cultural mainstream. That doesn't mean it can't change, but at this stage in its existence, it's unlikely to ever again change the world.

The Rise of the Avatar DJ
a.k.a. What music a DJ plays has become far less important than who they are, and more importantly, what they represent.

November 1, 2022

—

I think this might be one of the worst-titled pieces I've ever published. To be clear, it has nothing to do with the metaverse, nor does it have any connection to the film *Avatar: The Way of Water*, which was in the middle of its publicity campaign when the essay first went live.

Aside from that potential confusion though, this is another piece that distills many different thoughts I've expressed via the newsletter into something resembling a coherent thesis. When people say that dance music seems "different" after the pandemic, the dynamic described here is often one of the main things they're talking about—and struggling to make peace with.

———

Earlier this year, I was hired to put together an artist bio for a DJ. That in and of itself wasn't strange. I've occasionally written bios and promotional text throughout my career, and as pay rates for "real" music journalism have largely stagnated, taking on these side jobs has become increasingly necessary to pay the bills. (The ramifications—and potential ethical complications—of that are admittedly tricky and potentially concerning, but I'll have to save that conversation for another day.)

Writing a bio is generally a pretty straightforward affair. As the name implies, it's obviously meant to include key biographical details (e.g. place of origin, city of current residence, a summary of how the artist got started and found some level of success/

recognition, etc.), but it also serves a promotional function, and is frequently written to cast the subject in the best possible light. Newer artists are portrayed as fast-rising forces of nature that can't be ignored, while more established acts are described as iconic figures whose influence colors wide swaths of the musical landscape. In essence, it's a sales pitch, and as such, a bit of exaggeration is often employed, to the point where the average bio includes not only an accounting of career highlights, but also a fair number of florid adjectives and sweeping pronouncements about the artist's (supposedly) singular talent.

So what was different about this one bio I was commissioned to write? It too had a promotional function, and was stuffed with the DJ's background info and assorted accomplishments, including a rundown of the most prominent festivals and clubs where they'd performed. In many ways, it was a standard bio, save for one thing: it made almost no mention of what kind of music they play. Despite being a known quantity within the dance music world, the artist—who shall remain nameless, but is a critically approved act who plays at credible events all around the world—isn't really known for a particular sound. (To be clear, this isn't a "they play everything and so genre descriptors are meaningless" situation. It's just that write-ups of this artist generally include zero information about their musical selections.) And while that initially seemed odd, I eventually came to another realization: in today's DJ landscape, perhaps that kind of information no longer matters.

The withering of genre boundaries isn't limited to dance music of course, and is something that has only accelerated with the rise of streaming. We're now at a point where an entire generation of consumers has come of age in a media environment where notions of "mood" and "vibe" trump genre, and where larger historical contexts (i.e. where an artist comes from, what musical scenes they were a part of, etc.) are often entirely absent. Music culture and consumption has been flattened, and though it may disappoint older listeners who fondly remember their youthful days as diehard punks, ravers and metalheads, most teenagers long ago stopped primarily identifying themselves by their favorite genre.

This isn't necessarily a bad thing! In retrospect, the former rigidity of genres (and the ways that people organized around them) does seem somewhat ridiculous, and the idea of a modern teenager freely jamming crunk, classical and crust punk does sound—at least in theory—like a product of a world in which listeners are more open-minded. And when that kind of mindset finds its way to the dancefloor, it's not surprising that contemporary party people aren't necessarily interested in hearing house DJ X, techno DJ Y or jungle DJ Z. In all likelihood, their decisions about what artists to see and what events to attend have little to do with genre at all. In 2022, what music a DJ plays is far less important than who they are, and more importantly, what they represent. They've become avatars for the intangible, and have upended the dynamics of dance music fandom.

Dance music history is full of larger-than-life DJs, and there's little question that the appeal of artists like Larry Levan, Ron Hardy, Frankie Knuckles, Jeff Mills and countless others involved more than just the specific contents of their record crates. Although detail-obsessed trainspotters and record geeks have long been a part of the culture, nightlife has always been primarily about release and finding some level of freedom on the dancefloor. DJs have long been described—often with cringe-inducing language—as quasi-religious figures, their skills, selections and mere presence leading crowds to the veritable promised land. Notions of "mood" and "vibe" were predominant in the club decades before streaming services came along, so what's happening in today's dance music culture isn't a wholly new phenomenon.

At the same time, the dance music industry—particularly once it first began to grow into a global enterprise during the 1990s—has also spent decades focusing on the musical particulars of its participants. Some of this was pure marketing, as each new scene and subgenre presented an opportunity for labels, promoters and media outlets to stoke the hype machine and present certain artists as representatives of a hot new sound.

There's also the fact that dance music has often faced (cheap and uninformed) criticisms that it's not "real" music, and that its makers are merely pushing a few buttons on a computer. DJs, who are frequently dismissed as "just playing other people's music," tend to be viewed even less favorably. Up against those narratives—which are still prevalent, even today—it's no wonder that the industry has often filled its own messaging with language designed to boost the credibility of its artists and dance music itself. That messaging has often been incredibly serious (at times bordering on academic), asserting that dance music and the culture around it are important and worthy of thoughtful consideration.

For years, this approach—which was arguably rooted in a desire for wider validation—largely set the tone in dance music discourse and fandom. Given that so much of the culture initially unfolded outside of the mainstream, information about dance music (not to mention the music itself) was frequently scarce, which allowed musicologists and specialists (some might use less gracious terms like know-it-alls and gatekeepers) to frequently gain positions of relative power and influence. With these guys—and yes, they were almost always guys—at the helm, very specific and usually very serious ideas of what the genre (and being a fan of the genre) ought to look like took hold throughout the '90s and 2000s.

In that environment, it's no wonder that dance music was for so long such a nerdy enterprise. Fans and journalists would track the rise and fall of subgenres like the stock market, and every city with a few talented producers was examined as a potential hub of innovation (i.e. a "hot new scene," or even worse, "the new Berlin?"). When new artists and DJs emerged, their sound was often triangulated to an almost ridiculous degree, with self-styled experts practically concluding that someone's style was 20% classic New York house, 40% Drexciya, 20% breakcore and 10% progressive trance.

That last bit is obviously an exaggeration, but these kinds of breakdowns do still happen today, albeit increasingly in the context of music reviews that few people, including dedicated dance music fans, are reading. Contemporary dance music is full of these kinds of antiquated practices (and the crumbling institutions that perpetuate them), as the decision makers and agenda setters of old—a group that tends to include media outlets, old heads on social media and an assortment of other established entities within the industry—have held fast to their ideas about what dance music should be and how things should work. Meanwhile, a new generation has largely ignored those ideas as it gradually asserts itself and establishes its own way of doing things.

For now, however, many of the culture's old structures, hierarchies and priorities are still present—and in some cases, are still dominant—but they're also looking increasingly rickety, especially as dance music's separation from the mainstream has largely disappeared. Once a self-proclaimed bastion of futurism and innovation, dance music these days is essentially a known quantity, even amongst those who don't really like it. On a more basic level, there's also simply more of it than ever before, with more releases, more parties, more festivals, more artists, more labels, more radio shows, more mixes, more regions taking part, etc. Dance music may not be pop music—at least not all of the time—but it is the foundation of a fully global, multibillion-dollar industry that's often blatantly commercial in nature. Mass appeal has brought more money and more opportunities to the table, but it's also ushered in a new way of doing business, one in which the specific nature of the actual music on offer is far less important.

Some of this is just a matter of scale. Appealing to a wider crowd usually involves sanding down the rough edges of a product, ultimately delivering something that's safe and recognizable for the average consumer. That's certainly happened in dance music, where the industry continues to endlessly recycle sounds and styles from the '80s, '90s and 2000s, and in which the most celebrated contemporary "innovation" usually involves blending those sounds and styles with different forms of pop music.

At the same time, not everything that's happening right now can be boiled down to some version of "dance music is serving up safe tunes for the unadventurous average consumer." Perhaps streaming is to blame, but it feels like the importance of music—especially individual pieces of music—is declining across the board. Thanks to the internet, the supply of music is not only virtually infinite, but it's also essentially free. Engaging with a song, album or artist now costs basically nothing, and while that doesn't prevent listeners from still having profound experiences with music, it has unquestionably added to the disposability of the artform.

Within dance music, this is already having a real-world impact. Post-Covid raving has so far been defined by a litany of big, loud and colorfully exuberant tunes, but few have become truly ubiquitous. Songs come and go faster than ever before, and while making a "big tune" can still boost a producer's profile and land them some DJ gigs, it's not the same driver of success that it was pre-pandemic, let alone five or ten years ago. In a time where social media—and Instagram in particular—is at the center of everything, an artist's music has become almost secondary; it's their persona that fans are most likely to connect with.

Again, dance music isn't pop music, but as it's grown, it has undeniably copied several pages from the pop music playbook. In many ways, pop stars have always been a kind of empty vessel; they're avatars that can be adorned with whatever sounds, styles, aesthetics, fashions and buzzwords are making the rounds at any given moment. While an individual artist's level of agency in that process varies from one act to the next, there's no question that this has granted pop stars with a certain kind of flexibility and cross-cultural appeal. When thinking about someone like Madonna, Beyoncé or even Justin Bieber, their music isn't the primary product being sold; they themselves are, and that creates a very particular dynamic between those artists and their fans.

Dance music has occasionally flirted with that dynamic throughout its history, but once the EDM boom hit during the late

2000s and early 2010s, making hero-like figures out of artists like Skrillex, Avicii, Diplo and Steve Aoki, the floodgates were officially opened. Do these artists have some massive tunes? Of course, but it's also clear that their sustained appeal isn't necessarily rooted in the music they make. They're celebrities, and as such, garner just as much (if not more) attention for their antics, social media posts and associations with other famous people than they do for the contents of their catalogs. (For instance, Aoki's penchant for cake throwing is arguably better known than any one of his songs.)

In 2022, it's wild just how much this model has trickled down through the entire dance music ecosystem. (In fairness, almost all youth-oriented music cultures have been affected in a similar way.) Many of dance music's traditional markers of success (e.g. press coverage, good reviews, record sales, etc.) are either on the decline or largely irrelevant. Club and festival promoters now routinely make booking decisions based (at least in part) on Instagram follower accounts and who's gone viral on TikTok. Is it any wonder that even up-and-coming artists are spending as much time on their social media as they are in the studio?

It's easy to paint the artists following this path as shallow, and though critics (i.e. dudes on the internet) often aim their harshest critiques at young female artists (especially those they deem to be inappropriately dressed), this kind of image-first behavior isn't limited to that cohort. DJs and producers across the board are striving to do something, anything, that connects with audiences online, and while that most often takes the form of corny selfies and video clips of enthusiastically cheering crowds, there are no rules, and creativity in the medium is sometimes rewarded. Take French producer Bambounou: over the past year he's concocted a fake motivational speaker character who doles out dubious industry advice online, and has seen his bookings and notoriety jump as a result.

It's strange to think about an artist getting booked to DJ on the back of being "that funny guy from Instagram," but that's where dance music is at right now. Successful artists—especially young ones—need to represent something, and that something is often only tangentially related to music. Identity often comes into play here, and it's no surprise that the increased diversification of crowds has gone hand in hand with a major influx of Black, Latin, queer and female artists, along with acts that hail from other historically underrepresented groups and regions. Simply put, many people like (and feel empowered by) seeing artists who represent them and/or their worldview in the DJ booth, and while I'm absolutely not implying that anyone is getting famous solely based on their racial/ethnic/sexual identity, artists who vocally embrace their membership in minority communities do have a unique ability to connect with fans who, like them, have often been overlooked within dance music.

(For what it's worth, identity-based connections do extend to non-minority dance music participants as well, even when that identity is never specifically mentioned. It's probably not a coincidence that a huge part of Hessle Audio's fan base consists of straight, white, middle class men.)

On a more general level, an artist's appeal today often essentially hinges on one thing: their brand. It's not the most pleasant idea, let alone one that people generally associate with notions of genuine artistic creativity, but that doesn't make it any less true. Although an artist's brand can still be about music, it no longer has to be, and frequently isn't. Scrolling through the names on the average festival lineup—even the most credible ones—it's not difficult to sum up most artists' persona or "thing" in just a few words. If they're an amazing DJ or skilled producer, that's great and will likely be part of the mix, but if they're also uniquely funny, political, sexy, serious, outspoken or something else entirely, that's most likely what makes them a truly marketable commodity. And if they're affiliated with other established "brands" (e.g. artists, labels, crews, etc.), even better.

It's not just dance music artists who could be described as having a brand. Elijah, who does DJ but is arguably more of a behind-the-scenes figure, has become a benevolent, advice-dispensing industry guru. Mat Dryhurst works with Holly Herndon, but he's also the tireless Web3 and artificial intelligence enthusiast. Amongst music journalists, Philip Sherburne is electronic music's ambient dad, Simon Reynolds is the gold-standard dance music historian who can't stop coming up with new terminology and Gabriel Szatan is the irrepressible optimist who won't let his writing get in the way of a good joke (or even a dumb one).

All of these people are obviously more complex than the pocket-sized descriptions I've provided, but their "brands"—even if they weren't developed intentionally—nonetheless function as an effective kind of cultural shorthand. In a world where everyone is constantly bombarded with content, these kinds of shortcuts are often the only thing that can cut through the noise and make an impact. Why would it be any different with DJs? It may sound reasonable to say that all DJs should be evaluated purely on the content of the music that they play, but it's not clear that that framework makes sense for the culture as it stands now.

People head to the club for all kinds of reasons, but most of them are there for an experience, not to hear a specific collection of tunes. There once was a time where DJs could fly in, open their record box and offer a one-night-only gateway to an otherwise unavailable corner of the music landscape, but those days are largely over. Now that everyone more or less has access to everything, the only truly unique thing most DJs can offer is themselves. That is what audiences connect with, and it's a relationship that extends—at least in fans' minds—well beyond the confines of the dancefloor. Music is part of it of course, but so are Instagram posts, TikTok videos, photo spreads and whatever other bits of content the artist chooses to share. Memes, message board posts, whispered bits of gossip amongst friends... they all factor in as well. Call it celebrity culture or pop fandom, but it's now part of dance music too.

"What kind of music does that DJ play?" Many dance music fans no longer care.

"What do they represent?" That is the more relevant question.

II.
The
Broken
Music
Business

The Scene Isn't Worth Saving
a.k.a. The Covid-19 crisis has exposed the rot in the electronic music industry. Let's tear it out.

March 25, 2020
—

This is the most widely read piece I've ever published in the newsletter.

Much of that can likely be attributed to good timing. Written less than two weeks into the global Covid lockdown, collective fevers were running high and pretty much everyone had plenty of free time to gorge themselves on online content. This essay, which brazenly called for a wholesale teardown of entire pillars of the electronic music industry, tapped into both a collective sense of righteous anger and a naively optimistic belief that the pandemic represented a unique chance to remake the world in a better, more equitable version of its prior self.

Looking back, it's almost laughable how little progress was made in regard to all of the problems highlighted here. By the time that clubs and festivals properly reopened—approximately two years later—the revolutionary fervor expressed in this piece had largely been extinguished, and most people in the industry rushed to "get back to normal" as quickly as possible.

Reading my own words, it's also funny to see just how strident the newsletter was in that first year, with lots of righteous moralizing and seemingly no qualms about repeated use of the royal we. Although my perspective on electronic music's various problems hasn't changed all that much in the past few years, my discussion of them now tends to use more measured language, along with clearer distinctions that the thoughts expressed are my own. Does that mean I've grown? I'd like to think so.

———

Over the past few weeks, electronic music has come to a standstill. Clubs are closed, festivals have been postponed or canceled and many releases are starting to be delayed. DJs and dancers alike are stuck at home in self-isolation and music media outlets have largely stopped commissioning content that's not related to the coronavirus. (PR emails, however, keep coming unabated.)

This doesn't make our industry particularly special. People from all walks of life have had their lives put on pause, and frankly, many of them are in situations that are much more precarious. Yet that hasn't stopped the electronic music crowd from sounding the alarm about their plight, and while I certainly understand the impulse—as of this moment, I myself have very little work on the horizon for the foreseeable future—I've also found a lot of the discourse to be not just tone deaf, but remarkably limited in scope.

Last week, Resident Advisor rolled out a major campaign called Save Our Scene, which they kicked off with an open letter that has since been signed by more than 4000 people.[1] I encourage you to read it for yourself, but here are the major points:

• Dance music is in trouble.

• Dance music means a lot to us.

• We need to save dance music.

I don't mean to be glib, but that was basically it. Setting aside the fact that the letter included only a brief acknowledgement that maybe there are more important things to worry about right now (like, you know, people dying or the potential collapse of the health system), there also wasn't much in the way of actual proposals to help our industry. Sure, there were some vague calls to "hold each other up" and "channel the community spirit originally at the heart of dance music," but when it came to

1. "Save Our Scene: An Open Letter." *Resident Advisor*, March 19, 2020, https://ra.co/features/3641.

concrete suggestions of how the scene can be saved, this is what they came up with:

> *How can you help? Buy music and merchandise. Make a donation to support clubs and nightlife workers. Skip a refund to a canceled event. Do whatever you can. Your support makes a massive difference.*

A "massive" difference? Perhaps I have a different definition of the word massive, but these strike me as piecemeal suggestions that ultimately won't "save" anything. To be fair, RA has compiled links where people can donate to various clubs and initiatives, and has also put together a rundown of resources for those who want to give or receive help. They've even kept a running tally of virtual events for those seeking a bit of online engagement with electronic music. On a day-to-day, "here's what's happening right now" level, I have to admit that their editorial team has done an excellent job of staying on top of all the latest updates.

At the same time, RA's attempt to couch this work as part of a larger, community-minded Save Our Scene campaign rings hollow. What exactly are they trying to save? It's easy to get nostalgic and make vague allusions to PLUR and the magic of "dancing till dawn," but do those words really mean anything when they're coming from a ticketing company that was proudly touting its new partnership with Spotify just last month? The whole thing feels like a branding exercise, although that's likely a byproduct of its execution (there's even a dedicated logo!), but the campaign can perhaps be more accurately described as a grandiose act of buzzword-laden virtue signaling. It may be well intentioned, but it's also flaccid, which is perfect for a world in which low-stakes clicktivism allows people to feel good about themselves while accomplishing very little. Save Our Scene isn't about enacting real change; it's about getting by until we can return to the old status quo.

There's a logic to that approach, but I'd argue that the coronavirus pandemic has laid bare just how fragile the electronic music industry had already become. In most places, clubs have been closed for only a couple of weeks, and yet many of us are concerned that the whole industry might collapse. Even before the pandemic hit, it was clear that we were in trouble; producers' revenue streams were drying up, venues were closing, labels were struggling to sell records, festivals were crowding out local clubs and smaller promoters, music media layoffs were rampant, DJ fees were spiraling to unreasonable levels... the list goes on and on. Bit by bit, the electronic music ecosystem was rotting; we all saw it, and nobody was happy about it, but we kept on grinding anyway, because what other option was there? Thinking big wasn't an option most people even had time for.

Time, however, is no longer a problem. The whole world has been put on pause, and while many of us are rightly worried about simply keeping our heads above water, it's concerning how much of the discourse continues to frame this crisis as an unexpected bump in the road. The pandemic isn't a blip; it's a wake up call, and now is a great time to think about the big picture. I don't want to save the scene; I want to fix it, and enact structural change that allows us to build something that's both more sustainable and more rewarding for the electronic music community.

Given the scope of the industry's problems, I certainly don't have all the answers, but I do have some suggestions.

Disengage with exploitative streaming platforms

At this point, it's clear that Spotify, Apple Music and Amazon are a net negative for independent and underground music. From the microscopic royalty rates to the active commodification of music as a lifestyle product, these platforms foment the deterioration and destruction of independent and local music scenes. They most likely can't be stopped, but they certainly don't need to be encouraged and ought to be outright shunned.

Independent musicians and labels should stop engaging with these platforms, and should instead direct their work (and their fans) toward platforms that actually understand and appreciate their needs. Last Friday's Bandcamp sale was a great start, but in the grand scheme of things, the $4.3 million in sales it generated are just a drop in the bucket.[2] Consumers—even the ones who are avid fans of independent music—are never going to be convinced en masse to start buying music again, and streaming technology isn't going anywhere, so we need to find and/or develop platforms which cater to that without exploiting musicians in the process.

Disengage with the international festival circuit

With very few exceptions, festivals are not compatible with underground electronic music culture. Our community loves to fetishize small clubs and dark warehouses, and yet our DJs are spending half the year on giant stages, playing abbreviated sets for half-interested crowds. And why? Because it's profitable. That's it. Festival gigs pay a lot of money, so DJs play them, despite the fact that festivals (and their requisite exclusivity clauses) are suffocating local scenes. How are clubs and promoters supposed to compete? They can't, unless we take action. Artists need to stop taking those bookings, and their fans need to stop buying tickets. Independent media outlets should stop covering festivals, and ticketing outlets like Resident Advisor should stop selling tickets to them. Does this require sacrificing a lot of money? Absolutely. But with each passing year, we're moving dance music culture farther and farther away from its roots. When it comes to raving, bigger most definitely isn't better.

Reduce the scene's environmental impact

Electronic music is an environmental disaster. Every weekend, DJs are taking multiple flights as they hop from one party to the next.

---

2. The sale referenced here was the first time that Bandcamp waived its usual fees, allowing nearly 100% of sales revenue on the platform to be directed to artists during a single 24-hour period. In the wake of its success, additional sales days were announced throughout 2020, and the ritual now known as "Bandcamp Fridays" was born.

In the aggregate, we're talking about hundreds of flights per year, per artist; the impact on climate change is staggering, and it gets much worse when we also think about the thousands of dancers who are compounding the problem by jetting off to clubs and festivals all around the globe. For a scene that prides itself on progressive values, it's highly irresponsible, not to mention hypocritical.

Amplify local scenes

Of course, part of the reason that the volume of DJ flights is so out of control is that we've devalued local scenes. Allegiance to local parties and venues has declined, as electronic music fans increasingly just go wherever a certain international DJ is playing, even if it's a shitty megaclub or a giant festival. More and more, we're concertizing the party experience, which is maddening when we remember that DJs are quite literally playing other people's music. Don't get me wrong, I love DJing and value it as an artform, but in this day and age, when DJs largely all have access to the same music, is even the most talented selector going to be exponentially better than a skilled local? Most major cities are populated with plenty of talented DJs, but we continually overlook them in favor of a small pool of hyped (and significantly more expensive) fly-in talent; even worse, that hype usually stems from music that they produced, which is an entirely different skill set from DJing. It makes no sense, and it's also homogenizing local scenes, which increasingly take their cues from whatever is happening in major hubs like Berlin, London and New York. As much as increased connectivity brings us all together, it's important to recognize that amazing things can happen in (relative) isolation. Not all local scenes need to be the same, and we should encourage a diversity of approaches to music, parties and community building.

Break free of the Berlin-London-New York axis

The electronic music industry is largely concentrated in a few major cities, all of which have an outsized influence over the rest of the scene. Artists and narratives from these places take precedence over what's happening elsewhere, and journalists (who also concentrate in these cities) overstate the importance of what's happening in their immediate surroundings. Many artists can't afford—or simply don't want—to live in these electronic music hubs, but that doesn't mean their work should be given short shrift or, even worse, exoticized when the music media deems it worthy of coverage. Electronic music is a global enterprise; let's start treating it as such.

Rebalance revenue streams between DJs and producers

Simply put, DJs make too much and producers make too little. Although this stems from a larger shift in the music industry where revenue increasingly comes from the live arena, it's particularly problematic in a community where the live performers (DJs) are primarily playing music that they didn't write. Call it unfair, call it exploitative, call it whatever you like, but we can no longer justify a system in which the artists making the music (not to mention the labels who release it) aren't properly compensated. After all, if DJs want to keep making their money, then they need producers to keep making tunes, and producers can't do that if their only income is the minuscule trickle coming from streaming platforms. Whether we install some sort of revenue-sharing system or figure something else out, something needs to be done.

Fix the PRO system

Performance rights organizations are responsible for collecting royalties for music that's played in public, and they are badly failing electronic music. In theory, they should be a major revenue source for producers, but the problem is that they've done an awful job keeping track of what's getting played. Even with the growing power of music recognition technology (e.g. Shazam), PROs often struggle to identify what DJs are actually playing, and that's in the rare cases where they've actually done the work to engage with a festival or venue about making a real effort to do any tracking. DJs themselves could help out by self-reporting their playlists, but most artists either don't know this or aren't willing to make the effort. Producers too are part of the problem, as they often don't register their work with PROs, which means that they don't get paid, even when their songs have been properly identified. Education, organization and activism are absolutely needed here, as the PROs are already collecting money from venues and festivals; however, they have little incentive to change their practices and pay it out correctly. Unless our industry mobilizes to either advocate for change or set up their own royalty collection system, we're going to collectively continue to leave a whole lot of money on the table.

———

Anyways, all of this is just a start, and I don't mean for this to be some kind of manifesto. There's a lot to be done, and I'm fully aware that not everyone is going to like these suggestions. Hell, some of these ideas would downright jeopardize people's livelihoods, including people I count as friends and others whose work I deeply respect and admire. Regardless, let's at least have a serious conversation about it. I know that lots of us are concerned about basic survival right now, and basic questions like how the rent is going to be paid on April 1. But if we're going to talk about our scene, let's try to take a longer view, because we're not going to "save" anything by encouraging a few Bandcamp sales and pointing people toward livestreams in hopes that they'll make a donation. Our scene is under threat, but it was under threat long before the coronavirus hit. I say it's time to build a new one.

Fake It Until... Actually, Just Keep Faking It
a.k.a. The pressure to constantly project success in dance music.

May 3, 2022

—

Music fans often claim to want authenticity from their favorite artists, but is that really true? In the case of dance music, a genre whose obsession with fantasy and escapism can be traced as far back as the disco era, it's not clear that "realness" has ever been a top priority. Moreover, as its underlying industry has swelled into a global money-making behemoth, the facade it presents to the world has become even more elaborate.

Granted, the music industry as a whole has always been something of a smoke-and-mirrors enterprise, but in 2022, when dance music was struggling to get up and running again after two-plus years of pandemic-induced dormancy, the rosy narrative being spun became particularly uncoupled from reality. So when a prominent DJ (Peach) actually spoke up about the genre's bumpy road back to normality, it felt borderline shocking, and prompted me to take a harder look at dance music's concerning tendency to play pretend.

———

What does success look like in dance music? Concrete metrics are admittedly hard to come by, but both the industry and fans seem to have coalesced around a few key signifiers, including:

1. A busy touring schedule.

2. Adoring reviews in the press.

3. A lively Instagram account, preferably stuffed with envy-inducing travel updates, videos of packed dancefloors and stone-faced photos in front of Berghain.

That's just a partial list, but even in an expanded rundown, most line items will share one key trait: they all contribute to the impression that a particular artist is "killing it," regardless of whether or not that notion lines up with reality. Appearances can be deceiving, and when it comes to dance music, they quite often are.

Of course dance music isn't alone in this. The mantra of "fake it until you make it" has become pervasive in modern times, and looms particularly large in most creative fields. Dance music aggressively touts its DIY roots and the supposed "authenticity" of its mission, but it's not immune to larger cultural forces and trends. Celebrity worship, influencer culture, social media algorithms—these things affect everyone, and in a time when people often feel pressured to constantly present their "best life" to the world, why would DJs be any different? Given that their livelihoods largely depend on the opinions and perceptions of others, it's no wonder that so many artists are intent on presenting an "enhanced" version of themselves to the world. (This goes for unestablished/up-and-coming artists as well; society's widespread adoption of pseudoscientific ideas about "manifesting" success has certainly contributed to the current explosion of online fakery.)

Perhaps that's what made this admission by Peach—which she posted last week in her Instagram Stories—such a surprise.

Being entirely transparent about something a lot of promoters/venues/artists are talking about offline when i go to gigs – the reality is a lot of parties just arent selling tickets well, if at all. This is no shade to the lineups (this is happening to artists regardless of size) but it seems to be almost a change in priority for punters – perhaps people would rather be certain they can make the party before buying a ticket? maybe this is a symptom of clubbing after covid? maybe this is just a dance music thing? no one is really certain and the more i travel, the more i hear about this happening in other countries. In fact nearly everywhere ive been in the last 6 months has said the same.

Having said this – things do sell out, but it will be in days running up to the event (stressing out most of the people putting their finances on the line for the event lol)

In another slide, Peach went on to explain that her post was partially inspired by what was happening with Circuit, her ongoing residency at Wire Club at Leeds. The most recent edition was scheduled to take place last Saturday, and in the face of slower-than-expected ticket sales, she and the venue had decided to make the event completely free. That in and of itself wasn't all that unusual; given that clubs make most of their money from alcohol sales, entry prices will sometimes be reduced (or eliminated entirely) in an effort to simply get bodies through the door.

What was unusual, however, was that an artist—especially a headlining act like Peach, whose name theoretically provided the primary draw for the event—chose to openly acknowledge the situation. Even as an established artist, there was still an inherent risk in Peach publicly stating that tickets for her residency weren't selling as expected. Especially amongst promoters, it almost certainly raised an eyebrow or two, and while her future prospects likely remain very bright, it's not hard to imagine a few venues hesitating to book her down the line (or simply lowering their fee offers) because they're concerned that her draw might be faltering.

This gets to the crux of the problem. For all the lip service that's paid to the importance of transparency, speaking up (especially about money matters) is frequently not only not incentivized, it's a potential career setback, even when what's being said is the truth. Peach's observations might be anecdotal, but given that they're based on numerous conversations and experiences dating back six months, it's unlikely that she's the only one who's come across this issue.

It's actually promoters and venues who are most directly impacted by lagging attendance numbers, but they've largely been quiet, and for good reason—the pressure to keep up appearances is far too intense to allow honest communication with their audiences. Although appeals to solidarity and community might work on some people, especially if a venue is facing something particularly dire (e.g. imminent closure), telling average punters that a club's dancefloors have been half full lately isn't likely to entice them back through the door.

In any genre, the decision to attend an event is going to be multifactorial, but most of the time it revolves around one question: "Do I want to see X artist perform?" Dance music, however, is something of a different animal, and while certain high-level acts have a built-in draw, it's also true that a sizable chunk (and in some places, the majority) of a club crowd is there for reasons that have little or nothing to do with what DJs are on the lineup. One person might be there just because they like the venue or the party. Another maybe wanted a fun night out with friends and simply needed a place to dance. A different attendee could be someone who just hit the legal drinking age and wanted to go somewhere to have some cocktails, stay up late and get a little messy.

The options are endless, and in the wake of Covid, that's something of a perilous prospect for dance music. The club economy has always had an insanely high churn rate—only a fraction of dedicated clubbers last more than a few years in the scene—and in the wake of the pandemic, there are more reasons not to go out than at any time in recent memory. How many potential clubgoers simply aren't comfortable being in an enclosed, tightly packed space for hours on end? How many former club regulars spent the past two years staying at home and realized they liked it? (The number of premature, pandemic-induced clubbing "retirements" is probably quite high.) How many young people who would have started clubbing during the past two years never got the chance to go, and now don't see the point?

Covid majorly derailed nightlife, and with the entire industry now attempting to make up for all that lost time (and lost revenue), it's hard to fault anyone for acting like everything is just fine while quietly hoping things return to "normal," whatever that looks like. Yet surely some kind of readjustment is in order, and perhaps that's what's happening now, even if nobody is talking about it. Maybe expectations and economic models need to change, and in some cases, be downsized. Maybe different kinds of artists and genres need to be embraced within the clubbing space. When it comes to making decisions about booking, event planning and how the larger industry works on a day-to-day level, maybe new metrics need to be applied.

It's not like the old metrics are all that reliable anyways. A busy DJ schedule might make it seem like an artist is really popular, but it can also be a reflection of something far more mundane: bookers following trends and copying one another. It's no secret that many venues simply follow whatever venues like Berghain and Fabric are doing, or recycle names they spotted on the latest Dekmantel, Sónar or Dimensions festival lineup.

Others might follow whatever the press is covering, but is that an accurate representation of audience sentiment? Something like DJ Mag's annual Top 100 DJs list gets a lot of traction, but it's a notoriously rigged creation largely populated by artists whose teams have stuffed the ballot box and openly campaigned for votes. Those seeking something more credible might look at which artists are being featured on Resident Advisor, or who's been reviewed well by Pitchfork, but even that has its limits; the days when glowing press coverage directly translated to real-world fandom are largely over.

There once was a time when landing something like an RA podcast or a FACT mix could majorly level up an artist's career, but nowadays those things are usually just another blip on an overcrowded content radar. And as media outlets increasingly move away from click-based ad models, instead embracing brand partnerships and other revenue sources (e.g. RA's ticket sales) to stay alive, their content is thankfully getting less clickbaity, but that shift also means that even supposedly high-profile coverage can't be relied upon to draw all that many eyes.

With music media's influence waning, many industry decision makers have shifted their focus to social media instead, factoring things like follower counts into their booking calculus. On the surface, this seems like a reasonable, *Moneyball*-esque approach, one that brings quantifiable statistics into a world that was previously run on gut instincts, vibes and personal relationships. There's just one problem: the numbers being used are often bogus. In a space plagued by bots, fake followers, overly curated posts (more on that later) and plateauing user engagement (at least on any platform that isn't TikTok), the idea that an artist's Instagram, SoundCloud or Twitter account accurately represents the size of their fan base feels ludicrous. Spotify and other DSPs perhaps provide a bit more accuracy, but given the lean-back nature of how users engage with those services, it's fair to assume that there's a pretty sizable gulf between an artist's streaming numbers and the number of fans willing to actually purchase a ticket and attend an event featuring said artist in a particular market.

What about money? More clarity about what things cost and how much people are being paid would undoubtedly be useful for industry decision makers, but financial transparency is almost impossible to come by in dance music. Fans often assume that any artist whose name has been mentioned on a music website is pulling in obscene amounts of cash, but that's not necessarily true. Which DJs are making $500 per gig, and which ones are making $5000, or $50,000? Only a relative handful of people know for sure, and they by and large aren't sharing that information with the public. And while it's DJs who often catch the most flak when it comes to money matters, it's not like other industry players (i.e. promoters, venues, festivals, managers, booking agents, labels) are on the whole any less opaque about their finances.

During his recent run as a guest editor at Resident Advisor, Butterz co-founder Elijah commissioned an article in which three promoters broke down the financials of their events.[1] Those breakdowns were far from complete, and key details were either left vague or omitted entirely, but it's nonetheless telling that getting anyone to speak on the record about this stuff—even in a limited fashion—felt borderline revolutionary. Real financial transparency in dance music is still a long way off, which means that money is yet another area where large sectors of the industry are effectively working in the dark.

Even if accurate metrics did exist, the idea of an industry based entirely on statistics and algorithms sounds wholly unappealing. There's an artistry to booking and event planning, and it ought to be preserved. At the same time, it's still concerning how much of dance music—especially in its supposedly independent "underground" corners—continues to operate in a veritable fantasy land. While there's an element of fantasy in almost all music fandom—and when it comes to dance music, most people aren't hitting the club for a gritty dose of reality—problems are bound to arise when industry professionals (i.e. people who supposedly are better informed) are making decisions based on information they know to be incomplete or inaccurate.

With so many people propagating the idea that everything in dance music is hunky dory, existing problems will likely go unaddressed until they become too gargantuan to ignore. What Peach posted was revealing, but it's also telling that Eglo Records co-founder Alexander Nut recently tweeted a suggestion that Resident Advisor do a feature highlighting DJs with day jobs. There's an obvious disconnect between how the contemporary dance music world is being presented and the far less glamorous realities its participants are facing on the ground.

Is this rift merely part of a post-Covid hangover, or has some kind of larger, more permanent shift taken place? It's hard to know for sure, though the upcoming summer months and festival season should provide some clarity, but in the meantime, the

---

1. "Lawson, Michael. "How Much Does It Cost to Throw a Club Night?" *Resident Advisor*, March 17, 2022, https://ra.co/features/3983.

fact that so few people are willing to acknowledge (let alone discuss) that there might be a problem surely isn't helping matters. Following a difficult few years, it makes sense that folks want to focus on the positive and get back to partying (and making money), but in the rush to reopen, it seems that many of the industry methods and practices that were commonplace in 2019—and were deeply flawed, even before the pandemic hit—are simply being reinstituted. Lineups may look a bit different, and in some cases, are notably more diverse. That's a good thing, but it ultimately doesn't matter who's playing if people aren't buying tickets and interest in the music (and/or how it's being presented) has dipped. Is that possibility not at least worth considering?

Even if the attendance situation that Peach described is ultimately only temporary, there's no reason that the spirit of her message—being open and honest with her fans and the public, even when it comes to financial matters—can't be more widely adopted. No artist can realistically be "killing it" all the time, no matter how successful or talented they are, so why should anyone feel pressured to constantly project an image of success?

That pressure has turned so many artists into dedicated content creators, and by now, their tactics have become familiar to anyone paying attention. Scrolling through the average DJ's social media feed, there's the new release announcement, the sharing of pre-release preview tracks, the actual release day announcement and of course, the eventual anniversary announcement somewhere down the road. There's also the monthly pre-radio show reminder and the post-show "the episode has now been archived" announcement, not to mention screenshots of any press coverage and scattered pics/videos from the studio, preferably involving some tantalizing images of pricey gear. Of course, all those things are just a warm-up for the tour posts, from the requisite airport and airplane pics to the drool-inducing "look at this amazing thing I'm eating in a foreign country" photo, plus a few snapshots with fellow DJs, a couple of pre-gig reminders, an overdesigned (and quite possibly illegible) flyer or two, some random festival announcements (usually made months in advance) and, perhaps most importantly of all, the post-weekend "thank you" post that reads like a graduation speech, earnestly expresses the artist's gratitude and inevitably includes video clips of crowds losing their shit to some of the DJ's masterful selections.

Why do artists do this? More often than not, because they feel like they have to. Every post is a little reminder to the world that they exist, and are doing something worth paying attention to. "Logging off" or opting out, even occasionally, may no longer be a viable option (especially for up-and-coming acts), and in a hopelessly saturated media landscape where people's available attention is generally in very short supply, this kind of constant engagement makes a perverse sort of strategic sense. At the same time, there's no way that it's healthy. Celebrity culture may be inescapable at this point, but the fact that some of its most toxic elements have somehow trickled down to DJs hosting an NTS show or getting written up in Mixmag feels both unnecessary and fairly ridiculous.

Dance music may not be as "underground" as it once was, but it's still a relatively niche concern, and everyone involved would be well served by recalibrating their expectations and reconsidering not only what success means, but what it looks like. There's a difference between elevating people's reality and perpetuating an unattainable (and often unsustainable) fantasy, and far too many people—including fans, artists and all the industry people in between—are opting for the latter.

So... Are DJs Actually Just Exploiting Producers? a.k.a. The income divide between the studio and the DJ booth is becoming harder and harder to ignore.

November 12, 2019

—

When I wrote this article back in 2019—and literally started it by taking issue with a provocative Twitter thread from Martyn—I had no idea that just a few years later, I'd be asking him to author the foreword for my first book. (That being said, the fact that we've been able to have these kinds of disagreements—and even hash them out in public on occasion—without hating one another speaks to why I respect him so much.)

What's also interesting about this piece is that many of the problems I laid out have since been addressed directly by veteran artist DVS1 via his Aslice initiative. (For those who aren't familiar, Aslice is a platform that enables DJs to easily share a portion of their fees with all of the artists whose music they play in their sets.) Although the project is still relatively young, I very much support its mission, and also appreciate DVS1's determination to forge ahead with it, despite all the potential obstacles, including me saying that I was "extremely dubious about the prospect of setting up some sort of new profit-sharing regime between DJs and producers."

It's good to know that not everyone in dance music is as pessimistic as I am.

———

I have to hand it to Martyn. Last week, he posted an online thread that he surely knew was going to rile up the Twitter brigade.[1]

---

1. At some point since this essay was first published, Martyn deleted the thread, but the thoughts he laid out are summarized (albeit in broad strokes) in the piece. **109**

For those who missed it, he basically took issue with a notion that had been advanced in Resident Advisor's recent "The Changing Economics of Electronic Music: Part 2" feature.[2] The idea that bothered him wasn't new, per se—especially for those of us who have been following the work, or even just the Twitter feed, of Mat Dryhurst—but it's still the sort of thing that stirs up a lot of emotions and opinions amongst supporters and opponents alike.

Without being too reductive, said idea is rooted in the fact that producers have seen their income shrink to increasingly minuscule levels in the streaming era. At the same time, DJs are making higher fees than ever while (usually) playing music that was made by other people. Even worse, in many environments—festivals in particular—DJs are often being booked for slots that once went to live acts, which means there are fewer opportunities for actual music creators to earn money from performing their own music. Given this discrepancy, some argue that something should be done to rectify the situation, and the "something" most frequently cited is the implementation of a new system where a portion of DJs' fees (ideally over a certain threshold) goes back to the artists whose music they play in their sets. In theory, that would restore at least some of producers' lost income streams and help sustain a healthier balance in the electronic music world, one in which producers—you know, the people who actually make the music—will more easily be able to sustain their craft without feeling like they have to become a touring DJ to survive.

I don't want to speak for Martyn, but his Twitter thread pushed back against this argument along the following lines:

1. This analysis undervalues what it is that DJs do. DJing is an actual craft, and doing it well takes skill and years of hard work.

2. There already is a system in place for compensating producers when their music is played by DJs. Royalties

are being collected by performance rights organizations (PROs), but they're not being distributed properly for a myriad of reasons. Shouldn't we focus on fixing/improving that system instead?

3. Once a DJ buys a piece of music, they own it, just like any other consumer. As such, they have the right to do what they want with it, including playing it in a DJ set.

So... who's right? I have to admit, when I first came across Mat Dryhurst's thoughts on this topic (many months ago), I reacted in the exact same way that Martyn did. I think it's partially a function of age (sorry Martyn, but I'm grouping both of us with the "olds" here), but as someone who's been involved in this culture for more than 20 years (yikes), I do inherently place a lot of value—some of it admittedly sentimental—on what DJs do. It's easy to say that "anyone can be a DJ," but while technology and the proliferation of digital formats has made that idea more true now than it was in, say, 1995 or even 2005, the fact is that being a good DJ is absolutely not something that anyone can do. While it is true that the current dynamic between industry hype and booking patterns does frequently propel inexperienced DJs onto the international club and festival circuit, even if their DJ skills don't necessarily merit the level of fees that they're earning, staying on that circuit isn't so easy. Unless an artist is capable of dropping an endless series of hot records or they can figure out another way to maintain their level of hype, they're going to have to be a good DJ to keep getting booked, and that involves actual talent, artistic vision and a whole lot of hard work.

Moreover, there's a basic logic to the argument that once someone buys a record, it's theirs to do with as they wish. Perhaps it's a result of growing up in a capitalist society, but most of us don't think collectively about our possessions, not even the digital ones. I don't know about everyone else, but I think of the songs on my iTunes as "my music," even though it's all been created by other people. Hell, I think of it as "my music" even though a huge portion of that music has been sent to me for free as promos.

Speaking of promos, I've rarely seen them brought up in these discussions, but they are something that definitely clouds the issue. Although it varies from one DJ to another, it's a safe assumption that a significant portion of music being played by the average touring DJ was sent to them for free in the form of promos. And at the most basic level, a DJ promo is an invitation to play the music, is it not? It may not involve a specific spelling out of rights, but I think most DJs see promos (whether they're coming from an official PR campaign or an informal email from a producer or label head they know) as a message that says, "I think you might like this, go ahead and play it in your sets if you do." Beyond that, there haven't been any clauses attached, other than the usual "don't share this link with anyone else," and even that gets broken. There's certainly no stipulation that says, "If you do play this, I expect you to pay me a percentage of your DJ fee for that set."

In the past, clauses like that wouldn't have even been considered, because the DJ world (like most creative industries) bought into the idea of exposure. The logic of exposure basically says that if a creator (e.g. an electronic music producer) provides something for cheap or free to an entity (e.g. another artist, a media outlet, a giant corporation) with a larger platform, the attention that the "something" will receive will trickle down to said creator, supposedly leading to more attention for them, more gigs, more income, etc. This argument is still used today, frequently in reference to artists like Aphex Twin, and goes something like this: "If Aphex Twin plays your track, you're going to sell a bunch of copies of that song (and probably other music from your catalog too), and it might even lead to you getting booked for gigs yourself." And in truth, this has actually happened for certain artists; the Twitter anecdotes about the blessed hand of Aphex Twin are numerous.

That being said, can we all just agree that the idea of exposure is bullshit? I'm not saying that artists should never do work for free or cheap—hell, I do it myself sometimes—and I do believe in the idea of people "paying their dues" (at least to a certain degree), but the entire exposure system is built atop the same logic that brought us trickle-down economics. I'm not an economist, but we're basically talking about a system in which economic actors with more wealth and resources quite literally convince those with fewer resources to do work at below-market value, in hopes that it might lead to an eventual move up the economic ladder. I know that exploitation is a loaded word, but still, all of this sounds an awful lot like exploitation to me.

What really boggles the mind is that even though most people in the electronic music world consider themselves to be progressive or at least left-of-center, we've somehow adopted (and continue to perpetuate) a conservative economic system that's actually more capitalistic and, yes, exploitative than the ones being executed by our own governments. There has to be a better way, no? Or at least a more equitable one?

Going back to the DJ booth, it's true that some of this inequity could be solved by PROs. I don't want to get too bogged down in what PROs are and how they work, but these organizations (which vary from one country to the next, only complicating matters further) are already collecting royalties from festivals, clubs and other venues where music is played. The problem is that the data that they use to then distribute those royalties to copyright holders is woefully incomplete, and when it comes to electronic music, often includes shockingly little information about what tracks and artists are actually being paid.

Can the data provided to PROs be improved? Yes. Absolutely. Will it actually be improved? I don't know. At present, the PROs don't have a whole lot of incentive to fix things. As a group, electronic music artists represent a small (and generally unorganized) portion of PRO membership. Many artists are unaware how PROs even work, and it's safe to say that many people running PROs have a limited understanding of DJ culture and how even the basics of the electronic music industry work. (At the extreme, I'm talking about people who don't necessarily understand what mixing is, or even that DJs are playing other people's music.)

Technology could help, but things aren't yet at a level where the music being played at venues can be automatically monitored; accurately keeping tabs of what actually gets played would be even more difficult. At some point, perhaps blockchain technology will allow exact track information to be encoded into every tune a DJ plays (at least the digital ones) and then tracked, but for now, we're still relying on a Shazam-like piece of software to figure out what a DJ is playing, even if they're playing three songs at once and running the mixer signal through an FX unit. Based on my iPhone's usual success rate when I try to Shazam something, I think we're a long way off from technology solving this problem. And even if the perfect technology does come into existence, there's also the issue of getting it into every club and convincing everyone to use it. It's not impossible to imagine, but again, I think we have a ways to go.

In the meantime, the only real hope for accurate reporting is that DJs will do it themselves, and the good news is that yes, this is actually possible, at least in most places. Although reporting a tracklist for an illegal warehouse rave probably won't help anyone, if a DJ performs at a licensed club or festival, they can usually go online and input their tracklists, leading to some sort of payout for every artist whose music was played. In truth, however, it's not every artist—only the ones who are registered with said PRO. And this participation issue is the main problem I have with the idea that PROs are going to save electronic music producers. These organizations have been around for decades, their operations are nebulous and their accountability is low. They suffer no real penalties if the money they collect isn't distributed fairly, and changing that will likely require either a major surge of altruism on their part or large-scale organization on the part of the members they're not serving properly.

In my opinion, both are unlikely. For all the jokes about "business techno," the fact is that most people in electronic music aren't particularly business savvy, nor do they want to be. Furthermore, there aren't a ton of incentives for DJs to really change that when the benefits are abstract (e.g. "helping the scene") and the economic bonus for many of those who bother to take the initiative and do something like manually submit their tracklists would be small or nonexistent. For instance, what motivation does a DJ (who's not also a producer or label owner) really have to report their tracklist to a PRO, other than their desire to do the right thing? That should be enough, but as good as "doing the right thing" sounds, it becomes a lot less desirable when it involves a bunch of data entry after a weekend full of travel, late nights, little sleep and who knows what else. On a more basic level, how many DJs can even remember exactly what they played?

So no, I don't have a whole lot of faith in the PRO system. I don't know how to "fix" this problem, but having looked at the status quo, I have to admit that I've increasingly come around to the logic of what folks like Mat Dryhurst are saying. As much as I love and value the art/craft of DJing, it's pretty clear that DJs are making their money—and sometimes it's a lot of money—using the work (i.e. music) of other people who are not being fairly compensated. And once streaming comes to the DJ booth (and yes, that's sadly already in the works), this income disparity will become even more unfair.

At the same time, I'm also extremely dubious about the prospect of setting up some sort of new profit-sharing regime between DJs and producers. It sounds good in theory, but barring some kind of international government regulations making it mandatory for everyone, how many DJs are going to voluntarily sign up to give a portion of their income to other artists? Given our scene's intensely competitive and capitalistic nature, I'm afraid that the answer would be a lot fewer than we'd like to think.

Beyond that, even if such a regime were put in place, how would it be enforced? Where would the income threshold be before DJs are charged? Should a DJ making $500 per gig be forced to hand over a percentage of their fee? Should it start at $1000? $5000? Is the percentage flat, or does it increase as DJ fees rise? Who's going to collect the money and ensure that the figures are accurate? What happens to money collected for artists who aren't registered with the new regime? What's to stop DJs from trying to avoid these payments by demanding that their DJ fees (or portions of their DJ fees) be paid in cash, off the books? Alternately, what's to stop certain DJs from avoiding these payments by instead just playing sets of only their own music, or maybe just music from their own label? How would labels figure into this? Are they going to start demanding a cut of this new income stream? Will it become part of contracts when someone is signed to a label?

I could go on, but I imagine that you're getting the idea.

I'm not opposed to change. The status quo is fucked and is getting worse. Producers need to actually make money, or electronic music is going to wind up in a shitty place. DJs, on the other hand, are making a lot of money, but those profits aren't trickling down to the people whose music they're playing. At the same time, pitting DJs and producers against one another feels counterproductive, especially when there are other parties who are also making a killing out there: festival promoters, certain clubs, massive tech companies, etc. A lot of the problems electronic music is facing are just a microcosm of what all creative industries are facing in the era of platform capitalism, and things are looking grim.

So yes, DJs are probably exploiting producers. But they're not the only ones, and they're not doing it on purpose. Change is needed, but it's not going to happen without our entire community getting its act together, organizing and doing a lot of work. DJs and producers should be allies; if they can't work together to tackle these issues, then we can all be sure that someone else will, and none of us is likely to be happy with the result.

The End of Vinyl?
a.k.a. Maybe it's time to re-evaluate our relationship with electronic music's favorite medium.

February 11, 2020

—

Of all the recurring music arguments that seem to get rehashed every few months on Twitter, few are more tiresome than those involving the relevance/importance of vinyl. I knew that even before I started this piece, so I guess I shouldn't have been surprised by the veritable hornets' nest it stirred up when it first went live.

That being said, given that the essay was prompted by news that a devastating fire had potentially disrupted the entire vinyl production market, addressing the topic seemed like the right thing to do at the time. In the end, that catastrophic prediction never really came to pass; even during lockdown, the large-scale production of vinyl continued, albeit at a slower pace, and several years later, the format shows few signs of slowing down. Despite that, I can't say that my personal feelings on the matter have changed all that much. I've never been an overly sentimental guy, and while I don't wish to spoil the contents of the piece below, I will say this: when it comes to vinyl, I simply no longer see the point.

———

Last week, a fire broke out at a warehouse in Banning, a small desert city located a couple of hours outside of Los Angeles.[1] The building, which ultimately wound up being a total loss, was home to Apollo/Transco, one of two lacquer production facilities in the entire world. Lacquer discs are essential to the vinyl pressing process, which makes this fire potentially devastating

1. Lui, Malachai. "Abbey Road Mastering Engineer Miles Showell Comments on Apollo/Transco Disaster." *AnalogPlanet*, February 8, 2020, https://www.analogplanet.com/content/abbey-road-mastering-engineer-miles-showell-comments-apollotransco-disaster.

for a significant swath of the music industry, especially smaller labels releasing vinyl in the United States. As of now, it's not known when—or if—Apollo/Transco will manage to get up and running again; their website states "We are uncertain of our future at this point and are evaluating options as we try to work through this difficult time." Even worse, the world's only other lacquer production facility, MDC in Japan, is not only smaller than Apollo/Transco, but is reportedly not accepting new clients at this time.

All of this is very bad news for the electronic music industry. There's an entire ecosystem of labels, distributors and stores that relies on vinyl to survive, and it's hard to imagine that network not being severely disrupted in the months ahead. Some labels will undoubtedly switch to a different vinyl production process, DMM (a.k.a. direct metal mastering), which doesn't require a lacquer disc, but global capacity is limited and there are also concerns about sound quality. The lower frequencies of DMM-produced records tend to suffer, which is obviously a problem for electronic music.

Even before the Apollo/Transco fire, vinyl production was facing serious problems; while recent years have seen a much-ballyhooed "return of vinyl," the business of actually manufacturing records has been creaky at best. Existing facilities—at all steps of the production process (and there are several)—are struggling to keep up with demand, their capacity often limited by old machines. Things are so fragile that when a machine breaks, replacement parts often aren't available, and instead have to be fabricated. Even worse, there's also a severe lack of people with the technical knowledge of how these machines and processes work; over the past few decades, many of the most knowledgeable folks have passed away, often taking their expertise with them.

Knowing this, it's no surprise that production delays have practically become standard operating practice. This is why vinyl release dates have become so fluid, especially for smaller labels, and even an orderly production process can often take six months or more. And while it's true that global capacity has slowly been increasing thanks to old machines being refurbished and new pressing plants coming online, the Apollo/Transco fire is a perfect example of the vinyl industry's pronounced vulnerability.

This is madness. I know that vinyl is practically a sacred medium for electronic music, but perhaps we've reached a point where it no longer makes sense to try and maintain this rickety status quo. Just yesterday, Scratcha DVA—an artist whose unique brand of wisdom is always entertaining—tweeted the following:

> *If ur finkin of doin vinyl jus bare this in mind. U cn hav sex an make a whole brand new human being b4 u cn make a song an get it bk in ur hand on a 12inch bit of plastic*[2]

He's right. The time required to make vinyl is borderline ridiculous. And why exactly are we still fetishizing this medium? It's expensive, both to make and to buy. It's a petrochemical product that's terrible for the environment, as *The Guardian* reported just last month.[3] It's also highly impractical, both for personal and professional use. Most DJs these days (especially the ones that tour regularly) don't even play vinyl. Obviously there are exceptions, but in the aggregate, most artists have switched to CDJs, and even the DJs who do buy vinyl regularly are often just ripping it to digital.

I understand the appeal of vinyl. I used to collect it myself. Those discs come with a lot of sentimentality, and they offer something more permanent than a folder of digital files. There's undeniably something satisfying about having a physical release in your hands, especially when an artist or label has gone the extra mile with artwork, liner notes, etc. Vinyl may be expensive, but some people see the cost involved as a sign that these releases are inherently more valuable, as the investment required supposedly helps ensure that only the best music is being pressed onto wax.

2. Smart, Leon (@ScratchaDVA). Twitter, February 10, 2020, https://twitter.com/ScratchaDVA/status/1226789421585965056.

3. Devine, Kyle. "Nightmares on wax: the environmental impact of the vinyl revival." *The Guardian*, January 28, 2020, https://www.theguardian.com/music/2020/jan/28/vinyl-record-revival-environmental-impact-music-industry-streaming.

That's a nice idea, but let's be honest—it's bullshit. Although the rise of digital production and distribution has undoubtedly led to a sizable increase in the overall quantity of music being released, the idea that vinyl releases are inherently better is not only dubious, but willfully ignorant of how music is being made and consumed all around the world. At this point, vinyl has become a luxury good, yet it's still being held up by "underground" music circles as a totem of legitimacy. Music journalists are certainly complicit in perpetuating this idea, as vinyl releases continue to be regarded as more "serious." Although attitudes are slowly changing, there's a lingering sort of disdain for digital releases, which are widely seen as less important and less worthy of consideration.

Don't believe me? Take a quick scan through the news or reviews section of any electronic music website, and see what percentage of the coverage is devoted to releases that are coming out on vinyl. It makes no sense. Thanks to the rise of streaming culture, most readers aren't actually consuming music on vinyl, yet the press is still using the medium as this odd benchmark of who deserves our collective attention.

Again, attitudes about this have been changing, especially as a generation raised on digital music and streaming continues to gain a foothold in the electronic music industry. But maybe it's time to significantly speed up the process. Making vinyl was already expensive and time-consuming before the Apollo/Transco fire; in the months ahead, it's bound to become even more costly. Recent years have seen the music industry repeatedly congratulating itself about the so-called return of vinyl, but in the electronic realm, the truth is that most labels are struggling to sell even 200 or 300 copies of their releases. The potential profit margin for a successful limited-run release is razor-thin, and many small labels are losing money every time they put out a record. Of course there are exceptions, but if we look at things through a wider lens, most small labels are only functioning thanks to the willingness of their owners to continue pumping in money, and that money usually comes from another source (e.g. DJing, a "real" job, being a rich person). Is this kind of economic barrier to entry really worth defending? Think about all of the music being made—especially outside of Europe and North America—that never gets taken seriously, just because releasing it on vinyl isn't economically feasible. (In many places, it's downright impossible.)

Things don't have to be this way. While I'm certainly not advocating for the death of vinyl, I do think it's time to consider a major re-evaluation of the medium. For starters, could we do with a lot fewer vinyl releases? Absolutely. I do realize that any sort of major reduction would negatively impact a lot of people, and while I bear no ill will towards label owners, vinyl distributors or record shop proprietors, let's stop kidding ourselves—the writing is already on the wall. The vinyl industry, in its current form, is not just unsustainable; it's impractical, elitist and out of step with many of the morals and ethics that supposedly underpin electronic music culture.

That said, fixing things isn't as easy as just ditching the vinyl format. Music culture has been eagerly tearing down gatekeepers over the past decade, creating a vacuum that has largely been filled by tech companies and their algorithms. We certainly don't need to give them more power, and simply eliminating the "vinyl = important" benchmark could easily do just that. (There's also the stubborn problem that digital streaming isn't exactly good for the environment either. As the saying goes, there is no ethical consumption under capitalism.)

Truth be told, I don't have a definitive solution, but perhaps we could start with a wholesale attitude shift. As members of the electronic music community/industry, we need to redefine what makes a release "valuable" or "important." We're all living digital lives, so maybe it's time to recognize that digital-only releases are no less legitimate than physical ones. And if we do want to continue fawning over physical releases, perhaps it's time to stop looking at tapes, USBs or other mediums as "lesser" formats. After all, if a physical release is just being purchased to look nice on a shelf (and let's be real, that's what's happening a lot of the time), then a cassette can do the trick just as easily as a piece of vinyl, and at a fraction of the cost. And for the audiophiles out there, digital storage has reached a place where even WAV, AIFF and FLAC files can be easily stored, swapped, sold and shared, and they all sound great.

It's funny, electronic music is supposed to be rooted in notions of futurism. We like to tell ourselves that our community is fair-minded and forward-thinking. But so many of our contemporary practices are tied to sentimentality and notions of "this is the way it's always been done." Traditions can be a good thing, and I'm not the kind of person who regularly advocates for "smashing the system," but when it comes to vinyl, we're long overdue for a change. The Apollo/Transco fire is a major bummer, but it might also be the catalyst we need to make some real changes.

The Dwindling Power of the Online DJ Mix a.k.a. The realities of an oversaturated marketplace.

August 17, 2021

—

Putting this book together, I couldn't help but notice that certain words popped up over and over again. "Oversaturated" is one of those words, and I think it speaks to something that most people have struggled to deal with in the digital age: the veritable firehose of content that we're blasted with every day. Perhaps younger generations will be better equipped to navigate this information onslaught, but in the meantime, the adjustment is wreaking havoc, both on our attention spans and the perceived specialness of any one piece of art.

DJ mixes have long been key to electronic music culture, even during the days when they were recorded on cassettes and reel-to-reel tape. Arguably the closest musical approximation of the club experience, they've primarily existed online during the past 15 years or so, and have become more or less ubiquitous in the process. Do they still matter though? And how did they become so prominent in the first place? This piece takes a look back, and ponders the pros and cons of a present in which the online mix options have become virtually infinite.

———

It's hard to pinpoint exactly when it happened, but at some point during the past decade, online DJ mixes stopped mattering much.

Perhaps that's something of an exaggeration. Online mixes obviously still retain some level of cultural cachet—which is likely why electronic music fans are practically drowning in them these days—but in the grand scheme of things, most fail to move the needle.

It's hard to imagine now, but 10 years ago, DJ mixes on the internet were relatively rare, at least in comparison to today's online landscape. Although electronic music culture has been very online since the earliest days of the web, and plenty of DJs were hopping on upstart internet radio stations as far back as the '90s, it took a while for the idea of curated mix series to really take hold.

Both Resident Advisor and XLR8R launched their weekly podcast series in 2006 (the former with a mix from Troy Pierce, the latter with a session from the Plug Research label). Rob Booth's *Electronic Explorations*, which began as a weekly radio show and later became a mix series, launched in 2007 with a guest mix from Milanese. FACT inaugurated its mix series in 2008 with a set from The Count & Sinden, and the now-defunct sites Little White Earbuds and MNML SSGS joined the fray that same year with mixes from Terrence Dixon and bvdub, respectively. In 2011, Groove magazine started its own series with a mix from Apparat.

This is far from a complete list—many media outlets and online mix series have come and gone over the past 15 to 20 years—and it's absolutely possible that Resident Advisor and XLR8R weren't the first organizations to get into the game. Nevertheless, by the end of the 2000s, those two publications, along with FACT and a handful of other sites and organizations, had established a new—and highly influential—kind of content template.

The timing of this wasn't coincidental. Although these mix series predated the current podcast boom, it's noteworthy that Apple introduced the iPod in 2001 and first added formal podcast support to iTunes in 2005, enabling audiences to more easily find and subscribe to their favorite series. This also dovetailed with a time when CD sales were taking a nosedive, a development that eventually spelled doom for most of the CD-based mix series out there. (During the latter half of the '90s, the format was omnipresent in electronic music, with series like *Global Underground* becoming bestsellers and magazines regularly bundling new issues with exclusive mix CDs they'd commissioned from popular DJs.)

With CD sales evaporating, a cassette revival years away from happening (not to mention unthinkable at the time) and listeners increasingly shifting towards digital consumption, the stage was set for online mixes to rise in prominence, and that's exactly what happened. During the late 2000s and early 2010s, doing a mix for a site like Resident Advisor, XLR8R or FACT felt like a genuine big deal, something that could instantly level up an artist's visibility and booking calendar. (Full disclosure: I myself curated the XLR8R podcast series from late 2008 until early 2015, so there may be some level of bias in my recollections.) Artists, labels, managers and PR agents began to incorporate these mix series into their promotional campaigns, and a genuine competition broke out between outlets as different sites jostled to confirm mixes from in-demand DJs at just the right moment.

Was this a perfect system? Absolutely not. First of all, these series were all driven by the idea of exposure, with artists providing content (i.e. work) for free in hopes that it might pay off somewhere down the line. There's an obvious, if misguided, logic to that—which is probably why the exposure model continues to be so prevalent today—but it doesn't negate the fact that these mix series (the most prominent of which were tied to for-profit media organizations) were relying on free labor to boost their profile and prop up their business. (There's also the fact that most of them completely ignored copyright laws and licensing requirements, which meant that the artists whose music was included in these mixes—without their permission—also went uncompensated.)

Looking back, it's also not difficult to argue that these relatively high-profile mix slots were being gatekept to a certain degree, especially when the curation was generally overseen by a relatively small number of decision makers (most of them white, male and concentrated in places like New York, London and Berlin). It's probably fair to assume that institutional, structural and cultural biases crept into the selection/invitation process, as did a growing concern over "would audiences click on this?," a notion which rapidly swelled in importance as the internet moved toward click-based economic models. Diversity (of race, gender, country of origin and even genre) didn't disappear completely—when you're curating a weekly mix series, at least some level of open-mindedness is required, if only to fill all of the slots—but it did frequently take a back seat to familiarity, name recognition and whatever sounds and trends were fashionable at the time.

Despite those imperfections—which, in retrospect, were numerous—the excitement around these prominent online mix series held firm during the early 2010s, at least for a time. I left XLR8R in 2015, and right up until my departure, the weekly podcast continued to be some of the most popular content on the site. (Considering that the series is still going, as are those of Resident Advisor and FACT, it's probably safe to assume that these mixes continue to draw significant traffic.) However, even before I left, that popularity did begin to waver, and it seemed clear that the influence of individual mixes was on the decline—a trend that has only accelerated with each passing year.

Why? There are many factors, but the main reason is simple: there are way more online outlets for mixes these days. Ten years ago, only a handful of sites were in the game, but nowadays, places like Resident Advisor aren't just competing with XLR8R and FACT; countless labels, festivals, promoters, clubs, crews and fans have gotten into the act, sparking exponential growth in the sheer volume of mixes that hit the web each week. (Dekmantel, which oversees one of today's most popular mix series, inaugurated its podcast in 2015, kicking things off with a DJ session from Marcel Dettmann.)

Much of this explosion can be traced back to the widespread adoption of platforms like SoundCloud and Mixcloud during the early 2010s, which allowed would-be curators to easily upload and share audio content online. Previously, the audio files for online mixes were usually hosted on curators' own websites and servers, a practice that proved to not only be expensive—particularly as a series' volume and audience grew—but also required listeners to visit individual websites when they wanted to listen to a particular mix. SoundCloud and Mixcloud flipped the script, adding a social media element while creating one-stop listening hubs where listeners could more easily find and share mixes they liked. And for those curating the content, these platforms were free (or comparatively cheap), allowing many of them to dispense with overhead and not bother with building a traditional website. (At some point, even mix series that did have dedicated websites also began hosting their content on SoundCloud and Mixcloud, taking advantage of those platforms' easily embeddable players.)

From a curatorial standpoint, if online mixes once revolved around gatekeeping, then that gate has been lowered significantly during the past decade. While the most popular mix series are still curated by a handful of prominent outlets, those places are no longer the only game in town. Far from it. There are now dozens, if not hundreds, of mix series out there, and that doesn't even include the similar content offered by entities like Boiler Room, not to mention the thousands of different online and community radio stations that now exist all around the globe.

Of these, London's NTS (founded in 2011) is perhaps the most noteworthy—at least in the electronic and independent music world—but the dozens of shows they broadcast each week are just a drop in the overall bucket. Its model—which also owes a great deal to Dublab, which has impressively been broadcasting from Los Angeles since 1999—has been emulated countless times in all sorts of different communities (both real and virtual), and these upstart stations all have a whole lot of time to fill, which means that even relatively novice DJs can probably get a radio show somewhere if they really want one. (In 2021, it's almost more difficult to find a DJ who doesn't have a radio show.)

Simply put, when it comes to online mixes, there are now more outlets than ever before, and even if an artist isn't invited to contribute to one of them, they still have an easy option at their disposal: recording a mix on their own and uploading it themselves. Numerous sites allow DJs to skip would-be gatekeepers entirely and speak directly to their fans, and with the help of platforms like Twitch and Mixcloud Live, they can even do it live. (Of course, building a fan base without support from existing outlets/organizations/etc. can be a very tall order, especially in today's ultra-crowded landscape, but that's a matter for another essay.)

So... this is good, right? In terms of sheer access, things have undoubtedly improved. If someone wants to put a mix together and get it online, there's no one to stop them, and if they'd rather have an outlet host their mix, there is no shortage of options out there. On the curatorial side, there's a ton of competition, and that—along with increased calls for more diversity and better representation, particularly during the last year—has prompted even the biggest mix series (e.g. Resident Advisor, FACT, XLR8R, Dekmantel, etc.) to widen their nets and platform a more varied array of artists.

In addition, with several of the more established series having already topped 700 mixes, they've already featured many of electronic music's more established "name" artists. Unless their curators start repeating themselves—a move which would likely be frowned upon—they have no choice but to dig deeper in search of new and different DJs to spotlight. (Oddly enough, from a competitive standpoint, having a less established mix series can actually be an advantage right now, simply because there are more recognizable names to solicit mixes from.)

All of this certainly sounds great. The doors are open and continue to widen, but there is one major drawback: the current glut of mixes has severely blunted their impact (and promotional value). Online mixes have become so prevalent that journalist Philip Sherburne has been doing a monthly *Best Mixes* column for Pitchfork since 2016. Another writer, Chal Ravens, has been doing something similar for several years—her *Monthly Mix Roundup* is currently hosted by The Face—and Resident Advisor also includes mixes as part of its monthly *Best Music* column.[1]

---

1. As of 2023, Sherburne's Pitchfork column has become a roughly quarterly exercise, while
Ravens' column no longer exists.

While this sort of content is partially driven by a need for clicks—lists and round-ups sadly do tend to perform better than most other articles—it's also motivated by the fact that even the most ardent listeners can't possibly keep up with even a fraction of the mixes on offer these days, let alone all of them.

The market for mixes has become saturated, and as a result, even the most prestigious mix series—which were once considered appointment listening, regardless of what DJ was being featured—often tend to generate more shrugs than cheers. In many ways, the situation is akin to what's happened with television, mirroring that medium's shift from broadcast networks to cable and now streaming. When there were only three or four major mixes dropping each week, huge portions of the electronic music audience heard them, or at least took notice of their existence. In the current landscape, that's impossible. Fans' consumption habits have splintered, and are now being catered to by more content sources than ever, and while that's been great for breaking down barriers to participation and boosting variety, it's also sapped individual mixes of the power they once had.

In 2021, being asked to do an RA podcast is something that will still make many artists happy, but in all likelihood, it isn't going to significantly alter their career trajectory. A great mix might prompt a slight boost in social media followers or an inclusion in one of the aforementioned round-up columns, but truly breaking through has largely become a question of volume (i.e. getting covered/mentioned in a multitude of different places). Mixes are now just one piece in a much larger stream of content, as fans often expect their favorite DJs to not only post mixes, but maintain an active social media presence (preferably a funny one), do interviews, host radio shows, drop new releases and basically be present at all times. (Of course, those same fans will then criticize artists who do "too much," which makes this creative balancing act all the more difficult.)

None of this is static, and 10 years from now, the status quo around online mixes will likely be completely different from today's situation. It's often tempting to look back at the past and say "things were better before," but regardless of whether or not that's true—and in many cases, it absolutely wasn't—it's perhaps more constructive to simply acknowledge that things have changed. Does the average online DJ mix feel more disposable now than it did a decade ago? Yes, and there's something unfortunate about that, a feeling that the culture has been cheapened somehow. At the same time, are more DJs than ever now being given an opportunity to showcase their skills? Also yes, and that's something to celebrate.

Do those two things balance each other out? I'm not certain, and the answer to that question is likely something that's ultimately dependent on who's being asked. And regardless of their answer, there is one inescapable truth: today's "balance" won't last long—not for online DJ mixes, and probably not for much of anything else in the electronic music world. Knowing that, perhaps it's best to just ride the wave and see what happens next. If nothing else, it'll be different.

Compilation Fatigue
a.k.a. Do we really need all of these compilations?

October 29, 2019

—

The following is the shortest piece in the entire book—published when the newsletter was less than two months old, it was written during a time when I was still figuring out exactly what First Floor was—and it's arguably the one that reads the most like a straight-up complaint. On the bright side, that means it includes a few snappy zingers; even so, it also comes off a bit more arrogant than I would have liked.

All that said, the primary narrative of the piece still feels relevant, and if anything, the growth of Bandcamp has only increased the volume of compilations in the world—and most of them aren't particularly memorable, let alone essential.

Mono No Aware is still amazing though. What a fantastic record.

———

Is it just me, or are there too many compilations these days? Maybe I'm just missing something, but do people actually like and/or value these things? Do they secretly sell tons of copies or generate gobs of streams? Do labels just like them because they're easier to promote? I would genuinely love to know.

To be clear, I don't have a problem with all compilations. Reissue compilations, for instance, especially ones highlighting a particular label, sound, scene or movement, can provide an incredible snapshot of music history. And even when a compilation is focusing on a current sound, scene or movement, they can also have real value, particularly when they provide an entry point to something that's happening outside of the electronic music mainstream (i.e. the things that Resident Advisor and other sites don't usually post about).

This "entry point" function is so important. Looking back at electronic music history, compilations have long served as a sort of gateway for listeners interested in learning more, and some releases have been massively influential. 1988's *Techno! The New Dance Sound of Detroit* played a huge role in spreading that music across the Atlantic, and those *Rio Baile Funk* compilations were essential listening during the mid 2000s. (I'd wager that plenty of listeners didn't even know what a favela was when those compilations came out, let alone that such incredible music was coming out of those communities.) Of course, there's also the famed mix CD; at one point, mix series like *Fabric* and *Global Underground* were arguably more important and influential than most artist albums—I know I wasn't the only one jamming Paul Oakenfold's *Tranceport* back in 1998—but those days are well in the past. In the face of endless online mixes, the relevance (and volume) of mix CDs has waned considerably.

But if we focus on just the past few years, how many truly memorable compilations of new music have been released? Personally, I can think of only one that has really meant something to me: *Mono No Aware*, a fantastic collection of ambient-ish music that came out via PAN in 2017. (Granted, as someone who's constantly inundated with new music, my memory is fuzzy and perhaps I'm forgetting some other quality compilations. Regardless, *Mono No Aware* is the only one that comes to mind immediately for me, which I think says a lot.)

Mono No Aware worked because it wasn't an empty gesture. The record featured 16 tracks by 18 different artists, but it still sounded like a proper album, as its litany of high-quality tunes coalesced into a cohesive musical statement. (It also included Yves Tumor's "Limerence," which is just a flat-out incredible song.)

If more compilations took this approach, I wouldn't be complaining. Unfortunately though, most of the compilations I receive feel like borderline random collections of disparate, loosely connected tracks. In a digital world, when most listeners have literally millions of tracks at their fingertips, these kinds of compilations have no real purpose. And no, I don't think a label's anniversary automatically qualifies as a "real purpose." It's not that I don't understand the impulse—as someone who's started and run multiple labels myself, I know just how hard it is for a label to survive even one year, let alone five or ten.

At the same time, celebrating these kinds of anniversaries should go further than simply throwing together a "greatest hits" collection or a sampling of throwaway tracks from artists who've previously contributed to the imprint. Yet that's what usually shows up in my inbox, whether it's a label celebrating its fifth year, its fiftieth release or some other arbitrary milestone. (Having just received a raft of ADE Sampler compilations, which came on the heels of numerous Ibiza 2019 compilations, I can assure you that the bar for these "milestones" is now ridiculously low.)

In labels' defense, it is extremely difficult to get artists to contribute their top-shelf material for a compilation. Why would they? Few artists these days work with only one label anyways, and in an environment where producers have to constantly think about "building their brand," there's little incentive to lend some of your shine to someone or something else, even if it's a label you like. Even for new artists, is it really worth signing over your best stuff to a label when it's just going to end up as one of 15 tracks on a compilation? Most of the time, the answer is no.

In the end though, the fault here does ultimately lie with the labels. If you're a label owner putting together a compilation, and the tracks coming in aren't that special or just plain don't go together, does it not make sense to just scrap the release? Is there really no other way to commemorate your label's birthday or whatever it is that you're trying to highlight or celebrate? Putting out a compilation might be an easy way to drum up some interest in your back catalog and/or get a publication to write a news story, and it's probably the easiest way to get 12 (or more) different artists all tweeting at the same time about your label's new release, but unless it's curated with care, its musical value won't add up to much. In that case, it's basically just noise, and we already have more than enough of that.

The Album You Made Might Have Been a Giant Waste of Time
a.k.a. The trouble with big projects in a time of short attention spans.

November 8, 2022
—

Although I'm hesitant to describe anything I write as controversial, I will admit that this essay caused a whole lot of consternation when it was first published. Given the title, one can certainly make the case that I was asking for it, but it was also illuminating to see the degree to which certain people—artists and fans alike—are still emotionally invested in the album format. (Interestingly enough, very little of the most vocal pushback came from the realm of dance music, but considering that albums have never really been the genre's primary currency—especially for DJs—perhaps that's not surprising.)

In his foreword to this book, Martyn wrote, "Seasoned musicians often forget to question the things they have been doing for years," and that observation gets to the heart of what so many of my First Floor writings are about. The following piece isn't a diatribe against albums. I love albums! It is, however, a critique of the music industry's tendency to keep doing the same things over and over, ignoring the fact that said things quite possibly first sprouted out of conditions that ceased to be relevant years ago.

———

Back in September, I had the pleasure of interviewing Bambounou, and while most of the conversation focused on his unorthodox (albeit successful) approach to social media, the French producer also said something interesting when asked whether he had any plans to make a new album:

> *People have short attention spans, and although I don't necessarily want to constantly be releasing music, I also don't want to work on an album for five years just so someone can listen to it for 15 seconds and say that it's shit. What's the point of that? I'm not saying I'll never do an album again, but not right now.*

He's likely on to something.

A borderline absurd amount of music is being released these days. Just a few weeks ago, it was reported that 100,000 songs are now being uploaded to streaming services every single day.[1] (Let's assume those 100,000 songs have an average runtime of three minutes; a person would have to spend more than 208 days listening, 24 hours a day, to get through them all.) Consumers—even those who consider themselves dedicated music fans—are being bombarded with content, and when the onslaught of television shows, movies, news, books, podcasts and social media is factored in, very little room is left for new music.

Even I, a person whose career literally revolves around keeping tabs on just one relatively small corner of the music world, have a hard time keeping up. Every week, I receive hundreds of promos, and am alerted to dozens (sometimes hundreds) more by Bandcamp notifications, social media posts and news reports on various websites. Keeping track of them all is a gargantuan task, and even when I try to limit my scope to only those electronic music releases I personally think might be noteworthy or interesting, I'm still often left with more than 100 albums/EPs/singles to consider each and every week. (And when a week includes a Bandcamp Friday, that figure often shoots even higher.) Writing about them all would be impossible, and even mentioning all of the ones I genuinely like is frequently out of the question.

(For what it's worth, somewhere between 10 and 20 tracks from new releases are usually highlighted in the 'New This Week' round-up that appears in the Thursday edition of First Floor,

---

1. Ingham, Tim. "It's Happened: 100,000 Tracks Are Now Being Uploaded to Streaming Services Like Spotify Each Day." *Music Business Worldwide*, October 6, 2022, https://www. musicbusinessworldwide.com/its-happened-100000-tracks-are-now-being-uploaded/.

and that number of reviewed releases holds relatively steady across most music media outlets. Even Pitchfork, which built its entire publication on the back of album reviews, generally only runs about 20-25 reviews per week, and that's across all genres, utilizing both its sizable staff and large freelance pool.)

In this environment, securing press coverage—let alone getting noticed by music fans who aren't actively on the hunt for new music—is something of a crapshoot, especially for new, unestablished and underresourced artists. Being on a big label, being affiliated with known talents/scenes and having the help of a manager/PR company can of course help, but even then there are no guarantees. Having a plan—not to mention a budget—can absolutely give someone a leg up, but in the end, a lot of getting noticed boils down to matters of luck and timing.

Knowing that, maybe making an album isn't the best way to go. When every release is essentially a roll of the music industry dice, what's the point of slaving away on albums and only throwing those dice once every few years?

I like albums. I grew up on albums. They've been the music industry's predominant format since at least the mid 1960s, and have long been marketed as artists' best—and perhaps only—way of making a genuine creative statement. Tradition dictates that singles (and to a lesser degree, EPs) are largely disposable, while albums are weighty tomes worthy of thoughtful consideration. This is rather ironic, especially given that the format itself (i.e. the length of music that constitutes an album) is something that stems from the physical limitations of how much music could be pressed onto vinyl back in the day. Although digital media has essentially eliminated those limits, the album format continues to be placed on a pedestal; when journalists and other industry types chart the course of an artist's career, albums are often the benchmark moments, with particular LPs defining an entire era of a musician's work and accomplishments.

This album-centric worldview wasn't necessarily created with malicious intentions, but it is something that has served the music industry well for decades. Most specifically, it drove album sales, and during the pre-internet era, prompted consumers to pick up LPs and CDs, even when they actually were only interested in a song or two. That was highly profitable, and with that economic engine roaring during the latter half of the 20th century, the entire music industry oriented itself around a model in which the album was at the center. When it came to marketing, the format allowed those doing the selling to deliver a concentrated promotional push, one focused on a single, long-form work of art whose arrival was sold as an "event," much like the arrival of a new blockbuster film.

Journalists have certainly been complicit in pushing the album-as-event narrative, and have continued to champion the format, even as consumers increasingly shift toward singles and playlists in the streaming era. Sentimentality is undoubtedly part of that, but there's also a practical benefit. After all, what's more likely to attract readers (and advertisers)—coverage of "big," supposedly world-changing works of art (and the artists who made them), or steady dispatches about musical movements whose output largely appears in dribs and drabs? It's not a coincidence that the mainstream music press has historically struggled to cover more singles-based genres like hip-hop, dancehall and dance music, and during a time when media outlets have largely gone online and hitched their economic wagon to web traffic and click rates, the pressure to publish content focused on "big" (i.e. familiar) artists and their "big" releases has only intensified. (That may change as revenue-starved outlets increasingly turn to brand partnerships, but for now, most publications remain stuck on the "what will get people clicking?" model.)

Even now, when—thanks to the rise of streaming—album sales are by and large no longer a reliable source of revenue, the format remains a key cog in the industry's money-making machine. For major labels and top-tier artists, a new LP will likely boost streaming income (at least temporarily), but even for smaller and independent acts, albums provide something even more important: a reason to tour. Live performance has supplanted sales as the primary source of income for most artists, and while touring is often presented as a time when artists go on the road and present their latest material, it's probably more honestly framed as just a pretext—especially for more established acts—to travel around, play the hits, sell some merch and collect some cash. (In a sadly ironic twist, even the prospect of making a living via touring now seems to be at risk, particularly in the face of potential Covid infections, rising travel and logistic costs and the predatory practices of corporate-owned venues and ticketing companies.)

Where does that leave the album? Of course it can still be a meaningful, long-form musical statement, but in practical terms, it's basically a business card. It's something that artists create—usually with no expectation of directly making money from it—in hopes that people, both inside and outside the music industry, take notice and theoretically pay for something else down the line. However, in a hopelessly overcrowded content marketplace, the truth is that most of the time, most people won't take notice, and even those that do won't pay attention for long. Think about it: how long do the most successful releases, regardless of genre or format, remain a focus of the cultural discourse? A few days? Less than that?

Late last month, Rihanna—easily one of the biggest pop stars in the world—dropped "Lift Me Up," her first new song in six years, and it took the internet approximately one day to decide the song was mediocre and move on. (It's telling that her subsequent decision to cast Johnny Depp in a fashion show has generated far more sustained conversation.) If someone like Rihanna can barely cut through the noise with a new track, what chance does a new or emerging artist—or even an established one—have of breaking through, even within their own bubble?

Connecting with audiences is harder than ever, and while the music world continues to think of itself as a bastion of artistry and creativity, it's also true that individual artists' popularity, notoriety and longevity increasingly have little to do with the music they make (or in the case of a DJ, what music they play). Getting noticed now often has more to do with ubiquity than individual artistic achievement, which makes the prospect of spending years on a long-form album seem wildly risky. Sure, it might hit and be hailed as a masterful collection of music, but it's far more likely to be ignored. Even if it's enjoyed by a select group of fans and listeners, their attention is likely to be fleeting, and given the way that most people now consume music, that attention will almost surely be focused on just a handful of tracks—or maybe just one track. Streaming has flattened the listening experience, and on most platforms, a 12-track album—or even a 28-track double album—is presented on most artists' pages as no different than a standalone single or three-track EP.

Given that, wouldn't a series of smaller releases make more sense than an album? The benefits are not just practical, but psychological too. When a single or EP comes out and doesn't make waves, it'll likely be far less devastating for the artist than an album flop, and it also leaves them with room to quickly follow it up and try again. No one will complain about an artist releasing three EPs over the course of six months, but when someone drops two full-lengths in the span of a single year, talk of them "putting out too much music" often begins to surface amongst all but the most dedicated fans—even if both albums were largely ignored.

Albums have a sentimental place in the hearts of older music lovers (myself included), and spent decades as the foundation of the entire music industry, but they no longer reflect the way that most people—music lovers included—experience and consume recorded music. Why then, does the music world remain so fixated on the format? Perhaps it's a matter of perception. Artists are often not taken seriously until they've delivered an album, and the music press does continue to devote a disproportionate amount of its coverage to acts in the middle of an album cycle. It's easy for artists to see this and plan their careers accordingly, but they'd likely be better served by realizing that these patterns—like many things in the media and music industry—are rooted in an antiquated way of both making art and doing business.

Although the album format is unlikely to disappear anytime soon, it is on the decline, and for artists simply looking to get noticed—and hopefully build a sustainable career—there are other, more effective ways that they can invest their time and energy. Those ways are frequently derided as vapid and unartistic—and in fairness, they often can be, especially when social media is involved—but they don't have to be. Music and creativity can—and ideally should—still be part of the process, but tying that process to a particular format is shortsighted. If someone genuinely wants to make an album because it's the best way for them to express a particular artistic statement, then they absolutely should. But in an era when most artists' resources are limited, there's no reason for everyone to follow an old blueprint.

Pull Your Music Off Spotify
a.k.a. Bandcamp is the kind of platform we ought to be cultivating.

May 5, 2020
—

I've written a lot about streaming over the past few years, and for good reason—the technology has completely reshaped not just the music industry, but the way that people make, market and consume music itself. It's changed the nature of artistry and devalued the idea of ownership, and even as conversations about the streaming economy (and its many inherent problems) have risen in prominence, it still feels like the impact of streaming has yet to be fully understood. That's likely why I've returned to the topic again and again, and probably could have devoted this whole book to it.

However, in deference to my readers' sanity, I've instead whittled my many streaming-related missives down to just three essays. Written in three different years, I think they demonstrate how my perspective on the issue has evolved over time—this first one, written during the early days of the pandemic, is definitely the most strident of the bunch—but also show how my underlying opinion hasn't changed much. Streaming, despite being extremely popular, was not designed with independent music culture in mind, and will likely always be fundamentally incompatible with creative communities that exist outside the commercial mainstream. Reckoning with that is arguably the music world's largest ongoing challenge, and coming up with effective solutions has proved to be exceedingly difficult. (Even supporting Bandcamp, which is lionized here, has become morally complicated since the company was sold to Epic Games in 2022.)

On a lighter note, it's also hilarious that this piece includes the phrase, "I tend to be wary of donation- and subscription-

based models." In my defense, I hadn't yet turned on paid subscriptions for First Floor, but looking back now, I'm sure glad that I did.

I had a different essay planned for today.

All last week, I was convinced that the second Bandcamp Friday was going to be a disappointment. Although the first one in March had been a massive success, pulling in $4.3 million in sales,[1] I figured that the novelty of the platform giving up its usual 10-15% commission for 24 hours had already worn off. I tend to be wary of donation- and subscription-based models anyways, and knowing that most consumers out there probably had even less disposable income available than they did six weeks prior, I imagined a scenario in which Bandcamp Friday #2 showed a lot of moxie, but ultimately fell a bit flat.

I was wrong.

It only took 14 hours for Bandcamp to match its sales total from March, and yesterday the platform announced a total haul of $7.1 million for the entire event.[2] That's an increase of 65%.

Now, this doesn't mean that I'm going to declare Bandcamp the savior of the music industry. $7.1 million sounds like a lot, but the global music industry brings in tens of billions of dollars of revenue annually. The Bandcamp Friday phenomenon may be encouraging, and it's generated some feelgood anecdotal stories about artists being able to buy groceries or pay their rent, but it's not going to rescue us.

It is, however, a sign that an appetite exists for platforms that truly value the interests of artists and labels, particularly those who operate outside of the mainstream. Barker summed it up nicely (albeit angrily) in a tweet:

---

1. Diamond, Ethan. "Update on Friday's Campaign to Support Artists During the Covid-19 Pandemic." Bandcamp, March 23, 2020, https://daily.bandcamp.com/features/update-on-fridays-campaign-to-support-artists-during-the-covid-19-pandemic.

2. Bandcamp (@Bandcamp). Twitter, May 4, 2020, https://twitter.com/Bandcamp/status/1257357467148746752.

> *While @Spotify are still trying to turn a profit flogging you cheap library music playlists, @Bandcamp are casually taking days off from making money for themselves while being a very real support to artists. At this point Bandcamp are basically funding Spotify content.* [3]

That message was just the beginning of a much longer thread, in which Barker talks about how the Leisure System label (which he helps run) removed its catalog from Spotify earlier this year, and how that subsequently triggered a rise in Bandcamp sales, even before the coronavirus hit.

I think he's onto something. Artists complain about Spotify (and other streaming platforms) all the time, and most of us have seen the ridiculous charts displaying just how little money a stream generates. And yet, artists and labels continue to engage with these platforms, seemingly resigned to the notion that although the situation sucks, it's better to have your music available on Spotify, Apple, Amazon, etc., because that's where the listeners are.

This is just another version of the "exposure" myth that already plagues the music industry. I suppose there's a certain logic to the idea that listeners might "discover" an artist's music on a streaming platform (presumably by hearing it on a playlist), and that could theoretically build momentum that eventually translates into more streams, more merch sales, more gigs and maybe even some actual record sales. In reality though, how often does that happen? And does the success of a tiny fraction of artists justify the fact that everyone else is essentially providing free (or very cheap) content to a platform that's barely compensating them in return? The legitimacy of Spotify and these other streaming platforms is based upon the idea that listeners can log on and find "everything," and that claim, despite being inherently ridiculous, is only bolstered every time that a new artist or new label signs up.

There's an argument out there that artists need to demand higher pay rates from these streaming giants, and it's not without merit.

3. Barker, Sam (@samvoltek). Twitter, May 1, 2020.
   https://twitter.com/samvoltek/status/1256174446903275520.

There's an obvious absurdity to the idea that a company like Google (which owns YouTube and somehow gets way less flak than Spotify) can get away with paying rates that ultimately work out to less than .002 cents per stream. At the same time, it's unlikely that these companies' business models are ever going to change significantly, because it simply wouldn't make financial sense. Although places like Apple and Amazon can comfortably operate their music divisions as a sort of loss-leader, losing millions while ostensibly drawing in customers to their more profitable products and services, streaming leader Spotify has no such luxury, and it's already paying out approximately 70% of its revenue as royalties, mostly to major labels like Universal, Sony Music and Warner. The company may be inching toward profitability, but it's currently still operating at a giant loss (hundreds of millions per year), even as its user base approaches 300 million people worldwide.

Barring some sort of major shift in its business model, Spotify simply won't be capable of paying artists more, and other large platforms are unlikely to take that initiative on their own. Knowing that, there's only one option that makes sense for independent artists and labels: removing their music from streaming platforms.

Perhaps this seems like a call for independent musicians to cut off their nose to spite their face. After all, I've spoken with multiple label owners who've told me that streaming actually accounts for a larger percentage of their income than actual sales. (And yes, these are electronic music labels that presumably are still selling significant quantities of vinyl to DJs and engaged fans.) Given the current state of the discourse in electronic music circles, it's not exactly fashionable for them to say that publicly, but that doesn't make it any less true.

In the long run though, there's little to be gained from continuing to participate in an inherently flawed and unfair system. Some artists and labels may be profiting now, but are they profiting as much as they would have 10 or 20 years ago when people were actually buying music? And what about all of the artists and labels who aren't profiting in the current system?

Shouldn't we do something better for them?

This is where Bandcamp comes in. Again, I'm not saying it's a savior and its platform is honestly far from perfect, but at least its values seem to align with those of independent music communities. Writer Liz Pelly, as she tends to do, put it a lot more eloquently in the following tweet:

> *i hope the excitement of bandcamp days is a reminder for anyone who needs it of what it would feel like to divest from exploitative systems in music generally + focus on more meaningful exchanges (buying music, supporting artists directly/regularly, wherever u choose to do that)*[4]

It's important to remember that the streaming giants are platforms of scale; they are literally designed for the mass market and the commercial mainstream. There may be a lot of bullshit narratives and dewy-eyed nostalgia about "independent" music, but at its core, it's an idea that's not rooted in mass consumption. Spotify thrives on passive listeners (i.e. the folks who simply hit "play" and let music stream endlessly in the background), but passive consumption is antithetical to the idea of independent music, which generally requires listeners to dig a little deeper and seek it out. (If we're being honest, the scarcity and exclusivity of independent music is also part of what makes it fun.)

That's what makes a platform like Bandcamp so appealing. At least for now, it's not geared towards the mainstream. It may not be on the radar of the "average" listener, but maybe it's time for independent music culture to stop caring about the "average" listener. It's silly for an experimental noise artist to be operating in the same sphere as Drake, but that's what's happening on Spotify. Why don't we cultivate spaces that cater only to the folks who really want to be there? Bandcamp is one of those spaces, and unlike many of the streaming giants, its operation is already profitable. This is the kind of self-sustaining ecosystem that we should be supporting and growing—sustainably, of course.

---

4. Pelly, Liz (@lizpelly). Twitter, May 2, 2020.
   https://twitter.com/lizpelly/status/1256590958579286017.

I don't think Spotify is going anywhere. Even if independent artists and labels everywhere suddenly pulled their music off the giant streaming platforms, those companies are going to be fine; most of their revenue comes from mainstream music anyways. When I advocate for artists and labels to stop engaging with Spotify, it's not because I think we're going to collectively take them down, or even prompt any kind of large-scale reforms. If that happened, it would of course be great, but in the meantime, I suggest that we leave them to do their thing and focus on building something better for ourselves.

The Monetization of Apathy
a.k.a. A bitter truth about what people are listening to and why.

April 12, 2022

—

This piece is ostensibly about fake artists on streaming platforms, but looking it over again, what I think it's really about is my own resignation to the idea that the streaming problem most likely won't ever be fixed in any sort of meaningful way.

When First Floor started, critiques of the streaming economy were less frequent than they are now, and many consumers simply weren't aware of the inequities baked into the system. One could believe that the listening public simply lacked all the relevant information, and that once informed, they'd want to do the right thing. Yet as the years wore on, and the streaming conversation became practically inescapable, even in mainstream music circles, nothing really changed. Spotify suffered through a lot of bad press, but there's been no major customer exodus, let alone major progress in terms of getting artists paid more. Seeing this unfold, I've increasingly found myself thinking, "Maybe the average consumer just doesn't give a shit about this issue." Perhaps that's unfair, and I don't mean to deflect blame from corporate bad actors, but as this essay lays out, the streaming economy thrives on listener apathy, and hoping to change that feels more like wishful thinking than a realistic plan for reform.

———

Spotify has a fake artists problem. That's not news. In fact, Music Business Worldwide first reported on the issue all the way back in 2016.[1] (It wasn't until a year later that the story really blew

1. Ingham, Tim. "Spotify Is Making Its Own Records... and Putting Them on Playlists." *Music Business Worldwide*, August 31, 2016, https://www.musicbusinessworldwide.com/spotify-is-creating-its-own-recordings-and-putting-them-on-playlists/.

up,[2] prompting Spotify to issue a fierce denial of the allegations and state: "We do not own rights, we're not a label, all our music is licensed from rights holders and we pay them—we don't pay ourselves.")[3]

The story has continued to develop over the past five years, and despite the rash of negative attention thrown Spotify's way, fake artists have continued to proliferate across all of the major streaming platforms. As detailed in another Music Business Worldwide story which dropped last month, it seems that much of the initial "fake artists" boom was not necessarily the direct work of Spotify, but something initiated by a group of small labels (many of them in Sweden) looking to game the streaming system.[4] For instance, Swedish label Firefly Entertainment, which has managed to get its music placed on nearly 500 first-party Spotify playlists (i.e. playlists run and curated by Spotify itself), has at least 830 fake artists on the platform, although it seems the the bulk of the music credited to them was created by as few as 20 songwriters, most of whom were presumably paid an upfront flat fee and/or a reduced royalty rate on the back end.

Why would Firefly do this? It's a numbers game, where labels flood the zone with cheaply created music that's been purposely designed to fit streaming platforms' mood- and genre-based playlists. If just a handful of songs land choice spots on popular playlists, they can generate millions—even billions—of streams, bringing in lots of income to the commissioning label, which doesn't have to then split those profits with artists at the usual rate. (On a related note, there's also an entire ecosystem of spammers working to exploit streaming platforms' search algorithms for profit, often by creating misleading[5] or flat-out

2. Raymond, Adam K. "The Streaming Problem: How Spammers, Superstars, and Tech Giants Gamed the Music Industry." *Vulture*, July 5, 2017, https://www.vulture.com/2017/07/streaming-music-cheat-codes.html.

3. Gensler, Andy. "Spotify on Non-Existent Artist Allegations: 'We Do Not and Have Never Created Fake Artists'." *Billboard*, July 7, 2017, https://www.billboard.com/music/music-news/spotify-fake-artist-allegations-response-7858015/.

4. Ingham, Tim. "Remember Spotify's Fake Artists? They're Still Going Strong – and Still Attracting Scandal." *Music Business Worldwide*, March 28, 2022, https://www.musicbusinessworldwide.com/remember-spotify-fake-artist-theyre-still-going-strong-and-still-attracting-scandal/.

5. Pahwah, Nitish. "The Artist Impostors of Spotify." *Slate*, May 10, 2021, https://slate.com/technology/2021/05/spotify-same-name-artists-impostors.html.

generic[6] artist names.)

These practices may be morally questionable (and that's being kind), but they've also been lucrative for at least some industry actors, which is why the major labels have also gotten in on the act. Rolling Stone reported back in 2019 that Sony had adopted an "if you can't beat them, join them" approach, creating its own fake artists and racking up billions of streams in the process.[7] And according to yet another recent Music Business Worldwide story—which admittedly consists of a list of allegations (some of them unproven) from an anonymous reader who claims to "have a pretty extensive background in the music business working for both rights holders and retailers"—the practice has only grown since then, with the likes of Warner and Universal joining in.[8]

As music industry schemes go, these streaming manipulations do feel particularly depressing. Although music has always been plagued by nefarious actors looking to game the system, what's happening now is more surgical than the corrupt practices of old. Writer Ted Gioia recently discussed the topic in his Honest Broker newsletter, and said the following:

> *This kind of scam wasn't possible before streaming. People obviously listened to music while studying or working, but they either picked out the record themselves, or relied on a radio station to make the choice. Radio stations were sometimes guilty of taking payola, but even in those instances a human being could be held accountable. But with AI now making the decisions, everything can be hidden away in the code.*[9]

6. Slattery, Peter. "Why Spotify Has So Many Bizarre, Generic Artists Like 'White Noise Baby Sleep'." *OneZero*, September 22, 2020, https://onezero.medium.com/why-spotify-has-so-many-bizarre-generic-artists-like-white-noise-baby-sleep-c9ce09dc9002.

7. Ingham, Tim. "'Fake Artists' Have Billions of Streams on Spotify. Is Sony Now Playing the Service at Its Own Game?" *Rolling Stone*, May 15, 2019, https://www.rollingstone.com/pro/features/fake-artists-have-billions-of-streams-on-spotify-is-sony-now-playing-the-service-at-its-own-game-834746/.

8. Stassen, Murray. "An MBW Reader Just Blew Open the Spotify Fake Artists Story." *Music Business Worldwide*, March 30, 2022, https://www.musicbusinessworldwide.com/an-mbw-reader-just-blew-open-the-spotify-fake-artists-story-heres-what-they-have-to-say/.

9. Gioia, Ted. "The Fake Artists Problem Is Much Worse Than You Realize." *The Honest Broker*, April 9, 2022, https://tedgioia.substack.com/p/the-fake-artists-problem-is-much.

Spotify didn't invent passive listening, as anyone who's encountered an unobtrusive "lite rock less talk" radio station can attest. Streaming has, however, accelerated the rise of passive listening, and in the process has exposed (and capitalized on) an ugly truth that diehard music fans will likely find hard to swallow: most people really don't give a shit about what they're listening to.

As easy as it is to demonize Spotify and the various profit-seeking actors in the streaming universe, it's worth noting that many of their practices simply wouldn't be possible if consumers were more interested in the contents of their listening diet. (When it comes to fake artists, most of them are incredibly easy to spot, provided that the user is actually paying attention.)

This apathy isn't necessarily a new development; while it's essentially impossible to measure the collective level of "caring about music" over time, it's unlikely that the appearance of streaming has single-handedly ushered in a precipitous drop in consumer interest. Passionate music fans obviously still exist in large numbers—and in many ways have become turbocharged by the internet (e.g. online stan armies)—but even if aggregate consumer interest in music has declined somewhat during the past 20 years, at least some of that can be attributed to the rise of the video games, social media, smartphones and all of the other things clamoring for our attention.

Without falling into a "blame the consumer" argument—the music industry is still the proverbial "bad guy" in this scenario —there's no question that people's access to music has definitely changed, as has how much they're being charged for it. In the pre-streaming era, even casual fandom required more active engagement. Thirty years ago, listening to music often necessitated physically going to a store and purchasing it; people back then may have followed corporate-driven charts and trends, but active selection on their part was nonetheless part of the process, regardless of their passion level. Granted, not everyone was purchasing new albums every week, but even if a person's entire music diet consisted of listening to terrestrial radio, the songs being played were all made by "real" artists and were selected by "real" people, as opposed to an algorithm. (Again, that system was far from perfect or fair; the payola that Gioia mentioned was definitely a problem, as was the major labels' stranglehold on playlists.)

Radio still exists of course, but its influence on music has now been dwarfed by streaming, where the royalty rates paid to rights holders are significantly lower. The problematic economics don't stop there either, as streaming platforms offer consumers access to a virtually infinite number of songs, and do so for a ridiculously low price. (According to music industry news and analysis outlet Music Ally, more than 50% of Spotify's 406 million monthly active users utilize the platform's free tier,[10] and while the company does have 180 million premium subscribers, those customers are only paying $9.99 a month in the US, and less in many other markets. Even when inflation isn't factored in, that is significantly less than how much a single album cost 20 years ago.)

When streaming's cost of entry is so low, the need for active engagement and thoughtful selection all but disappears, and individual pieces of music become effectively disposable. With an unlimited supply of music (not to mention a skip button) at their disposal, the average user faces no real consequences when they select a song—or even an entire album or playlist—that they don't like, so why not press play and let the platform run? If someone is just looking for something to fill the silence when they're working or making dinner, what does it matter anyways?

If streaming platforms had a fixed payment model (e.g. paying a set price per stream), perhaps their encouragement of this kind of passive listening wouldn't be so bad. After all, more plays would generate more money, regardless of how or why that play happened in the first place. Unfortunately though, things aren't that simple. Most companies employ a pro-rata payment model—where rights holders are paid based on their percentage of total plays across the entire platform—which means that as both the size of the total streaming audience and the total number of artists posting their

10. Dredge, Stuart. "How many users do Spotify, Apple Music and other streaming services have?" *Music Ally*, February 3, 2022, https://musically.com/2022/02/03/spotify-apple-how-many-users-big-music-streaming-services/.

music on these platforms continue to grow, individual artists often wind up earning less and less per stream.

This is why Spotify continues to push narratives—most prominently via Loud & Clear, an ongoing campaign to bolster the company's reputation that relies heavily on cherry-picked data—that say a per-stream rate isn't a "a meaningful number to analyze." (Given that Spotify is already paying out almost 70% of its annual revenue to rights holders, it also stands to reason that paying a fixed per-stream rate would potentially sink the company financially, barring major changes to its pricing and/or business model.) Although many in the music world have called for a switch to a user-centric payment model—in which rights holders are compensated according to the percentage of time that each individual user on a platform spends listening to their music—Spotify has also echoed reports claiming that the impact of such a change wouldn't be transformative for the industry at large. (For what it's worth, said reports haven't stopped other platforms like Tidal, SoundCloud and Deezer from adopting—or at least announcing plans to adopt—user-centric schemes, albeit in a limited fashion.)

Zooming out from the particulars of streaming payment models—the discussion of which can admittedly be somewhat mind-numbing—it's important to consider what the explosion of streaming truly represents: the transformation of the passive music economy. Spotify isn't making its money by converting dedicated fans of niche artists and genres into mindless playlist zombies; it's making money by offering a convenient, cheap and easy-to-use product to people who never cared all that much about music in the first place. It's true that in decades past, those passive consumers would have bought more records/tapes/CDs/MP3s, but only because they had to, not because they were truly dying to have the music in their personal collection. Music ownership these days is less about utility and more about having a personal totem that underscores an individual's emotional connection to an artist and their work. Most listeners aren't interested in that, so is it any wonder that so many of them have opted for streaming instead?

It's difficult to shed too many tears about streaming's impact on the musical mainstream. That ecosystem was corrupt and overtly commercial before, and it largely remains so now, even as its logistics have changed. The shift from Top 40 radio and corporate chain stores to Spotify and TikTok might be interesting to track on an academic level, but on an artistic level, that sphere is still largely producing shallow dreck, regardless of what your local poptimist might tell you.

What is worrisome, however, is how the unraveling of the pre-streaming music economy has impacted independent musicians and the communities they cultivated. The line between the commercial mainstream and independent music has long been fuzzy—and it's only gotten fuzzier during the past few decades—but there was a time where independent artists and labels could operate in a self-sustaining fashion, relying on income from the sales of (relatively) small-batch releases in tandem with touring. Few artists were getting wildly rich in the process, but they could eke out a decent living. Over time, the sales half of that equation has been eroded (primarily by streaming), and during the past two years of Covid, the touring half has been upended as well.

In fairness, it's unrealistic for artists and labels to expect that business models from the 1990s and 2000s should still be valid today. Things change, technology evolves and everyone—not just creative types—has to adapt. At the same time, the dominant streaming platforms clearly haven't catered their model to the needs and norms of independent music, and nothing else has emerged to properly fill the void. Subscription-based platforms (e.g. Patreon) have laid out a potential new revenue model for artists, and certain pockets of Web3 are also working to reset the music economy, but widespread adoption of these things has yet to materialize. In the meantime, artists are left flailing, forced to play a game (i.e. streaming) in which they are impossibly overmatched and have no real stake in setting the rules.

For those whose life and/or livelihood is tied up in music —especially independent music—all of this can be incredibly disheartening. Opting out would seem to be the obvious solution, but when streaming is effectively the only game in town—according to a report from the RIAA, it was responsible for 83% of US music industry revenues in 2020[11]— not engaging with those platforms can seem suicidal, especially for emerging artists.

There's no easy answer, and consumers—at least as of now —aren't really on artists' side. It's no secret that Spotify and other streaming giants are giving artists a raw deal, and yet their customer base continues to grow. These companies and all of the other profit-chasing entities in their orbit—including the various fake-artist factories out there—have recognized (some might say weaponized) listener apathy, reorienting the entire music economy around two basic principles:

1. People want convenience.

2. Said convenience should be as cheap as possible.

What about things like artistry, community and economic sustainability? Sadly, they don't make the list. Streaming has monetized some of consumers' least altruistic impulses, and has done so while brazenly claiming to have "saved" the music industry. People might complain about it on social media—and rack up tons of likes in the process—but unless consumers start expressing that same discontent with their wallets, the dynamics of streaming are unlikely to change anytime soon. Independent music may have the moral high ground, but it's going to be hard pressed to compete with consumers' desire to turn off their brains and simply press play.

11. Friedlander, Joshua P. "2020 Year-End Music Industry Revenue Report." Recording Industry Association of America, February 26, 2021, https://www.riaa.com/wp-content/uploads/2021/02/2020-Year-End-Music-Industry-Revenue-Report.pdf.

Streaming Should Pay More, But How?
a.k.a. Spotify and the rest obviously have other priorities, and it's far from clear that consumers have any appetite for price hikes.

March 14, 2023
—

If resignation was the driving force behind the previous essay, this third and final streaming piece is evidence of my full-blown exasperation with the streaming debate. Streaming is objectively bad for numerous sectors of the music world, and arguably for music itself, but that line of reasoning, at least so far, has by and large fallen flat with consumers, who continue to flock to platforms like Spotify in ever-higher numbers.

It's a maddening situation, and as long as streaming critics' strategy continues to primarily revolve around goofing on Daniel Ek (who, in fairness, does seem like a colossal dork), finding new ways to say "Spotify is bad" and floating economically impossible ideas for reform, the possibility of meaningful change often seems remote. This piece isn't a hopeful one, but it does present what I think is a realistic evaluation of the status quo, along with some thoughts about how independent artists might best approach streaming in the years ahead.

———

Almost a year has gone by since I last dedicated an edition of the newsletter specifically to streaming, and frankly, things haven't improved much since then. According to a report by the Recording Industry Association of America, streaming accounted for 84% of recorded music revenue in the US last year,[1] and yet companies like Spotify, Apple and Amazon continue to pay rights holders the equivalent of fractions of a penny per stream. Artists have

1. Friedlander, Joshua P. "2022 Year-End Music Industry Revenue Report." Recording Industry Association of America, March 9, 2023, https://www.riaa.com/wp-content/uploads/2023/03/2022-Year-End-Music-Industry-Revenue-Report.pdf.

now spent years clamoring for higher payments, but Spotify is actively going in the other direction, announcing just last week that it would be expanding its Discovery Mode program, in which rights holders accept even lower royalty rates in exchange for an algorithmic boost (i.e. better placement) on the platform. Between that and with the company's new TikTok-style vertical feed, which will place an even larger premium on algorithmically selected content than before, it's exceedingly clear that Spotify is far more interested in its own survival than that of the artists who provide its content offerings.

Of course it is! Spotify is a multibillion-dollar corporation operating at a global scale, as are its primary competitors. These companies might make the occasional noise about helping artists—Spotify's ongoing Loud & Clear campaign is perhaps the most prominent example—but no amount of "we really care" branding can obscure the fact that streaming is not an altruistically or artistically minded enterprise. It's a service, and a cheap one at that. It's not geared towards artists, or even music lovers; it's been optimized for passive listening (i.e. consumers who are perfectly content to be fed content options and let the algorithm do its thing), and with each passing year, it's starting to look more and more like commercial radio with a skip button. (If predictions that Spotify's new interface will lead to an uptick in the quantity of advertising on the platform prove to be correct, then the radio comparisons will be even harder to avoid.)

Less than three decades have passed since Napster, iTunes, MP3 blogs and filesharing completely upended the music ecosystem, and yet the industry has somehow circled back to a place where music consumption and distribution is largely controlled by just a handful of giant corporations. (In comparison to today, the '90s music landscape actually looks like a bastion of competition and free enterprise; there were more major labels and more companies that owned radio stations, not to mention a robust independent music ecosystem where artists outside the commercial mainstream could potentially carve out a modest living on record sales and touring alone.) The anger directed at streaming companies is totally understandable, and over the past few years, it's most frequently been funneled into two specific calls for reform:

1. Higher streaming royalty rates. The top demand in the Union of Musicians and Allied Workers' highly publicized Justice at Spotify campaign is for the company to pay "at least one cent per stream."

2. Switching to a user-centric royalty payment model. This is more complicated. Streaming companies are presently using a pro-rata model, in which all revenue is put into a single pot, and is then distributed to rights holders by calculating the percentage of total streams on the platform they've accumulated in a particular territory during a particular time period. For example, if 20% of all US Spotify streams are for Drake songs in a given month, then the rights holders of his music would receive 20% of the total American royalty payouts for that month. A user-centric model would take a different approach, calculating royalty percentages on a user-specific basis. So if a single subscriber listens to nothing but Aphex Twin for an entire month, then Aphex Twin would receive all of the royalties generated by that one user during that month. While studies on the potential economic benefits for individual rights holders within a user-centric model have so far provided mixed results, user-centric payments are still widely seen as inherently more fair, simply because they directly correspond to individual listening behavior. It's not a coincidence that the adoption of a user-centric payment model is the second demand in the UMAW's aforementioned Justice at Spotify campaign.

Have you stopped reading yet? The complexities of royalty payments alone are enough to get most consumers to start tuning out of the streaming conversation, which is perhaps why that conversation so often gets boiled down to "pay artists more." That demand sounds simple enough, and it's the sort of slogan that pretty much anyone can get on board with (and "like" on their favorite social media platform), but it ignores one major problem: Even if streaming companies wanted to pay more to rights holders—and to be clear, they don't want to—they couldn't.

Spotify lost €270 million during the fourth quarter of 2022,[2] despite the fact that its subscriber and active user numbers reached unprecedented new heights.[3] The company claims to already be paying nearly 70% of every dollar it generates to rights holders, with more than $3 billion total having been paid out during the last two years alone.[4] How much higher can those numbers realistically go? Perhaps the fact that Spotify recently laid off 6% of its global workforce will help the company's margins,[5] but considering the giant financial hole it's already in, it's unlikely that calls to effectively triple its royalty rate (which is what critics' oft-repeated "penny per stream" demand effectively represents) are financially feasible.

Streaming critics often point to Spotify's deals with podcaster Joe Rogan (reportedly more than $200 million[6]) and soccer team FC Barcelona (reportedly more than $300 million[7]) as signs that the company has plenty of money to spend. But let's say that all $500 million of that money was instead split equally between

2. Szalai, Georg and Vlessing, Etan. "Spotify Hits 205M Paying Subs, Grows Ad Revenue, But Loss Widens Amid Higher Expenses." *The Hollywood Reporter*, January 31, 2023, https://www. hollywoodreporter.com/business/business-news/spotify-earnings-subscribers-fourth-quarter-2022-advertising-1235312606/.

3. "Spotify Reports Fourth Quarter 2022 Earnings." Spotify, January 31, 2023, https://newsroom. spotify.com/2023-01-31/spotify-reports-fourth-quarter-2022-earnings/.

4. Aswad, Jem. "Spotify's Payments to the Music Industry Nearing $40 Billion." *Variety*, March 8, 2023, https://variety.com/2023/music/news/spotify-payments-music-industry-40-billion-1235547087/.

5. Dillet, Romain. "Spotify cuts 6% of its workforce, impacting 600 people." *TechCrunch*, January 23, 2023, https://techcrunch.com/2023/01/23/spotify-cuts-6-of-its-workforce-impacting-600-people/.

6. Strauss, Matthew. "Spotify Sources Say Joe Rogan's Deal Was $200 Million, Double What Was Originally Reported." *Pitchfork*, February 17, 2022, https://pitchfork.com/news/spotify-sources-say-joe-rogan-deal-was-dollar200-million-double-what-was-originally-reported/.

7. Shaw, Lucas and Gualtieri, Thomas and Bloomberg. "Spotify Camp Nou? FC Barcelona will rename its stadium in reported $300 million deal as it tries to climb out of a financial hole." *Fortune*, March 16, 2022, https://fortune.com/2022/03/16/spotify-camp-nou-fc-barcelona-rename-stadium-300-million-deal-financial-hole/.

all 200,000 of what Spotify's Loud & Clear campaign describes as "professional or professionally aspiring recording acts globally" on the platform. Each act would receive a one-time payment of $2500. That's not nothing, but it's not exactly life-changing money, let alone anything resembling a living wage. (And if some larger fraction of the more than 11 million total artists on Spotify were included in these theoretical payments,[8] the amount would drop even further.) Moreover, considering that these controversial Rogan and FC Barcelona deals were spread over multiple years and also generated revenue the company wouldn't have received otherwise, eliminating them wouldn't necessarily put Spotify in the black.

No matter how much cost-cutting Spotify and the other streaming companies do, there's likely only one way for them to increase revenue to a point where significantly higher streaming payouts would be possible: raising prices.

Apple has already gone this route, raising its individual monthly subscription price (in the US) from $9.99 to $10.99 last October. Spotify, however, remains at $9.99 per month, the exact same price it's had in the US since the company's launch there in 2011. (For what it's worth, Amazon Music is also $9.99 per month.) Especially in light of recent inflation, it's absurd that these companies—and especially Spotify—have maintained such low price points, even if it was done in an effort to build their respective customer bases and theoretically get consumers "hooked" on paying for music. It's true that the convenience, reliability and low price of services like Spotify have likely transformed at least some illegal downloaders into paying customers, but after more than 11 years, streaming has also given rise to a broad listening public that expects access to what they (inaccurately) see as all of recorded music for less than what a single album cost throughout the 1990s. More people may be paying for music now, but when they're paying so little, it's not hard to see that music as a whole has been devalued as a result.

Artists need consumers to pay more for streaming, but here's the question that even the harshest streaming critics often refuse

8. Stassen, Murray. "Spotify Added 3M New Creators to Its Platform Last Year... and 4 Other Things We Learned from the Firm's Q4 Earnings Call." *Music Business Worldwide*, February 3, 2022, https://www.musicbusinessworldwide.com/spotify-added-3m-new-creators-to-its-platform-last-year-and-4-other-things-we-learned-from-the-firms-q4-earnings-call/.

to ask: what if they don't want to?

When it comes to streaming, the proverbial genie is already out of the bottle. The technology is widespread, easy to use and well liked by most consumers, especially young ones. People under 20 have never experienced a world where purchasing music is the dominant form of music consumption, and though more dedicated fans can of course be nudged towards buying physical albums or purchasing digital music on Bandcamp, Beatport and other sales platforms, it's difficult to imagine a contemporary music ecosystem in which streaming doesn't play a significant (or even dominant) role. Streaming may not provide the most meaningful experience, but casual fans often aren't interested in that. For listeners who see music as just something to put on in the background, things like price and convenience take precedence, which is why even if Spotify was to go belly up tomorrow, other companies—most likely Apple and Amazon, who have other revenue sources and don't necessarily need their streaming operations to turn a profit—would happily step in and gobble up its market share. (There's also YouTube, which pays even lower royalty rates, is used by more than 25% of the planet every month and yet somehow never seems to attract much sustained criticism from the music world.[9])

Consumers didn't create this system, but in 2023, they are accustomed to it, and if their current spending habits are any indication, they don't seem terribly bothered by how streaming has negatively impacted artists or the larger musical landscape. Spotify has weathered literally years of bad press and vocal critiques from a number of verifiable musical icons, and yet the company's customer base continues to grow larger and larger. Perhaps that says something about our society's collective ethical failings or how "doing the right thing" is often not a priority in a capitalist system, but on a simpler level, music consumers are rational actors, and regardless of how they feel about Spotify or any other company, they likely recognize that when it comes to streaming, they're getting a pretty amazing deal.

9. Dixon, S. "Monthly active users (MAU) on selected social media platforms worldwide in 2022 and 2026." Statista, October 2022, https://www.statista.com/statistics/1350018/social-media-mau-global/.

Could streaming prices go higher? Absolutely, but where exactly do they need to be? Should streaming cost $12/month? $15? $20? $50? It's impossible to know, especially when any price increase will likely prompt at least some consumers to abandon these platforms altogether, especially when several companies continue to offer free, ad-supported tiers. If the past behavior of major media and communications companies (e.g. cellular service, cable television, internet providers) is any indication, the best way to minimize customer losses would be to implement price increases on an incremental basis. Apple already seems to be following that path, but even if companies like Spotify wanted to start meeting artists' demands for higher payments—and again, they don't—it's unlikely that an additional $1 per month is going to allow them to get to where they'd need to be to make that happen. For the sake of argument, let's say that $20 per month is what they ought to be charging; Spotify couldn't just double its prices all at once without losing a giant chunk of its customer base. Getting to that price point would take years, and in the meantime, more and more artists would be left to struggle to survive in a system that was never designed to benefit them.

Back in 2020, I wrote a piece titled "Streaming Can't Be Fixed," and my feelings on the matter haven't changed much over the past few years. Streaming might be framed as a bastion of listener choice and a way for artists to independently forge their own path, but it's ultimately successful because it works for A) the most famous/popular/established artists in the world, B) the bulk of the listening public, who are primarily interested in hearing those artists, C) the major labels who release music from those artists and D) the streaming companies who bring all these groups together. Things like independent artists and labels, local music scenes and music that isn't specifically designed to be easily and repeatedly consumable... they're not really part of the equation, at least not in any significant way.

That's a tough pill to swallow, particularly when so much of the music economy now revolves around streaming, and it's put companies like Spotify in an incredibly advantageous position. At the moment, there is no real viable alternative to streaming, which allows these companies to present themselves as saviors, touting an "it's us or illegal downloading" narrative that much of the commercial music industry has bought into. That narrative isn't completely bogus either; although streaming companies are probably more accurately described as "opportunists" than "saviors," it's not like file-sharing technology has magically disappeared during the past decade. Though it's true that illegal downloading is far too often used as a kind of boogeyman to justify streaming companies' behavior, if their prices were to suddenly spike dramatically, how long would it take for consumers—and especially tech-savvy young people—to start flocking to Soulseek and other comparable platforms? Not everyone would go that route of course, but blowing a hole in the music economy would only require a certain percentage of consumers to make the switch.

So what should artists do? Just give up? Of course not, but those grousing on the internet and hoping that Spotify and all the rest will someday collapse under the weight of public criticism will likely continue to be frustrated and disappointed. Personally, I'd advocate for the following:

Lobby for government regulation

This is already happening, most notably in the UK, where a parliamentary committee in 2021 opened a formal inquiry into the economics of music streaming. This has resulted in a report calling for a "complete reset" of the streaming market, and has elevated the pointed critiques made by likes of musician Tom Gray and his #BrokenRecord campaign, but it has yet to result in significant reforms or new legislation.

Over in the US, Congresswoman Rashida Tlaib last year introduced a resolution calling for the creation of a new streaming royalty. That generated lots of positive press and prompted more than 14,000 people to write their congressional representative and support the resolution, but it has yet to gain serious legislative traction. Back in 2021, US House Judiciary Committee Chairman Jerry Nadler and Internet Chairman Hank Johnson Jr. wrote a letter to Spotify, concerned about the potential "race to the bottom" effect of its Discovery Mode program, and those concerns were subsequently echoed by representatives Yvette D. Clarke, Judy Chu and Tony Cardenas in another letter that was sent last year, but again, no legislation has come out of these efforts.

Nevertheless, it is significant that governments have started to recognize the issues around streaming, and while translating that recognition into new laws and regulations will undoubtedly be difficult and time-consuming, it does perhaps represent a more realistic path toward concrete change. Public outcry hasn't prompted Spotify and other streaming outlets to significantly change their ways, and they're certainly not going to adjust their business model based on some kind of internal moral awakening. These companies exist to make a profit, and they're not going to change unless they're forced to change. Barring a mass consumer and artist exodus from their platforms—and neither of those seem likely—then government intervention will be the only way to get Spotify and the rest to alter their course and increase payouts.

Accept streaming for what it is

Streaming is unfair, for a myriad of reasons, and the experience it offers doesn't align with the values that most musicians—especially independent musicians—hold dear (or at least claim to). That said, it also doesn't seem to be going anywhere, which leaves artists and labels with a choice: engage with streaming platforms on their own terms, or take their music elsewhere. It's an undeniably shitty choice, but when concrete reform is likely years away (if it's coming at all), artists still have to make it.

Some labels require their artists to have their music available on streaming services, but musicians working on their own can actively choose where they do and don't want their music to appear.

(Even amongst those signed to labels, plenty of independent imprints would likely be amenable to removing an artist's music from streaming if said artist was adamant in their opposition to it.) Artists should ask themselves the question, "Is being on streaming platforms really worth it?" For many, the answer is probably "no." If streaming isn't bringing in much income, and it's also not fostering discovery of one's music, then what exactly is the point of working with these companies? It's true that Spotify and other platforms are where the bulk of the listening audience is currently located, but when that audience is mostly interested in major label stars, recycled old hits and unassuming background music, is that really where artists—especially more adventurous and left-of-center musicians who aren't concerned with finding mainstream success—want to focus their efforts?

There are consequences to removing one's music from Spotify, and doing so will undoubtedly prompt certain fans to complain about it on social media, but from a purely financial standpoint, the numbers can often make sense, particularly if eliminating the streaming option prompts even a slight uptick in sales via platforms like Bandcamp. If the average digital track costs $1 to purchase, that's worth approximately 300 streams; does the "discovery" aspect of Spotify and other streaming platforms really justify that disparity? Maybe not, especially when there are numerous other ways for artists to connect with their fans (and potential new fans); those ways (e.g. social media, Discord servers, media coverage, live shows) might take longer to build and ultimately have a lower ceiling in terms of potential reach, but they also present opportunities for engagement that goes a lot deeper than hearing a song on a random streaming playlist.

Streaming doesn't have to be an all-or-nothing proposition, either. Even amongst those artists and labels dissatisfied with the streaming status quo, plenty still want to have their music available on these platforms, simply for the sake of accessibility. If they're comfortable with that tradeoff—and clearly, many of them are—having their music on Spotify doesn't mean they have to orient their entire practice towards succeeding on that platform. (Considering that doing so would involve competing with literally the most popular artists on the planet, it's not the smartest strategy for independent artists anyways.) They can still drive their fans toward Bandcamp, create exclusive releases and merch that has to be purchased and build their fan bases through live shows, social media, collaborations and whatever else they'd like to try. Moreover, they can do all of that while publicly criticizing the streaming status quo. It might prompt a few cries about hypocrisy (e.g. "How can you complain about Spotify when your music is on there?"), but in a grossly imperfect system, following this dual path is sometimes what works best. There's obviously nothing wrong with artists advocating for changes to streaming, but accepting that real change is a remote possibility—at least for the time being—and making decisions based on the realities of the present day can also be healthy, especially when it leaves them with more time and energy to focus on promotional and creative methodologies that make sense for their own practice.

Righteous indignation is easy, and it certainly plays well on social media, but to date, it hasn't done much to improve the streaming economy for artists. Spotify and the other streaming companies aren't going to do the right thing, and it doesn't look like consumers plan to either. In the face of that, why should artists have to be idealists? Like everyone else, they're trying to make their way in the world, and though pulling their music off streaming platforms is an admirable stand to take, it's hard to fault anyone who doesn't want to step into that particular abyss alone.

The Cost of Passion
a.k.a. Musicians aren't magicians, and what they do is work.

November 29, 2022

—

What is music worth? In the streaming era, one could reasonably answer "not much." And what about all the people who work in music? More often than not, they aren't perceived as very valuable either.

Having worked in the music industry for more than two decades, I'm often struck by just how little the average person understands about how the proverbial sausage gets made. The fact that those details aren't public is, of course, part of music's allure—it's show business after all, and things like spreadsheets and royalty rates aren't particularly glamorous—but even as most people recognize that the music industry is a relatively dirty business, the (blatantly false) idea persists that everyone involved in it is joyously living some kind of fantasy life.

The following piece explores that contradiction. The music industry is broken, but many of its most exploitative practices simply would not be possible without the widespread indifference of the listening public.

———

The music industry runs on passion.

I know, I know. Aside from sounding like a total cliché, that sentence reads like something a branding agency might slip into a pitch deck. However, if we set aside all notions of vapid sloganeering, there's still a nugget of truth in there.

The music industry does run on passion, but not because those who work in it (or simply aspire to) are a uniquely driven bunch.

No, it runs on passion in the sense that music—like most creative endeavors—is something that most consumers (and even some artists) don't consider to be real work. Musicians usually aren't seen as laborers; they're thought to be "living the dream," and while exploiting/underpaying/undervaluing them isn't necessarily thought to be okay, it's rarely regarded as a serious problem.

Journalist and artist manager Brandon Stosuy hinted at this in a tweet earlier this year:

> in the music industry everyone wants to get paid and nobody wants to pay anybody[1]

It's not as though consumers are intentionally looking to screw artists over. Many of them likely want to support artists, but they usually wind up falling short. Why? Because they've been led to participate in systems that were set up to capitalize on their apathy. Take streaming for example. Most people would never walk into a record shop and steal an artist's latest album, but they will go and stream that same album online, even when they know that the artist will likely only be paid a few pennies as a result. They might not feel great about it—some might even rail against the evils of Spotify on social media—but few will feel bad enough to cancel their subscriptions or go purchase the music instead.

Streaming companies know this, and while the low cost and general convenience of their product are certainly key to its appeal, there's also a psychological component at work. Thanks to these platforms (not to mention the proliferation of digital production software and DIY distribution services), music is now more plentiful and readily available than ever. That's frequently spun as a good thing (and it can be), but there is a downside: music has lost much of its perceived value, and those who make it are increasingly regarded as a sort of eminently replaceable workforce.

That's not entirely new—celebrity has always had a certain level of disposability—but it's nonetheless ironic that in a society

1. Stosuy, Brandon (@brandonstosuy). Twitter, April 5, 2022, https://twitter.com/brandonstosuy/status/1511338917181669376.

obsessed with fame, and in which the most successful artists are often placed on ridiculous cultural pedestals, the bulk of the creator class is still seen as expendable. Artists are generally regarded as "lucky" to be doing what they do, and if they dare to speak up and say that they're not happy with their working conditions or that they're not making enough money to survive, it usually doesn't take long for someone to point out that there are countless others who would happily step in and take their place.

This attitude is pervasive throughout the music industry, and helps explain how exposure has for so long been regarded as an acceptable form of compensation. Artists—especially those who are newcomers—are routinely approached by larger platforms (e.g. festivals, brands, magazines, more established acts) and asked to perform/create/contribute (i.e. work) for little or no money, with the justification that the exposure they'll receive will potentially create more lucrative opportunities down the line. Of course there are no guarantees that those opportunities will actually emerge, but that's something for the artists on the receiving end of these offers to worry about; in the meantime, they're still expected to not only effectively work for free, but also to be thankful for the chance to do so.

It's a ludicrous system, but again, it reflects a collective disregard for music, art and those who make it. Artists aren't treated as laborers in need of support; they're basically seen as content creators, their value largely stemming from the staying power of their most recent project. Although being an artist has always been precarious, it's odd that even now, during a time when social consciousness is arguably at an all-time high, their needs and concerns so regularly fall on deaf ears.

Touring is a prime example. Costs have gone through the roof in 2022, forcing many artists—including numerous high-profile acts—to cut down their dates or get off the road altogether, and while that's generated small pockets of uproar, little in the way of substantial change has taken place. Fans aren't necessarily to blame here—many of live music's most serious problems can be traced back to the market-manipulating tactics of companies like Live Nation and Ticketmaster, along with smaller things like venues taking a cut of artists' merch sales—but barring a large-scale shift in consumer behavior (or significant government intervention), the powers that be are unlikely to change their ways.

Capitalism is an obvious scapegoat here, and though it's likely not going anywhere, it does help to explain the occasionally ruthless, all-against-all mentality that defines much of the music industry. Even in its nominally independent and "underground" corners, the music business is very much a business, and while artists are perhaps the most likely to get the short end of the proverbial stick, it's worth noting that they too can be exploitative, especially when it comes to more established acts demanding exorbitant fees from venues and event promoters. (DJs—and their representatives—can be particularly bad on that front, and when promoters are also stuck with the rising costs of flights, hotels and transport, along with booking agents' 15% fee, it's no wonder that so many clubs and parties struggle to make the numbers work.)

Music journalists sit even lower in the overall hierarchy. (Admittedly I'm a little biased on this topic.) The occupation has never been lucrative, but in recent years the pay has become almost laughably low, to a point where even prominent and celebrated writers routinely hold other jobs and/or take non-journalism gigs to help pay the bills. (Making things worse, many publications also follow the exposure model, and though larger media outlets should theoretically have bigger budgets and more resources at their disposal, it's not uncommon for them to offer low fees, knowing that their prestigious byline alone is often enough to get writers to say "yes.") A genuine exodus from the field is underway, and while journalists were once a valued part of the musical ecosystem, their present-day work rarely garners much respect. On the contrary, it's frequently regarded as a borderline worthless vestige of the past, even amongst dedicated music fans.

There's a lot of ugly behavior out there, and seeing the difficulty of the overall landscape, it's worth asking: who is actually making money in the music industry at this point? Sometimes, it feels like the answer is "no one." That's obviously not true, but outside of what feels like a small circle of hyper-successful figures at the top, many people are struggling. Artists, venues, promoters, journalists, labels, publicists... the list of wobbly institutions is long, and even community radio, which has grown to almost unprecedented levels via the internet, isn't really a sustainable enterprise. People look at stations like NTS, which pulls in brand partnerships with companies like Adidas (and, much more controversially, cringey NFT hub Bored Ape Yacht Club), and think it's a smashing success, but the station—like most online broadcasters—also relies upon thousands of hours of unpaid volunteer labor to survive. And while that's kind of beautiful in a community-oriented, "we're all in this together" way, it's probably not a viable long-term model, especially for less well-known radio outposts.

Some might argue that it doesn't matter. After all, making music isn't supposed to be about making money, and focusing too much on the business or industry side of things can only corrupt the creative process. There's some truth to that, and most people in music (rightfully) mistrust anyone who holds themself up as a "I can help you unlock the secrets of the industry" expert. At the same time, idealism has its limits, and treating the music-making process as some kind of passion-fueled mysticism ultimately feeds into the notion that what artists are doing isn't work. In this telling, they're not laborers; they're magicians and conjurers whose creations emerge from the ether, fueled only by untainted creativity and sheer force of will.

That's a lovely idea, but despite its romantic appeal, does it actually serve artists, beyond inflating their egos? Making music is work. Writing about music is work. Organizing events is work. Running a venue is work. Putting out releases is work. Building a career in any of these fields (or even attempting to) is often incredibly difficult. What's wrong with acknowledging that? Do artists and other folks in the music industry not deserve a sustainable existence? Of course they do, and simply advocating for a change in perspective shouldn't be regarded as some kind of betrayal to the cause.

Passion is important, and music would be painfully dull without it, but passion alone is also easy to exploit, both by consumers who don't know any better and industry types who do. It's helped birth a musical ecosystem in which artists routinely aren't paid what they deserve, aren't respected as workers and often aren't missed when they (understandably) flame out. Maybe it's time to re-evaluate.

III.
The
Electronic
Music
Press

Critique vs. Curation
  a.k.a. A look at music reviews in 2021.

November 2, 2021
—

What is the job of a music journalist? Even I'm not certain anymore. I have an idea of what I think it ought to be, but in the modern media landscape, that often bears little resemblance to the soul-crushing content grind that the job has largely become. Of course the general public also has its own conception of what music journalism entails, which makes the formulation of a proper job description even more difficult.

Things haven't always been so complicated. In the most traditional sense, music journalists are critics, and for decades, the reviews they wrote carried real weight. It wasn't that long ago that a high-profile review could potentially alter the trajectory of an artist's career, but today? Most barely move the cultural needle. In the era of streaming and social media, when access to music is virtually unlimited and there's no shortage of opinions on offer, it's fair to ask, "Do we still need music reviews?" And if not, what exactly should journalists be writing about?

———

Last month, I conducted the first-ever First Floor readers poll, and while I'm still poring through all the data, one stat definitely surprised me. Amongst those who responded to the survey, more than 60% listed the newsletter's music reviews/ recommendations (a.k.a. the "New This Week" section) as one of the parts of First Floor that they like the best. (For reference, only the essays and interviews were more popular, and not by that much.)

Why did this surprise me? Well, for years now, I've been under the impression that within the realm of music journalism, the importance of music reviews is rapidly declining. That's not just a hunch or something I made up—even back when I was running the editorial at XLR8R (a job that ended in early 2015), the site's reviews section had been slumping for years, and now that I regularly follow the numbers for First Floor, I can confirm that that same downward trend appears to have held firm (or perhaps gotten worse). Simply put, people don't click on these things.

Other media outlets—particularly those that focus on electronic music—seem to have come to a similar conclusion. Despite the fact that the volume of new releases is arguably higher than ever, the number of reviews being published has undoubtedly shrunk in recent years. XLR8R last ran an album review in 2019, and Stamp the Wax appears to have halted years before that (although the site does continue to publish a lot of track premieres). Mixmag stopped doing reviews when its print edition was paused last year, and has since attempted to pick up the slack through monthly online round-ups of the "best" new albums and tracks.

Crack and Inverted Audio still publish reviews, but have scaled back their offerings to just a handful each month. Resident Advisor, which previously had one of the most robust review sections in electronic music, has also undertaken a significant drawdown, usually running one album review each weekday, along with a few single write-ups. That's still more than most other electronic music outlets, but it's telling that the word "reviews" was literally removed from RA's main menu as part of the site's redesign earlier this year. (Reviews are now filed under "Music," where they're listed alongside podcasts, "Mix of the Day" and themed playlists.)

The Wire still runs pages and pages of reviews each month, but as a publication that relies on paid subscribers and remains primarily focused on its print edition, it's arguably playing by a different set of content rules than its more online counterparts. That said, The Quietus also remains committed to reviews (one is published each weekday), and so does DJ Mag—at least in its print edition, which runs dozens of reviews each month. Online, however, those reviews are rarely prioritized; although the magazine's "Album of the Month" does get published as a standalone feature, the rest of the reviews are generally split up into three different categories (EPs & Singles, Albums and Compilations) and combined into unruly (and not easily searchable) bulk posts.

What does all this mean? What prompted this reduction? There are many factors at work, but at the most basic level, people just don't read reviews anymore, at least not online. (A more complex reading might surmise that although some people still read reviews, they don't do so in large enough numbers to justify the time and money required for publications to do them properly.)

Of course, here is where cynics usually jump in and say something like, "People don't read reviews because they're tired of pompous gatekeepers" or "People don't read reviews because the quality of writing has gone to shit." Are there elements of truth in those sentiments? Sure, but they also leave out significant chunks of the story.

More than anything, people don't read reviews anymore because in many cases, they no longer really need them. That wasn't the case 20 or 30 years ago. In the pre-Napster, pre-streaming era, when vast swaths of music were virtually inaccessible (especially if they existed outside of the mainstream), reviews could be a legitimately useful tool for discovering new music. Back then, finding new artists and releases often required both the know-how to identify and track them down and, more importantly, the money to buy them. Given most listeners' limited information and resources, reviews (and the radio) could be practically invaluable, providing a sort of road map to music fans who wanted to know what releases were out there and actually worth their time.

Was this a flawed system? Yes. Were the music journalism ranks overstuffed with straight white guys? For sure (and yes, that's still a problem). Were music critics overly deferential to rock tropes while being needlessly dismissive of pop, hip-hop, R&B, electronic music and numerous other genres? Absolutely. Even if you're not a poptimist or a fan of the current music media landscape, there's no question that the old way of doing things was far from perfect.

What then is the point of music reviews in 2021? Access to music is instant, cheap and widespread, which means that we're now living in a time when listeners can literally fire up a streaming platform, listen to almost any piece of new music and decide how they themselves feel about it. Reviewers' opinions used to help music fans determine whether something was worth buying, but now that most people aren't actually buying anything, that particular question has been rendered moot.

In truth, many of the most basic functions of reviews have largely been rendered obsolete. Listeners no longer need journalists' help to know what a record sounds like either, but that hasn't stopped writers—myself included—from continuing to slip nuts-and-bolts musical descriptions into their work, specifically mentioning how a song's "soaring guitar melody" interacts with its "thundering drum beat." Old habits die hard, and while the best journalists use illustrative metaphors or employ verbiage that's a whole lot more compelling than the examples I've provided, there's undoubtedly something a bit odd about attempting to capture the literal dynamics of a song with words when the music itself is often so readily available.

To avoid this, many modern reviewers have shifted away from rote sonic descriptors, attempting instead to place the music they're evaluating in a larger historical or social context. If "what does this record sound like?" was once the primary question to be answered, it's now frequently supplanted by "What does this record mean in the grand scheme of things?" and "How does this release relate to the world that the artist (and the rest of us) live in?" Although these more global kinds of questions have always been part of the music reviewing recipe, one could argue that they've now become the primary ingredient.

This is particularly true for an outlet like Pitchfork, one of the few English-language publications that still prominently centers reviews within the scope of its editorial. As the site has increasingly embraced pop sounds (and, more generally, genres outside of indie rock) over the past decade or so, its reviews have also become more contextual, often weaving in commentary about larger social, historical and cultural trends. This likely rankles some traditionalists, especially within the increasingly vocal "anti-woke" crowd, but Pitchfork's reviews frequently take stands about what values—creative, aesthetic, cultural, historical or political—are important (at least according to the writer and the site's editors), and back up that position with a (somewhat arbitrary) score out of 10.

The music itself is still important, of course, but in today's cultural landscape, so is what an artist and their music represent—and it's the latter half of that equation that usually generates the most conversation, especially when social media is driving the discourse. When it comes to artists like Lana Del Ray or Kanye West, there are listeners out there who are content to tweet about which songs they like best on the new albums, but the folks who tend to gain the most traction online (i.e. the people who post constantly, stoke conflict and tend to generate a whole lot of clicks) are those who would rather dissect an artist's entire character and debate their value as human beings—with strangers, no less.

Emotional responses are the lifeblood of today's internet, simply because they get people to engage. Think about it: if someone sees that their favorite artist has been reviewed on Pitchfork, they're probably going to click the link, just to check the score. (Yes, there's a reason that the scores aren't visible on the home page.) For that person, checking out a review isn't about discovery or finding out whether or not the album is any good—it's about seeing how an outlet's opinion matches up with their own. Thanks to streaming and the immediate access it offers, they've probably already heard the music anyways, so all they want is to see the score and say, "That's bullshit" or "Oh cool, I was right."

It's the same psychological phenomenon that has led to the rise of clickbait headlines and an infinite number of dashed-off hot takes: in an oversaturated content environment, the stuff that most easily makes an impact is that which gets our blood boiling or tugs at our heartstrings. That's a high bar to clear—and given our collective outrage fatigue, it's arguably getting higher every day. For most people, an old-fashioned review (i.e. one that simply describes what a record sounds like and maybe slips in a few comparisons and influences), even if it's well written, probably isn't going to cut through the daily noise of the internet.

This isn't to imply that Pitchfork is purposely seeking controversy or rigging its scores to get audiences fired up and clicking. (Having seen how vicious online fan bases can be when their favorite artist gets anything less than a rave review, only the most cynical of editors would intentionally unleash their fury.) As an occasional contributor, I'm obviously biased, but I think a lot of excellent writing gets published on the site, and its expanded approach to reviewing has prompted all sorts of deeper, more thoughtful discussions about music, the artists who make it and the people who consume it. (It's also produced some narrative clunkers, along with occasional bout of rhetorical overreach and/or seemingly sandwiched-in sociopolitical commentary, but such are the dangers of swimming in these waters, especially for an outlet that's publishing four long-form reviews each weekday, plus more on the weekend.)

Moreover, Pitchfork's approach to reviewing isn't exclusive to them. In many ways, it's become the dominant form across the industry, and yet, this style of review hasn't gained much traction with audiences for more niche genres like electronic music. It's not that thoughtful electronic music writing doesn't take place, but even when narratives are expanded beyond solely discussing the music, the reviews themselves rarely catch fire online—or seem to make much of a difference at all. Perhaps that says something about the nature of more specialist music fans, or maybe it's merely a function of the total audience size being significantly smaller.

After all, only a handful of "underground" electronic artists are truly big enough to crack the wider cultural conversation, which means that even the most provocative acts are unlikely to trigger sprawling discussions and social media battles.

On an even more practical level, electronic music media outlets these days generally don't have the time or resources to nurture high-quality reviews. It's not like writing reviews for a place like Pitchfork is a super lucrative gig, but at most electronic music publications, the freelance fees are laughably small. I've been quoted as low as $10 or $20, and maybe that's okay for a writer who's starting out and is trying to build a resume, but for someone more experienced who's actually trying to eke out a living as a music journalist, there's really no point. (It's not a coincidence that many of the reviews at places like Resident Advisor are now being done by staff writers.)

Regardless of what genre you're working in, writing a proper review is difficult, time-consuming work, and most likely requires at least a little research, especially if you're looking to place a release within a larger historical or social context. (This is also why writing reviews isn't really an ideal job for a novice journalist, especially if they're not working with an experienced editor—something many specialist outlets don't have.) These days, agreeing to write a review also comes with a huge potential for grief. If you write a negative review (or sometimes even one that's not overflowing with praise), there's a decent chance that the artist (and/or their fans) will flood your social media with abuse and generally make your life miserable for a day or two. Is that the end of the world? Not necessarily (unless people start trying to dox you, which does happen in extreme cases), but it's still hard to make that cost-benefit math add up when you're being paid a pittance.

That's likely the main reason why reviews these days are so overwhelmingly positive. Music journalists are a notoriously grumpy bunch, but somehow their collective output has gotten to a point where even middling reviews are often hard to come by. Most writers refuse to engage (on the record) with releases—including those from high-profile artists and labels—that they're not openly enthusiastic about. Although negative reviews do still happen on occasion, they're usually aimed at "safe" targets (i.e. artists who tastemakers have decided are okay to criticize, a judgment that often has little to do with their actual music). In electronic music, this means it's open season on an act like Disclosure, but someone making equally bland house/garage for a "cool" label is usually spared from critique, or more likely ignored altogether.

At this point, most reviews fall into one of two categories:

1. Reviews of the latest release from widely known artists that most readers of the publication are already deeply familiar with. (These are usually positive, but will occasionally be negative.)

2. Reviews of the latest release from relatively unknown (usually up-and-coming) artists that many readers of the publication won't know much about. (These are almost universally positive.)

For those expecting a more complete critical landscape, the above list might seem imbalanced or incomplete, but not everyone sees this situation as a problem. There's certainly an argument to be made that with so much new music being released all the time, there's no point in spending time criticizing the stuff that's not up to par, particularly when it's coming from less established artists. As an example, is anything constructive accomplished by panning a new EP from a relative unknown? Not really. From a cynical perspective, reviews of unknown artists rarely generate much traffic, but even if those reviews are viewed through a purely journalistic lens, it can seem mean-spirited to specifically take the time to take down an act that most people have never heard of.

There's a definite logic to this "positive reviews only" mindset, and in many ways, it's one that I've followed with First Floor.

The write-ups in the "New This Week" section of the newsletter aren't really reviews in the traditional sense; they're essentially blurbs about tracks that I've deemed to be my favorites of the week. I generally listen to around 100 new releases each week, and although most of them aren't particularly good, that ratio isn't reflected in the newsletter. On the contrary, nothing that I don't like—or even feel lukewarm about—ever finds its way into my recommendations. Is that honest critique? Maybe not in the traditional sense, but in the current media environment, where genuinely curious fans are often seeking a few guideposts through an overcrowded music landscape, perhaps it's a more constructive approach.

Reviewing music has always been a subjective exercise, and gone are the days where most publications had large staffs that could theoretically debate the relative merits of a release and come to some sort of collective agreement about its worth. (The word "theoretically" is important here. The degree to which these kinds of socratic discussions actually happened back in the day is something that's absolutely up for debate.) Nowadays, it's rare that more than two people (the writer and maybe an editor) are involved in the publication of a review, a reality that only makes the form's subjectivity all the more evident.

It's nice to imagine that a writer could approach a piece of music with a critical blank slate and provide totally unbiased judgment, but that's a fantasy. There's no such thing as a completely objective music journalist, so who's to say that a record that one writer doesn't like won't be adored by someone else? Should one writer's take really be registered as the official stance of a particular publication, especially when that take hasn't been vetted by a larger editorial body? And when the lack of diversity (not to mention experience) at most modern publications is factored in, there's an argument to be made that even with vetting and proper editing, the review process is always going to have an unacceptable amount of bias baked in.

Oddly enough, some of the most trusted reviews in electronic music these days come not from a publication, but from an online store—Boomkat. There's no question that the writing on the site is thoughtful and deeply knowledgeable, but it's also almost universally positive, even when it's delivered with a fair amount of snark. Boomkat reviews may not read like typical marketing or promotional text, but there are no bylines and the reviews aren't being promoted as "content" in the same way that reviews from music publications are—they are designed to sell records. Unlike other outlets, Boomkat isn't chasing likes or shares; the only engagement they really need is for people to click the "buy" button. When it comes to their reviews, expressing bias is arguably the whole point, and the site's editorial slant, which mostly manifests in what records they choose to write about and highlight, is a strong selling point for most of their readers (who might be better described as potential customers).

Although the Boomkat audience remains an outlier—plenty of listeners are content to follow whatever personalized paths are offered up by the algorithm of their preferred streaming platform—the site's approach to reviews does offer some important lessons. While the average music fan no longer needs reviews as much as they used to, those looking to go beyond the obvious still need help, and what they're looking for usually isn't critique, but curation. They want voices that they trust to provide them with shortcuts through the musical wilderness, most often in the form of recommendations. Those recommendations don't all have to be unfamiliar, either; sometimes it helps to simply get a confirmation that the latest release from an artist you already know about is worth a listen.

In many ways, music journalists have been transformed into little influencers, especially as more of us unhitch ourselves from established platforms (or start our own). When I think about First Floor, it is a sort of journalistic enterprise, but it's also rooted in the basic idea that my personal perspective is not only worthwhile, but actually worth paying for. As scary as it sounds, I myself am arguably the primary selling point of the newsletter, and according to more than 60% of the folks who responded to my readers poll, the track recommendations I put together each week are a major part of what makes First Floor worth reading.

Does that make me unique? Of course not. Even journalists on staff at established publications deal with this evolving reality; there's a reason that almost every single music writer is on Twitter, and it has a lot to do with the need to build a professional "brand," as gross as that sounds. Editors might have the steady jobs (as long as the outlets they work at manage to stay afloat), but established writers are often the ones who garner the most attention and loyalty. How many electronic music fans probably scoff at Pitchfork but still read every review that Philip Sherburne writes?

It's an unusual state of affairs, and one that speaks to the increasing atomization of content offerings across the board. When everyone wants to read and consume things that cater to their specific tastes and worldview, how could any one writer be expected to write a review that resonates with everyone? There may have been a time where that sort of concern didn't matter (or was simply ignored), and reviews chased some (ultimately unattainable) objective ideal, but that approach no longer squares with how people engage with music, or really culture of any kind.

Is this good or bad? I don't know, but it's probably some of both. As a longtime music journalist, it does seem unnatural to contribute to an overly sunny critical landscape that in many ways has become a glorified form of cheerleading. It seems obvious that not every new release is great, or even mediocre, but music reviews on most outlets might lead someone to think otherwise. At the same time, how many people are actually basing their own opinions on published music reviews in 2021? Not many. Listeners want to form their own opinions (or at least they think they do), and a writer declaring from on high that a particular album is amazing or sucks is unlikely to change many minds these days.

For now, reviews remain in a state of flux, but it's nonetheless difficult to imagine them taking on greater relevance in the years to come. Although music writers will likely always be around in some form, the percentage of their work specifically devoted to evaluating artists' output is likely to shrink, and maybe that's okay. In the meantime, however, I'll continue to write the occasional review and put together the track recommendations in the newsletter each week. Churning out varying forms of "this is great, check it out" isn't necessarily what inspired me—or, I'm guessing, most other music writers—to get into this racket, but in today's music environment, it's strangely become one of the most useful things I can do.

The Overwhelmingly British Music Press
a.k.a. What happens when the vast majority of electronic music media is based in the UK?

November 23, 2021
—

As a longtime writer and editor myself, of course I care (probably too much) about the quality of music journalism on offer, but the longer I spend in the field, the more I find myself thinking that another component of the job is potentially far more important: which stories get told in the first place.

The Brits have pretty much always had an oversized presence in music journalism, and when it comes to electronic music, they've arguably dominated the narrative since the late 1980s. The biggest dance music magazines have always been British, and as the media has noticeably contracted during the past 15 years, we've reached a point where almost all of the genre's dedicated publications are based in the UK, and even the ones that aren't often rely heavily upon British writers.

The following piece isn't some kind of anti-UK screed, and I'm well aware of the irony of an American complaining that *anyone* else has too much control over the discourse. Yet in a time when dance music has gone fully global, one country is disproportionately driving the narrative, and no matter how well intentioned its journalists are, there's just no way the full story is being told.

———

Last week, DJ Mag announced the nominees for its upcoming Best of British awards. Described as an "annual celebration of UK talent," the awards are something the publication has been doing for the past 15 years, and unlike its ghastly Top 100 DJs list, the artists recognized actually represent an encouragingly diverse array of British dance music. (It's certainly hard to imagine any other awards show honoring acts like Mala, Joy Orbison and Anz.)

So what's the problem? Some might argue that there isn't one. House and techno were born in the American Midwest, but it was the UK that most loudly sold it to the world. It was 1988's *Techno! The New Dance Sound of Detroit*, a compilation spearheaded by English DJ/journalist/A&R man Neil Rushton, that famously first introduced the genre to massive European audiences, and more than 30 years later, there's no denying that the UK has long been one of electronic music's most vital hubs, arguably embracing the genre, along with its artists and culture, in a way that the US never has. Moreover, the country has made countless contributions of its own, many of them vital; jungle, drum & bass, dubstep, grime and basically the whole hardcore continuum are all sounds with distinctly British origins (even if they do owe a major debt to Jamaican soundsystem culture), and the smiley-faced aesthetics of the UK's late-'80s rave culture continue to loom large today.[1]

This kind of large-scale "borrowing" is something the British music industry has been doing for a very long time, and regardless of whether it's categorized as appropriation or simple cultural exchange—the appropriate label absolutely depends on the specific context and the actors involved—it's reshaped the global music landscape. Perhaps it began with the British Invasion of the 1960s, when a flurry of mop-topped artists dominated pop charts around the world with what was essentially a rehashed version of American rock & roll (which itself was rehashing—some might say stealing from—rhythm and blues and other distinctly Black genres).

In the decades that followed, the UK music industry would follow the same playbook again and again, championing genres like soul, punk, dub, reggae, disco, house, techno and dancehall. These styles didn't necessarily upend the mainstream in the same way The Beatles once did, but they all had a major cultural impact. And while the histories of these sounds are often framed as a prolonged "exchange" across the Atlantic—a notion that's not without some merit, especially considering the increasingly fluid

---

1. "Hardcore continuum" is a term coined by music writer Simon Reynolds, and is based on the idea that the many variants of UK bass music are all part of a lineage that can be traced back to hardcore, an early-'90s British mutation of American house and techno.

nature of culture in recent decades—it's nonetheless telling that when the music involved is traced back to its source, it almost always seems to originate outside of the British Isles.

Knowing that, it's tempting to throw out words like "colonizers" and "cultural extraction," labeling the British as the proverbial "bad guys" in the story and calling it a day. The country's imperial past certainly factors into the larger narrative here, and is something worth exploring, but what DJ Mag's Best of British awards got me thinking about wasn't actually the "taking" aspect of the UK's musical history. Although the country has undoubtedly developed a stunning (some might say concerning) capacity for repackaging and recontextualizing others' music and subsequently selling it back to the places from which it came—a strategy helped along significantly by the British press and its tendency toward grandiose, tabloid-style blagging—what's perhaps even more remarkable (or worrisome, depending on your perspective) is how the UK has secured a place as that music's preeminent storyteller, record keeper and tastemaker.

Electronic music culture isn't a monolith; the US can lay claim to most of the O.G. heroes and still has plenty of say in the conversation (especially when its comes to social justice issues), Berlin is still regarded as techno paradise (and also seems to produce all of the best memes), and the Netherlands (or maybe just Amsterdam) always seems to have a seat at the table too. That said, the UK arguably dwarfs them all when it comes to setting the international electronic music agenda, and as I looked over those Best of British nominees, the question that came to my mind was, "What does it mean that DJ Mag, a magazine with global reach that literally franchises its brand and publishes different editions in various markets around the globe, has determined that the UK, its home country, is most deserving of its own electronic music awards?"[2]

Now, is DJ Mag uniquely at fault here? Of course not. DJ Mag is just one title in an electronic music media landscape that happens to be overwhelmingly British in orientation. Don't believe me?

---

2. At the time this essay was first published, DJ Mag also had dedicated awards for China and North America, but the former had started only the year prior and the latter had been on hiatus since 2019. **191**

Let's take a quick survey of the outlets who regularly cover "underground" (i.e. non-EDM) electronic music and where their businesses are primarily located:

Resident Advisor—UK
DJ Mag—UK
Mixmag—UK
The Wire—UK
Crack—UK
The Quietus—UK
FACT—UK
Dazed—UK
Dummy—UK
The Ransom Note—UK
Inverted Audio—UK
Stamp the Wax—UK
Test Pressing—UK
Attack Mag—UK
Pitchfork—US
Bandcamp Daily—US
FADER—US
Beatportal—US
XLR8R—US
5Mag—US
Electronic Beats—Germany
Groove—Germany
Les Yeux Orange—France

Admittedly, I've probably missed a few websites and magazines (especially ones of the non-English-language variety), and it's worth noting that many of these publications, especially the more prominent ones, do have offices, staff and/or contributors in other countries. That said, there's still a whole lot of UK on that list, and though the US does have some real heavy hitters, three of the American outlets mentioned (Pitchfork, FADER and

Bandcamp Daily) only devote a fraction of their overall coverage to electronic music.

What happens when so much of the dance music press is concentrated in one place? How does it affect what artists, labels, trends and stories are not just covered, but even deemed important enough for people within the industry to pay attention to? Even if you assume that music journalists are doing their work in good faith—and for the record, I think that most of them are—they're still human beings, bound by the limits of their own biases, extended social circles and media diets.

Media concentration is a big part of why electronic music publications will regularly feature relatively unknown producers and labels from Bristol, Manchester or London, while simultaneously leaving entire countries (and sometimes continents) ignored. It's why nightclubs in London, via sheer repetition in the media, become veritable household names amongst electronic music fans, but places like Croatia and Morocco only seem to get mentioned in the context of the (mostly British-run) festivals that happen there each summer. It's why every minute development concerning Covid lockdowns and the closing/reopening of clubs in the UK has been extensively reported on in the dance music press, while other countries' situations often receive only passing mentions, and even then, only if they are in Western Europe or North America.

These kinds of sleights and preferences are constantly (and often unknowingly) woven into the narrative, but even if they're not the result of intentionally malicious behavior on the part of the media, they still represent a problem. Inherent bias is real, and if a publication's staff is full of people whose musical universe is largely limited to London, Berlin, New York and an annual trip to Barcelona for Sónar, that experience (or lack thereof) is going to shape their notions of what matters.

Maybe there was a time when more regionally focused approaches made sense (or at least more sense than they do now). Back in the 1990s and 2000s, more countries (and cities) had their own publications that could specifically cater to local audiences, but in the years since the bottom fell out of print media, most of those outlets have shut their doors. The publications that are still around—including the ones in the UK—may be survivors, but they aren't exactly flying high economically; ad revenues are down, staffing levels have been cut and resources are more limited than ever, all of which further limit their capacity for expansive reporting.

That doesn't stop journalists from trying of course, and in recent years there's been a visible effort to cover more electronic music happening outside of the usual London-New York-Berlin axis. It's heartening to see (an admittedly limited amount of) coverage devoted to labels and collectives like Uganda's Nyege Nyege and Shanghai's SVBKVLT, but even then, human factors come into play—it's rarely noted that both of those entities are headed up by expats from Europe and the UK, respectively. (Pro tip: if a scene, label, party or collective outside of Europe and North America is regularly getting attention from the dance music press, there's a good chance that an expat with connections back home is involved.) That doesn't invalidate the work they're doing or the music they're releasing, but it surely gives them an advantage when it comes to communicating with the wider music industry.

Truth be told, there are just so many ways that biases can come into play. Take South Africa. Compared to its neighbors, the country has always been well represented in electronic music circles, but would genres like kwaito, gqom and amapiano have received as much attention if they hadn't come from a former British colony that's full of English speakers? Probably not. Latin America, a region that has been appearing more frequently on the international electronic music radar over the past few years, provides another illustrative example. It's probably not a coincidence that most of the industry's attention has been given to electronic music artists located in trendy vacation spots (e.g. Mexico City, Buenos Aires, Bogotá) for globe-trotting Europeans and Americans, and even then, there's a clear slant toward members of the upper classes, most of whom can speak English and communicate in the creative language of the increasingly UK-centric media.

Electronic music, even if it's limited to just the "underground" stuff, is now a global, multibillion-dollar enterprise, and yet one relatively small island nation continues to have a massive sway over the narrative. Who's the most influential electronic music writer of all time? Probably Simon Reynolds, a London native. (The more intellectual set might say Mark Fisher, another Englishman, while the digger crowd might mention Bill Brewster, who—you guessed it—is also from England.) French duo Daft Punk are arguably the most influential electronic music outfit ever, and who's authoring books about them? Two guys from the UK: Ben Cardew, whose *Daft Punk's Discovery: The Future Unfurled* dropped earlier this year, and Gabriel Szatan, whose *After Daft* is due out sometime in 2024.

Am I disparaging the work of these guys? Of course not. They've all earned their accolades and are worth reading, but taken together, there is an obvious homogeneity at work. (And yes, if you want to expand the definition of that homogeneity to "white men writing about electronic music," you could absolutely file me right alongside these guys. The problem clearly runs deeper than mere geographical borders.)

I'm not suggesting that the UK take a back seat so that the existing US music media structure can step in and steer the ship instead. There's some obvious irony in an American like myself complaining that someone else has too much sway in the conversation, especially when electronic music is one of the only genres where the US doesn't set the agenda and dominate the discussion. Given that, any proposal to extend American hegemony over another facet of cultural discourse—especially if the constitution of that hegemony remains homogeneous in terms of gender, race, class, etc.—probably isn't the best move. The US has never been known for its measured global perspective, and while there have been calls for Americans to reassert their ownership of the narrative around this music that was first created on their soil, it's worth noting that the discussions coming from places like New York and Los Angeles (i.e. the scenes which tend to speak loudest online) can often seem just as insular as what their counterparts in the UK and Europe are saying.

There are no quick fixes here, especially when English is increasingly the universal language of the internet. Even if a publication wants to focus on music from the non-English-language world, staying economically viable these days (especially for a niche electronic music outlet) usually requires building an international readership, and what's the easiest way to do that? Publish in English. And if you're publishing in English, where is it easiest to find competent (or even semi-competent) writers? The US, UK, Ireland, Canada, Australia, New Zealand and South Africa, and of those countries, only the UK has something resembling an extended electronic music media infrastructure that can actively recruit, train and platform journalists. Is it possible to find English-speaking writers from other countries? Of course, and it's something publications should do more often, but even the best non-native speakers are usually going to require additional editing attention, and that can be an issue when most outlets have limited time and resources to begin with.

The problem is further compounded on the supply side, as the glut of UK-centric media has given rise to an extensive, similarly UK-focused PR apparatus. So many electronic music publicists are based in the UK, and even the ones that aren't are often staffed by British people living in Berlin or other cities around Europe. Once again, language is an issue here, and if your firm is tasked with marketing music—even music that's not from the UK—to journalists and editors who work in English and are frequently based in the UK themselves, there's a good chance that you'll wind up hiring English speakers to do the job, and in Europe, that often means hiring a British person (or someone who can actively cater to their tastes and sensibilities).

The deeper you dig into the issue, the clearer it becomes that this situation is both complicated and self-reinforcing, and few in electronic music are immune to its effects. I myself cover a ton of UK music in my work, despite the fact that I'm not British and have never lived there. Why? I'm definitely not pursuing some pro-UK agenda, and I do actively seek out music from elsewhere, but as a journalist, part of my job also involves keeping tabs on the most "relevant" artists, labels and trends. Relevant is obviously a subjective term, but regardless of how it's defined, there's no avoiding the fact that many of electronic music's most influential entities—both historical and modern—are based in the UK, and their importance is only being amplified by the country's uniquely megaphone-like press and music industry. Over time, that amplification trickles down to new generations, giving rise to fresh crops of artists, labels, parties and scenes that are either in the UK or forged in its image, all of them demanding similar levels of attention. Meanwhile, electronic music scenes in other parts of the world especially ones whose output has little to do with techno or the hardcore continuum—are frequently left twisting in the wind, hoping that someone will take notice.

It makes sense that the UK press would want to big itself up, celebrate local heroes and tell stories that are close to home, and in a healthier media ecosystem, that kind of behavior would be happening around the world, with robust outlets scattered around the globe, publishing content from a diverse cast of contributors. Unfortunately though, that's not what today's electronic music media landscape looks like, which means that the places left standing (most of them in the UK) are now expected to shoulder a burden they likely don't want—and aren't really built to handle. Is that fair? Probably not, and it's honestly a bit ludicrous to expect the UK music press to properly tell the stories of electronic music from all around the globe, but if they don't take on that responsibility, it's not clear that anyone else will.

When it comes to storytelling, it's easy to say, "Just make more diverse content," but doing so haphazardly is a quick way for a media outlet to hasten the demise of their business; it doesn't matter what kinds of stories are being told when the audience isn't bothering to click on them. Journalists can trot out narratives and nudge audiences in certain directions, but their power isn't absolute. Online media these days is economically dependent on engagement, and succeeding in that system usually requires catering to familiarity and headlines that immediately provoke an emotional response; running stories that say "here's an interview with an artist you've never heard of from a place you've never been" is unlikely to be a winning strategy with most readers—especially ones already accustomed to a certain editorial point of view.

So why not find new readers and build a bigger, more open-minded audience? Well, there's an unfortunate sort of chicken-and-egg scenario at work; attracting new audiences often requires new kinds of content, but creating that new content requires taking risks and making sustained investments in things that aren't guaranteed to work. Audiences can't be forced, and for editors who are constantly under pressure to deliver clicks—and are probably worried about the stability of their job to begin with—sticking their neck out for the sake of what might be regarded as a healthier content offering can be a tall order.

At the same time, the status quo clearly isn't working, and as many electronic music media outlets continue to play it safe and cater to their own shrinking audiences, the discourse can sometimes look like a bunch of Brits bigging up their friends and telling each other how awesome they are. It may not be intentional, but for folks outside the UK, something like the Best of British awards isn't exactly inviting, and absolutely adds to the sense that the industry is unfairly tilted towards certain kinds of artists from a small list of places.

That said, is electronic music media concentration—or any of its deleterious side effects—specifically DJ Mag's fault? No. There are worse things out there than the Best of British awards, and even if they were canceled tomorrow, the electronic music press—and honestly, the entire industry—would still have plenty of work to do. People love to point fingers, but this mess can't be pinned on a single publication, or even a single country; even so, an inability to specifically assign blame shouldn't absolve those with the capacity to make positive change from taking action. Electronic music is a global undertaking, and there are amazing things happening all around the world, but it's on everyone—artists, labels, journalists, promoters and even fans—to step outside of their bubbles (or in the case of folks from the UK, their home island) and take notice.

Will that actually happen? Probably not, but it's something to aspire to.

The Welcoming of Brands into Music Journalism a.k.a. Thoughts on Resident Advisor's new creative agency.

August 16, 2022
—

My first real job in music journalism was at XLR8R. I started there in 2008, and at the time there were something like 15 people on staff, which was actually pretty small for an internationally distributed print magazine. Before long, however, things would get a lot smaller. Less than a year after I was hired, a global recession hit. Ad sales dried up, the print edition was eventually suspended and layoffs whittled the team down to virtually nothing. By the time I finally left in 2015, there were literally two employees left, and the other guy wasn't even full-time.

This story isn't unique, especially in the world of niche culture publications, but it does illustrate a profound shift that took place—and from which the music media has never really recovered. For more than a decade now, outlets have struggled to find new sustainable business models, and the answer most seem to have settled on is something that once would have been anathema in many independent music circles: brand partnerships. The following piece looks at how that happened, and considers its potential ramifications on the quality (and kind) of electronic music journalism we'll be seeing in the years ahead.

———

Resident Advisor has taken its fair share of lumps in recent years, and while it's unclear whether the company's reputation will ever fully recover—accepting a £750,000 government grant during the pandemic isn't something people will forget anytime soon[1]—it

1. Bakare, Lanre. "Dance music platform Resident Advisor defends £750,000 government grant." *The Guardian*, October 14, 2020, https://www.theguardian.com/music/2020/oct/14/dance-music-platform-resident-advisor-defends-750000-government-grant.

nonetheless remains active, and has arguably retained its status as the world's most prominent electronic music publication. More importantly (at least from a financial standpoint), Resident Advisor also continues to serve as an online ticket-selling portal, and as of last week, a new branch has been officially added to the company's scope of operations: its own in-house creative agency. As reported in Adweek, the new venture is called 23:59, and will be led by RA's "recently appointed chief brand and creative officer Kazim Rashid, with Italian fashion house Bottega Veneta as one of its founding clients."[2]

Launched as "an incubator for ideas, creativity and culture" and touted as "the leading solution for brands wanting to connect with the huge global electronic music and nightlife community," 23:59 might seem like a significant (and potentially eyebrow-raising) addition to RA's mission. In reality though, the change may ultimately be more cosmetic than concrete. Looking at the company's newly designed brand partnerships page, the 23:59 name and associated messaging are new, but much of the highlighted work—which includes collaborations with Nike, Asahi, Absolut Vodka and Rockstar Games—dates back years.

Nevertheless, the launch of a creative agency (or "creative studio," as 23:59 is billed on the RA website) is absolutely the kind of thing that will rankle electronic music purists and traditionalists, particularly those with ties to the genre's DIY roots and community-oriented foundational values. Admittedly, those ties have become tenuous over the years as dance music has grown into a global, multibillion-dollar industry, but that hasn't stopped Resident Advisor from positioning itself on its website as an organization "dedicated to shining light on the passionate people and communities around the world that make electronic music tick." It's a compelling narrative, and one that RA hasn't cultivated alone; back in 2015, a New York Times profile hailed the company as a "staunchly independent" enterprise, citing its "devotion to the 'underground' side of the

2. Lepitak, Stephen. "Music Platform Resident Advisor Builds In-House Creative Agency." *Adweek*, August 12, 2022, https://www.adweek.com/media/music-platform-resident-advisor-builds-in-house-creative-agency/.

culture that is at odds with the music's mainstream popularity."[3]

Although words like "underground" have become rather vague—some might say entirely meaningless—in today's music landscape, they still carry conceptual weight, particularly for brands in search of entryways into various pockets of youth culture. For them, "underground" is often just a code word for "passion," and their need to access that passion—and hopefully direct it toward the buying of certain products—is often at the heart of brand partnerships, and media outlets have been able to cash in. How? By utilizing their knowledge of (and standing in) various creative communities, the Resident Advisors of the world can serve as a bridge between artists—many of whom are themselves struggling to make ends meet, especially in a music ecosystem increasingly characterized by the limited financial returns of streaming—and the multinational corporations who want to tap into their devoted fan bases.

From the outside, this might seem nefarious—it certainly doesn't feel very journalistic, let alone DIY—but it's also a reliable revenue source during what's undeniably a tough time for online media. Ad sales might have paid the bills back when publications only existed in print, but once most media shifted online during the 2000s and 2010s, it didn't take long for advertisers to realize that digital ads weren't particularly effective, no matter how much clickbait outlets churned out in an attempt to boost their pageviews (and fulfill all of the impressions they'd sold to advertisers). With each passing year, digital advertising sales are increasingly dominated by outlets that offer scale above all else, meaning that tech giants like Google, Facebook and Amazon routinely pull in giant shares of online ad revenue while more niche outlets (e.g. music publications) are left with dwindling returns.

Knowing that, it's not surprising that a media company would look to bolster its brand partnerships business, and Resident Advisor is far from the first publication to do it. Vice has been working with brands since the mid-2000s, and has its own in-house agency called Virtue. Dazed has Dazed Studio, which

3. Sisario, Ben. "Influential Site Inhabits Fringe of an Electronic Dance Music Culture." *The New York Times*, July 12, 2015, https://www.nytimes.com/2015/07/13/business/media/influential-site-inhabits-fringe-of-an-electronic-dance-music-culture.html.

aims to "create innovative and award-winning co-branded and white label campaigns across the luxury and lifestyle sectors." Crack might be a niche publication, but it also launched its own creative agency last year, Crack Creative Company (CC Co.), which built upon the magazine's prior work with clients such as New Balance, Apple, Burberry and Sonos. The list of in-house creative agencies is endless, and it's not something that's solely restricted to music and culture publications. Even the New York Times, arguably the most respected media outlet on the planet, has its own "branded content studio," T Brand, which has been active since 2014.

From a business perspective, Resident Advisor is actually arriving late to the party, a delay that was likely only possible because the company for so long was primarily fueled by another revenue source: ticket sales. The pandemic obviously blew a giant hole in that business model, and the recent explosion of mobile ticket platforms like DICE—which notably bolstered its editorial/curatorial profile by acquiring Boiler Room late last year—likely hasn't been good for RA's bottom line either. Leaning into brand partnerships (and formalizing something the company has already been doing for years) is probably one of the few potential growth areas for Resident Advisor, so the creation of 23:59 makes good economic sense, but what does it mean for the site's future as a bastion of electronic music journalism?

In the short term, it probably doesn't mean much of anything. Again, brand partnerships are nothing new for RA, which means that the site's non-branded content—at least for now—isn't likely to be any more compromised than it was previously. (Granted, opinions about the quality of that content, and just how compromised it may or may not be, vary widely.) Furthermore, the idea that any major media outlet in 2022 is offering "pure," completely uncorrupted journalism, is borderline laughable. Even at places where the editorial teams are completely siloed from the business side of things (e.g. ad sales, brand partnerships, etc.), it's hard to view any publication as completely clean. Whether they're selling ads to alcohol companies, publishing discreetly labeled sponsored content, partnering with exploitative multinational corporations or are simply owned by a noxious parent company, there's a good chance that there's something less than noble happening at nearly every significant media operation.

That said, the mere presence of this ethical dirt doesn't automatically preclude the creation of quality content and the execution of respectable journalism. The Red Bull Music Academy might be the best example of this, and while I do carry a certain amount of bias as a longtime contributor, there's no question that the operation—which was essentially an elaborate, 20-year-long brand activation by a global energy drink company—was responsible for some truly phenomenal content, particularly when it came to the documenting of (often untold) stories from obscure corners of music both past and present. Now, was that content ultimately tainted by the political views of Red Bull's CEO, who publicly criticized European migrant policy and espoused a populist worldview? In the minds of some people, absolutely, but regardless of that, it's also clear that during the years since RBMA was shuttered in 2019, no other outlet has really stepped in to fill the void it left behind.

Of course, RBMA wasn't a media outlet in the purest sense of the term, and its ties to a corporate patron meant that the organization's resources often dwarfed those of regular publications. Regularly making quality content isn't cheap or easy, and while outlets like Resident Advisor and Crack will occasionally partner with brands like Apple and Nike—and those collaborations are surely lucrative—it's unlikely that the money from those projects adds up to annual editorial budgets that rival what RBMA was working with. Moreover, while those working at RBMA—who often came to the initiative after making a name for themselves at other creative and cultural organizations—were given a relatively free hand when it came to editorial and curatorial choices, media outlets are rarely given the same sort of freedom when working directly with brands. Regardless of whether the partnership involves content creation, developing creative strategy or executing some sort of live event, the ultimate end goal is meeting the client's objectives, not doing quality creative and/or editorial work. (In an ideal scenario, a brand partnership can accomplish both, but when push comes to shove, the client's needs will usually win out.)

So, does this mean that Resident Advisor is now hopelessly compromised? Of course not. RA, Crack, Dazed, Vice and pretty much all of the places that engage in brand partnerships have still published work worth reading in recent years, and it's hard to fault any company for developing alternate revenue sources during a time when so much of online media is struggling to simply keep the lights on. At the same time, this brand partnership work is something that audiences should be aware of, especially because most media companies do their best to keep it relatively quiet. (Even in a culture where concerns about "selling out" have largely receded into the background, there's nothing particularly cool about working with giant corporations.)

It's unlikely that RA will suddenly start publishing a rash of sponsored content—although it's worth monitoring whether there's an uptick in its frequency during the months and years ahead—but regardless of what shows up on the site, it's important to remember that most music and culture publications have limited editorial resources. And while a place like the New York Times might be big enough to completely silo its brand content teams, smaller publications will often call upon their regular writers, editors and designers to assist with branded work. From an ethical perspective, that's less than ideal, but even on a practical level, it often means that those people wind up having less time to devote to their usual journalism work (i.e. the stuff that they were supposedly hired to do).

In fairness, although music and culture journalism do have "journalism" in the name, the field has never really been journalism in the traditional sense of the word. Even when most publications were in print and had a lot more money to work with, their business models relied upon the idea that they were presenting a collection of stories and images that appealed to a certain consumer demographic. That objective hasn't really changed much over the years, and while quality storytelling still occurs, it's a stretch to describe any culture publication as a proper news outlet. Most of the time, music and culture journalists aren't breaking news or engaging in real reporting. That's not necessarily bad; cultural commentary has value, and not every piece of content needs to be an eye-opening investigative report, but audiences still ought to be aware of the larger forces at work.

When media outlets increasingly rely upon brand partnerships to survive, it does—or at least should—raise questions, the first one being, "Who are they really serving?" Are music and culture publications genuinely a source of quality information and storytelling for the reading public, or are they simply an adjunct to the marketing efforts of giant corporations? In practice, the answer of course isn't one thing or the other, but the fact that the truth lies somewhere in between—and is so rarely acknowledged in the "discourse"—is already cause for concern.

The Other (Bigger) Dance Music
a.k.a. The unexamined stories of EDM, tech house and dance music's commercial sphere.

August 9, 2022

—

People sometimes ask me why I always put the word "underground" in quotes. Quite frankly, it's because I'm not really sure what it means anymore, at least in reference to dance music. I suppose it functions as a kind of catch-all that signifies "everything that's not EDM," but now that even middle- and lower-tier DJs often have managers, booking agents and PR firms helping them to secure high-paying gigs and build a marketable "brand," calling them underground no longer feels appropriate—hence the quotes.

During the past decade, a massive wave of commercialization has swept through dance music, and yet the genre's most prominent media outlets seem determined to pretend that the culture is still primarily unfolding in clandestine warehouse raves. Even as much of the music journalism sphere has pivoted towards pop and more commercial sounds, the dance music press has chosen to effectively ignore many of the genre's most economically successful (and, at least in theory, culturally impactful) corners. That's a bizarre choice, and while the aging raver in me would love to think it's because these publications are determined to "keep it real," this piece attempts to dissect what's really going on.

———

Dance music is a global, multibillion-dollar industry. According to this year's IMS Business Report, the sector's value topped $6 billion in 2021, and that's actually down 20% from its pre-pandemic high in 2019.[1] And yet, even with all this money floating around, dance music's media landscape feels incomplete.

It's not that there aren't a variety of publications out there. They might be overly concentrated in the UK (and overrepresent UK writers/perspectives), but between Resident Advisor, DJ Mag, Mixmag, Crack and another dozen or so outlets, a whole lot of dance music-related content is being created, even at places (e.g. Pitchfork, Bandcamp Daily, Dazed, The Face) where dance music isn't the primary focus. The quality of said content isn't always great—although that's arguably true in pretty much every corner of music journalism these days, regardless of the genre being covered—but even if what's being published is largely throwaway and surface-level stuff, there are enough writers and publications out there to present something resembling a comprehensive look at what's happening in dance music at any given moment.

A comprehensive look, however, is not really what's being provided. Scanning across different outlets, it quickly becomes clear that not only are these publications frequently covering the exact same things, but that those things usually constitute only a misleading fraction of the overall dance music ecosystem. If a dance music novice was to flip through the virtual pages of Resident Advisor, they might be left with the impression that Berghain is the most important club in the world, Dekmantel is the top festival and places like Ibiza exist only as a punchline, unless someone like DJ Harvey visits the island. Of course there are other bits of content on offer, and it's admirable that RA—and other prominent outlets—have made a concerted effort to diversify the artists and stories being platformed during the past two years, but at the same time, it is strange that dance music's most well known (and most frequently referenced) publications often act as though the genre's more blatantly commercial sphere (i.e. its biggest songs, artists, clubs and festivals) simply don't exist.

In fairness, First Floor isn't much different. Although I would never bill the newsletter as "the voice of global dance music and culture"—as Mixmag very much did in its promotional 2021 media pack for potential advertisers and brand partners—I do frequently ignore the areas of dance and electronic music that don't interest me, assuming that analysis of the latest Deadmau5 single likely wouldn't entice my readers either. This is something that most media outlets do; time and resources are limited, so instead of covering everything, most publications instead stake out a particular editorial niche and stick to it, working to establish themselves as go-to "experts" in their corner of the industry/culture.

What is odd though is that when it comes to dance music, so much of the industry is essentially being ignored. While a handful of outlets (e.g. Dancing Astronaut, Your EDM, EDM.com) do dedicate themselves to covering EDM and the other more pop/commercial corners of dance music, they're rarely held up as bastions of serious music journalism, and don't tend to serve as launching pads for writers and editors toward bigger outlets and more wide-ranging careers. (Billboard, where Katie Bain is currently the director of dance/electronic coverage, might be the lone exception, although the publication—which clearly focuses on a variety of topics and genres—does seem to have deactivated its dedicated Billboard Dance channel.)

As a fan, I don't personally care all that much about this, and it's unlikely that a lack of coverage about whoever is in the Beatport Top 100 bothers most other dance music journalists either. Although dance music is no longer the purely independent/DIY phenomenon it once was (literally decades ago), a certain "underground" mentality (or at least a remnant of it) remains woven into its DNA. Things like EDM, tech house, and so-called "business techno" might be hugely popular (not to mention profitable), but they're not necessarily perceived as "cool" or "authentic," and that makes them anathema to most people (including journalists and other tastemakers) who consider themselves fans of "real" dance music and its supposedly high-minded origins/traditions.

In 2022, the exact definitions of terms like "underground" and "authentic" have become increasingly fuzzy, particularly as dance music has grown into a global behemoth, yet they still carry conceptual weight, especially in a social media-driven culture where perception often trumps substance. On a more concrete level, these ideas also carry a lot of economic weight, particularly in the publishing world, where many outlets only survive by selling themselves to consumers, advertisers and corporate sponsors as bastions of cutting-edge culture. Sites like Resident Advisor and DJ Mag might have news sections, but it's important to recognize that presenting a well-rounded, wholly complete picture of dance music isn't really their main goal.

In that sense, these outlets (and their primary competitors) aren't all that different from the thousands of other culture publications out there. What is strange, however, is that so few outlets have attempted to swoop in and fill the void in what's being covered. EDM and tech house are massive. The live music industry figured that out long ago, and accordingly adjusted its practices to capitalize on that reality, but the culture commentator class (which includes journalists, along with other tastemakers, influencers and the kinds of people who incessantly post on Twitter) has largely responded to commercial dance music with abject derision, or by simply ignoring it altogether.

Considering how music journalism has shifted during the past 10-15 years, this is bizarre. The rise of poptimism has largely dispatched the indie snobs of old, and looking down one's nose at Beyoncé, Rosalía or any other pop star is now seen by many as retrograde, closed-minded thinking, at least when the dismissal of their work is solely based on their fame, commercial appeal or the type of music they make. Regardless of whether or not this is a good thing—and for what it's worth, it's had a lot of negative side effects, including a wholesale validation of star worship and stan culture—it's simply the state of affairs at this point.

Yet even as the music press—and the music industry at large—has come to embrace the biggest pop stars in the world, dance music's most commercial acts haven't been welcomed into the tent. Maybe that's because so much of the pop music conversation is dominated by the US, a country whose misunderstanding of (and frequent animosity towards) dance music dates back decades. Maybe it's because so many of the leading dance/electronic music writers are older people with connections to the genre's more "underground" days, and they bring that perspective (some might say bias) into their work. Some might even say that EDM and tech house aren't genres whose fans have much interest in "discourse," and while the idea that those musical styles are rooted in mindless hedonism does hold a certain amount of water, that kind of wholesale dismissal seems both short-sighted and snobbish. (It's also the kind of thing people used to say about genres like hip-hop and reggaeton, and we've seen how that turned out.)

At this point, perhaps the "why" doesn't matter. Somehow, we've arrived at a place where a form of massively popular music (and the culture that surrounds it) has been largely unexamined for more than a decade. I personally may not be interested in the artists playing at festivals like Ultra and Tomorrowland, but it's nonetheless weird that by and large, there's almost nothing written about them, even in more mainstream music media outlets. Take a look at Pitchfork's recent electronic music reviews; for every Odesza who gets featured, there are a lot more artists like Kuedo and Vladislav Delay garnering coverage. The divide is even more striking in Resident Advisor's review section, which finds room for the new Beyoncé album and will occasionally reach for other mainstream pop stars, but largely ignores EDM/tech house entirely, instead highlighting smaller acts, many of which aren't even at a level where a site like Pitchfork would take notice.

These editorial decisions do ripple out across the music industry (and pop culture at large). Although the music media's days of setting the cultural agenda are more or less over, what gets coverage feeds into prevailing notions of what artists, trends, subcultures, etc. "matter." Culture tends to trickle from the bottom up, but that trickle is almost always facilitated by tastemakers and decision-makers in positions of power and influence, and right now those folks are heavily skewed toward certain sectors of dance music. Artists who appear on Resident Advisor, DJ Mag, Crack, etc.—and, if I'm being honest, in First Floor as well—are often presented to the world as "independent" and/or "underground" acts, but what does that really mean when many of them have managers, PR reps, booking agents and labels pushing that narrative?

Of course, many EDM and commercial dance artists also have sizable teams of their own (not to mention connections with giant booking agencies and high-level event organizers), but whatever hype exists around them, it's usually not being generated by journalists or other industry tastemakers. What these acts are doing might be garish, tacky, derivative or simply in service of terrible music, but in some ways, their trajectories are more organic and "DIY" than whatever fashionable new act is being pushed by XL or Warp Records this week. Knowing that, why are these artists not also part of the cultural conversation?

Again, I myself am not clamoring to read about Skrillex, Tiësto, Steve Aoki or whatever other acts are rocketing up Apple Music's Dance Pop Hits playlist, but considering the global popularity of their music, somebody probably is, especially if it's written about in a thoughtful way. It's delusional to think that these artists aren't profoundly influencing and shaping culture, and have been for years. (The rise of hyperpop is many things, including a clear confirmation that EDM aesthetics have firmly sunk into the fabric of pop.) Younger generations of dance music journalists have already begun to let down their guard when it comes to pop music—case in point: Carly Rae Jepsen is on the cover of the current issue of Crack—but why does that reach past the "underground" canon only seem to extend to most obvious Top 40 acts? Is there honestly nothing of creative value happening in the entire EDM and tech house sphere? Even if there isn't, is it not a large enough cultural phenomenon to examine seriously?

There are countless stories being left untold, and for anyone interested in what's going on musically and the forces/factors driving it, that's unfortunate. Moreover, in an era when so many journalists and media outlets have reoriented their craft toward covering and dissecting pop music, the industry's ongoing "ignore it and hope it goes away" attitude towards commercial dance music also feels something like hypocrisy.

Beyoncé and Drake Aren't Reviving Anything
a.k.a. House music isn't in need of saving, and major labels aren't interested in that anyways.

June 28, 2022
—

The mainstream press has never been great with dance music, especially in the US, but every once in a while, the media's ignorance of the genre really comes to the forefront. The summer of 2022 was one such time, as Beyoncé and Drake both had new albums rooted in dance music (or, more accurately, albums that were simply billed as such), and publications—many of which usually ignore the genre altogether—immediately responded with their usual bevy of star worship, trotting out wildly inaccurate narratives and ahistorical claims about the "revival" of house music.

The particulars of those narratives (and my frustrations with them) were laid out explicitly in this piece, and while what the music press was saying was pretty egregious at the time, their words look even worse in retrospect. Although Beyoncé's *Renaissance* did receive all sorts of accolades (including a Grammy for Best Dance/Electronic Album), there has been no resulting house music boom in the pop sphere, and the average person remains largely ignorant of the genre, its history and its contemporary culture.

When the mainstream and a vibrant subculture collide, it rarely goes well for the latter. It's something I've seen many times before—which, on the plus side, did allow me to slip in some punk/emo references in this essay's opening paragraph—but it's still a bummer to watch it play it out.

———

Over the weekend, I finished a book called *Sellout: The Major-Label Feeding Frenzy That Swept Punk, Emo, and Hardcore (1994–2007)*. Released last year and written by Dan Ozzi, it spotlights 11 different bands—the likes of Green Day, Blink 182, Jawbreaker, At the Drive-In, Thursday and My Chemical Romance among them—and specifically focuses on each of their major label debuts. As someone who came of age during this time and spent a fair chunk of the late '90s at various emo, indie and punk shows—for what it's worth, I was also going to raves during those years—the book had a certain nostalgic appeal. However, it also provided an interesting look back at the post-Nirvana era, showcasing both the machinations of major labels in search of "the next big thing" and the internal politics of punk rock and independent music, which fractured in the face of giant checks and the sudden interest of the cultural mainstream.

In the wake of Drake's *Honestly, Nevermind* album and the Beyoncé single "Break My Soul"—both of which borrow from house music—the cultural mainstream is once again rubbing up against a music culture and community that largely exists outside the Top 40 pop landscape. Dance music has been through this before of course—most notably during the "electronica" boom of the late '90s and the EDM explosion that followed about a decade later—but where past surges often involved a bottom-up push in which new/relatively unknown/"underground" acts were being actively marketed to wider audiences, what's happening now is a byproduct of the biggest artists in the world suddenly dabbling in the genre.

Given the world's obsession with anything Drake or Beyoncé does, it's no surprise that their new releases have prompted an uptick of interest in dance music, especially amongst those (critics included) who previously gave the genre little more than a passing thought. Unfortunately, much of the resulting "discourse" has had all the depth of a children's wading pool, particularly amongst the more American corners of social media, where comparing the Drake and Beyoncé records to the music one hears in the dressing room of an H&M apparently constitutes both high comedy and insightful analysis. The commentary provided by the professional music press often hasn't been much better, and while I'm not inclined to compile all of the dreck here, the list that The Face recently slapped together of "The Best Pop-House Tracks to Get You Dancing This Summer" feels like a good example of the opportunistic, surface-level and (most importantly) click-friendly content that many outlets have churned out during the past two weeks.

In fairness, paper-thin Drake and Beyoncé articles have been a music media staple for more than a decade. The only difference is that now those articles are referencing dance music, a world that most pop, hip-hop and R&B writers aren't particularly well versed in. As such, the past week has produced some occasionally cringe-worthy copy, including the following line from that above-referenced piece in The Face: "like it or not, house music is having a *massive* mainstream moment." (The italics are theirs.)

That claim may or may not prove correct in the weeks and months ahead, but that hasn't stopped the media from repeating it over and over. Here's a sampling of recent headlines:

- BBC News: "Beyoncé, Drake and the Revival of 90s House Music"

- The Atlantic: "Beyoncé and Drake Reimagine the Rave"

- El País: "How Beyoncé Resurrected House Music"

- Mother Jones: "Beyoncé Is Bringing Back House Music—and Not a Moment Too Soon"

- The Guardian: "House Music Had Its Black Roots Ripped Up—Now Drake and Beyoncé Are Reclaiming Them"

- Refinery29: "House Music Has BEEN Black—Beyoncé Is Just Bringing It Back"

While it's encouraging to see a few mainstream outlets loudly touting the Black roots of house music—a fact that many people are still unaware of, even in the US, despite the genre's distinctly American origins—the larger narrative here has little to do with setting the historical record straight. What's emerging instead is a tale in which uber-famous pop artists are being cast as the saviors of house music, a genre that had, at least according to this story, apparently disappeared or died altogether. It's not necessarily a purposeful mishandling of the facts—ignorance and star worship are much more likely root causes—but the narrative being spun remains woefully inaccurate all the same.

Dance music may not be a staple of the US pop charts, but it's far from dead. On the contrary, it's at the heart of a global, multibillion-dollar industry. And while that industry includes several different styles of music—including EDM, which is likely more familiar to the average Drake and Beyoncé fan—house music remains one of its foundational pillars, and continues to be one of the most popular genres in the world, especially outside of the US. The idea that it was in need of "resurrection" is ludicrous.

Both people working in dance music and dedicated fans already know this, and there's been some minor pushback, mostly in the form of grousing on social media. At the same time, there's also been a wave of optimism, with hopeful artists positing that perhaps the Beyoncé and Drake albums will lead to some sort of trickle-down effect, with pop fans eventually discovering "real" house music and major labels enlisting credible independent artists for high-profile production work and big-budget remix projects. It's a nice thought, especially considering how difficult it is for the average house music producer to earn a living these days, but in reality, the chances of turning back the clock to 1995, when acts like Masters at Work were cranking out three major label remixes a week and getting five-figure checks for each one, are slim.

Perhaps things could change, but at the moment, artists like Drake and Beyoncé aren't reaching deep into the "underground" to produce their latest work. The only genuine house music artist on *Honestly, Nevermind* is Black Coffee, a South African producer who's previously collaborated with Drake, and whose commercial bent has literally made him one of the biggest DJs in the world. On Beyoncé's "Break My Soul," her primary songwriting collaborators are Tricky Stewart and The-Dream—who are both incredibly talented, but neither one comes from house music. The track does sample the Robin S. classic "Show Me Love," but the repurposing of a '90s anthem that's been ubiquitous enough to power several generations of bar mitzvahs and drunken karaoke excursions can hardly be considered a subversive (or particularly innovative) act. I'm no Kanye West fan, but his song "Fade"—which sampled Mr. Fingers' "Mystery of Love," Hardrive's "Deep Inside" and Barbara Tucker's "I Get Lifted"—dove significantly deeper into the house music canon, and that came out back in 2015.

It's nice to imagine that mainstream interest will somehow elevate the entire dance music sphere, but looking back at the history of major label interaction with cultural subgenres, has that ever really happened? Even in the most successful cases (e.g. punk, grunge), the major labels haven't invested broadly in music communities; they show up, scout for talent, throw money around, skim from the top and eventually move on once audience interest and/or the potential to make a profit dries up. Along the way, a handful of acts get big checks and maybe the chance to make a big-budget record they wouldn't have been able to do otherwise, but the notion that it's a net positive for the entire scene is highly debatable.

That's especially true when so much of the current house music hype remains centered on global pop stars, as opposed to artists who come from an actual house music lineage. If this remains the dominant paradigm, whatever "opportunities" that come along for independent artists most likely won't involve actually getting signed to a major label; if anything, they'll look a lot more like the recent remix albums from Dua Lipa and Lady Gaga. To their credit, those releases did enlist some credible artists; the former, 2020's *Club Future Nostalgia*, was executive produced by The Blessed Madonna and featured the likes of Moodymann, Mr. Fingers, Paul Woolford, Jayda G, Masters at Work, Yaeji and a slew of other acts. Lady Gaga's *Dawn of Chromatica*, which dropped last year, included remixes from Arca, LSDXOXO, Shygirl, Charli XCX and A.G. Cook, Doss, Jimmy Edgar and a number of other producers.

That's a fairly impressive collection of dance music talent, and it's good to know that these acts—some of which have been around for decades—presumably got both a decent payday and a bit of mainstream promotion. At the same time, it's not an accurate snapshot of what's popping in dance music's most innovative circles. Almost every artist involved is someone who was already a staple of the international club and festival circuit, and many of them were already plugged into the major label system in some fashion. In terms of curation, these releases are only impressive in the sense that "these aren't bad for major label pop remix albums," and that's a low bar to clear.

It's also worth noting that outside of the discourse they've generated, none of these recent releases have had much of a lasting musical impact. Both *Club Future Nostalgia* and *Dawn of Chromatica* briefly topped the Billboard Top Dance/Electronic Albums chart, but they quickly faded into the ether, and now feel more like curios than collections of bona fide bangers. The response to Drake's *Honestly, Nevermind* has been lukewarm, especially amongst American audiences, and while the ultimate legacy of "Break My Soul" hinges on the reception to Beyoncé's forthcoming *Renaissance* album, the cultural conversation to date has focused on lot more on the "reviving house music" angle and what Beyoncé is supposedly trying to say about the Great Resignation than the quality of the song itself.[1] Simply put, the pop world may be attempting to sell house music to the masses right now, but it's far from clear that the average music fan is actually interested in buying it.

1. The lyrics of "Break My Soul" mention the recent quitting of an exhausting job, and were widely interpreted as a reference to the much-publicized wave of resignations that took place in 2021/2022 as pandemic restrictions were lightened and people were expected to return to in-person work.

It's too soon to know whether this renewed mainstream interest in house music will develop into anything concrete. Given the speed at which culture moves nowadays, it could easily become a "remember when?" moment within a matter of months. But even if it does take off, and house music becomes the hottest new trend in pop, it's unlikely that will be something to celebrate, and not because it violates some (largely antiquated) notions of "selling out" the culture.

This isn't the '90s, and the major labels aren't looking to lure artists out of the basement with huge checks and promises of becoming a star. In truth, they're not really looking to corrupt or transform anyone; they no longer have to. Animosity to mainstream pop is lower than it's been in decades, and major labels by and large aren't looking to sign niche independent artists anymore. They'd rather take notes from those artists' creative toolkits and then pass that information along to their established properties (i.e. people like Drake, Beyoncé and all the other pop stars looking to follow in their footsteps). In a very real way, the modern-day pop machine is a kind of pyramid scheme, and while getting artists at the bottom to participate might require spending a little money, or doling out the occasional songwriting/production credit, it's ultimately an extractive enterprise.

In the eyes of major labels—and the wider cultural mainstream —house music is simply another resource to be mined in the service of contemporary pop stardom. "Reviving" the genre is not on their to-do list, and supporting the wider house/dance music ecosystem in any kind of sustainable, long-term fashion isn't even part of the conversation. Independent artists, many of them starved for resources, income and attention, might go along for the ride anyways, but in most cases, neither they or their fans are likely to be happy with the end result.

The Latin Music Gold Rush
a.k.a. A closer look at electronic music's current fascination with Latin sounds.

January 24, 2023
—

I'm Latin. Half Latin, to be more exact. (My father was born in Cuba.) It's not something I discuss very often in my work, but it is part of who I am, and as such, the following piece is perhaps a bit more personally charged than many of the other writings in this book.

It's not about me though. It's about the sudden embrace of Latin artists and sounds that's taken place within the electronic music world during the past year, and how that embrace sometimes feels less like progress and more like a perpetuation of stereotypes of what "authentic" Latin culture entails. It's about how despite this surge of interest, those who seem to be benefiting most aren't actually those in Latin America, but diaspora kids and culture vultures. It's about how the electronic music industry—and the press in particular—makes a big show out of its commitment to diverse storytelling, but ultimately chooses superficial gestures over meaningful engagement.

I'm thrilled at the prospect of Latin electronic music finally getting the attention and respect it deserves. I'm not yet convinced that's what's actually happening.

————

Last week, the ACA label announced its first release. A joint venture between Phran (a Venezuelan artist based in Barcelona) and NAP (a Colombian artist who came of age in Canada and currently resides in Mexico City), the new imprint will officially debut in March with *The Tribe* (*Baila*), an archival EP from DJ

Babatr, a veteran producer from Caracas who's credited with developing the "raptor house" sound.[1] Within days, news stories about the forthcoming record appeared on Resident Advisor[2] and DJ Mag[3], both of which hailed Babatr's status as a raptor house "pioneer."

A few days later, Hyperdub—a label that's practically synonymous with the concept of the UK hardcore continuum—announced the forthcoming release of *Eslabón,* an EP from Houston producer Santa Muerte. Said to be "inspired by the mythology and religion of Mexican culture crossed with the bass-heavy sound of the city's hip-hop scene," the record looks to be the first overtly Latin entry in the storied label's catalog. That same day, I received an email from a UK-based PR rep who literally led her pitch with the fact that the record was coming from a Colombian artist on a Colombian label, and went on to describe the forthcoming release as "another shining example of the sounds of LATAM breaking out into the global underground scene."

Something is going on here, and while it's been bubbling up for a while, it's pretty clear that the attention paid to Florida producer Nick León is what truly threw open the floodgates. His breakout 2022 tune "Xtasis"—a collaboration with the aforementioned DJ Babatr—was named the track of the year by both Resident Advisor and Crack, and also prompted electronic music tastemakers to take a fresh look at Miami. Once the butt of countless jokes (many of them related to tech house and bottle service), the city—and specifically, its Latin-influenced new generation of artists—has as of late been widely christened as the hottest up-and-coming scene in dance music, and Latin rhythms, with a major assist from the press, have suddenly become electronic music's biggest hype. (Need proof? TraTraTrax, the Colombian label which released "Xtasis," was recently described as 2022's label of the year by Resident Advisor, with writer Andrew Ryce

1. Native to Caracas, raptor house (a.k.a. changa tuki) first emerged in the early '90s as an outgrowth of the city's local soundsystem culture, and combines elements of house with Latin/Caribbean rhythms to form a unique (and bass-heavy) variant of dance music.

2. Hawthorn, Carlos. "Caracas's Dj Babatr, pioneer of raptor house, announces first vinyl EP." *Resident Advisor*, January 18, 2023, https://ra.co/news/78370.

3. Eede, Christian. "DJ Babatr, Venezuelan raptor house pioneer, announces debut vinyl release, 'The Tribe (Baila)'." *DJ Mag*, January 18, 2023, https://djmag.com/news/dj-babatr-venezuelan-raptor-house-pioneer-announces-debut-vinyl-release-tribe-baila.

going so far as to say that the imprint "feels like it could be this decade's Hessle Audio."[4])

That's great, right? Throughout its history, the electronic music industry has generally held firm to a resoundingly UK and Eurocentric focus, and while some of that attention has since been shifted over to the US, regions like Latin America have often been left completely out of the conversation. The electronic music press has been especially disappointing on this front. Prior to last year, the only mention of the phrase "raptor house" in Resident Advisor's editorial offerings was a single 2011 news story.[5] (In truth, even calling the piece a news story is generous, as the post provided zero context and merely pointed listeners toward a short piece on the genre that writer Dave Quam put together for the now-defunct publication Cluster Mag.) DJ Mag's record is even worse; before 2022, it seems to have published exactly zero mentions of the term "raptor house." Given that history, the fact that DJ Babatr—a working-class artist who's been active for more than two decades but has never achieved widespread recognition—is suddenly someone whose latest release is automatically newsworthy does feel like something to celebrate.

At the same time, what's really driving this sudden surge of interest? Is electronic music truly looking to broaden its musical (and geographical) horizons, or is what's happening now just the latest "hot new thing" in a subculture that's always been susceptible to fleeting trends? It's not really clear, and even if questions about those motivations are completely set aside, it's nonetheless concerning that both the economic success and perceived artistic validity of Latin artists continues to be so highly dependent on the whims of European, UK and US decision makers—particularly when the relevant knowledge base of said decision makers does little to warrant such a responsibility.

As much as the music press (and the wider industry) has worked to present the latest wave of Latin electronic music as a new phenomenon, that's a fiction. Electronic music has been

4. Ryce, Andrew. "Various (TraTraTrax) - no pare, sigue sigue." *Resident Advisor*, December 19, 2022, https://ra.co/reviews/35216.

5. Keeling, Ryan. "Venezuelan raptor house." *Resident Advisor*, May 11, 2011, https://ra.co/news/56178.

present in Latin America for decades, often in forms that aren't terribly different from the house and techno sounds that have long been a staple of the European, UK and US scenes. Why then have the artists making those sounds historically gained so little traction? Is a house record from Uruguay or a techno record from Nicaragua inherently inferior to its European or American counterparts? Obviously not, but aside from rare occasions—usually when a particular scene happens to be located in a place (e.g. Mexico City, Buenos Aires, Bogotá) that's become a trendy tourism destination—Latin American electronic music that conforms to European/UK/US genre norms rarely seems to garner much attention. More often than not, the prevailing attitude seems to be, "We already have that here, so why would we care about a Latin version?"

It's not that electronic music tastemakers haven't fallen in love with Latin sounds before. They have, many times, and while the examples are too numerous to list in full, a couple of the most prominent include Brazilian baile funk and electro-cumbia (primarily from Argentina and its ZZK label, but also from places like Mexico and Colombia), which helped kickstart a wave of "global bass" excitement during the late 2000s. More recently, the "deconstructed club" trend of the 2010s helped usher Mexico's N.A.A.F.I crew into the spotlight. For whatever reason, the wider electronic music world only seems to acknowledge that Latin America exists every five or ten years—a ludicrous proposition considering how central music and dancing are to the region's culture and history—and when it does happen, folks only tend to be interested in musical movements that exude some kind of perceived authenticity.

"Perceived" is the key word there, because what European, UK and US audiences consider to be "authentic" is often rooted in stereotypes and imagined ideas of what Latin culture is all about. Viewed through this oversimplifying lens, Latin music ought to be vibrant, colorful and overtly sensual. The drums should be polyrhythmic. The presence of mystical (i.e. indigenous) elements is a plus, and if the musical style in question can be tied to marginalized and working-class communities (preferably contemporary, although historical will suffice), that's even better. It's exoticism, pure and simple, and this kind of exultation/ objectification of the proverbial "other" has been capturing the imagination of Western audiences for centuries. Moreover, in modern times, it's enabled those audiences—and well-meaning progressives in particular—to congratulate themselves for their diverse listening habits and interest in foreign cultures.

Today's electronic music scene would likely struggle to cop to that kind of behavior, as most tastemakers would probably frame their current excitement about Latin rhythms as part of their ongoing interest in bold new sounds. But let's be real; when it comes to supporting Latin music, the electronic music world has never led the way, and embarrassingly lags well behind the commercial pop sphere. Artists like Daddy Yankee and Pitbull were topping the global charts more than a decade ago, but it's only in the past few years that the average techno fan has realized that maybe there's something interesting about reggaeton. Aside from the fact that elements of reggaeton, cumbia, baile funk and other Latin sounds are now suddenly being heard in new contexts (e.g. European, UK and US clubs that previously devoted themselves strictly to house and techno), there's very little that's genuinely "new" about any of this music. (And no, combining a reggaeton beat with a pitched-up Britney sample and some Rusko-style wobble bass doesn't really qualify as new either.)

In fairness, labels like TraTraTrax have fostered the creation of some new hybrid sounds, but they'd more accurately be classified as variants than anything resembling a fully-formed genre. At a fundamental level, Latin music simply hasn't changed all that much, regardless of what the present hype says; it's just that electronic music audiences in Europe, the UK and the US are now more willing to hear it. That's fine, and the development of more open-minded dancefloors is something to be encouraged, but it's still maddening when people in electronic music—and especially those in positions of influence—act as though they've been on board with Latin sounds all along. Publications like Resident Advisor and DJ Mag might casually throw around terms like raptor house now, but as detailed above, a quick look at their archives makes clear that they've both arrived extremely late to this particular party.

Granted, this kind of fakery isn't specific to these media outlets, or even an interest in Latin music. Tastemaker types have always had a tendency to feign expertise. (After all, few things are less "cool" than admitting to not knowing about a particular sound, trend, style, scene, etc. that other folks are talking about.) Even so, it's a dishonest practice, and when committed by what are two of electronic music's most prominent publications, it represents a fairly gross distortion of not just musical history, but those entities' role in shaping it. If press outlets are now going to act like they all along knew that raptor house, reggaeton, cumbia or any other style of Latin music was something great, how can they square that with the fact that they barely bothered to cover it? And why did the limited attention they did pay to Latin sounds rarely last longer than the music's fleeting hype cycles in Europe, the UK and the US, particularly when those cycles rarely corresponded with the music's actual relevance and popularity in the region where it was born? It's not like cumbia stopped being made when people who first read about it in the FADER in 2008 stopped paying attention to the genre.

The main answer is simple: market forces. Although the electronic music industry has gradually become a worldwide enterprise, its home base—and core audience—has always been (and continues to be) located in Europe, the UK and the US, and electronic music fans in those places have never had much of a sustained interest in Latin music. Resident Advisor may bill itself online as "the world's leading platform for electronic music discovery and connection" while DJ Mag touts its status as "a global multimedia brand," but neither outlet has ever devoted serious resources to engaging with Latin America, let alone covering the region's music scenes with any kind of sustained depth. (Of the two, RA has arguably done a better job—past features on Mexico City's sonidero culture, Colombia's techno scene and Brazilian grime come to mind—but dropping a long-form article every year or so can't really be classified as comprehensive coverage of a region that spans two continents and is home to more than 600 million people.)

Even if these publications wanted to provide a more substantive look at what's happening in Latin America, achieving such a goal is borderline impossible for a niche outlet operating in today's media landscape. During the past two decades, music journalism has been hollowed out by the internet and social media, and in a time of shrinking revenue streams, diminished resources and more artists/releases coming their way than ever before, electronic music publications barely have the bandwidth to cover anything outside of the London-Berlin-New York axis. Does this result in horribly slanted narratives? Absolutely, but when the genre's dedicated outlets don't even have a proper handle on what's going on in established electronic music hubs like Barcelona, Manchester and Montreal, it's laughable to think that thoughtful coverage of what's happening in Buenos Aires and Lima is somehow in the cards.

It is true that the visible Latin presence in contemporary electronic music culture is bigger now than it's been in decades. In 2023, names like DJ Python, Nicola Cruz, Matías Aguayo, DJ Florentino, Cardopusher and Nick León are likely familiar to those who are even mildly engaged with the current electronic music landscape, and the shadow cast by someone like Arca extends even further, tipping over into both the fashion world and the pop mainstream. This does represent a level of progress, but before the electronic music crowd rushes to pat itself on the back, perhaps a closer look is warranted. Scanning these names, how many of them are some combination of white, male and upper class? More importantly, how many are already based in Europe, the UK or the US? These artists, talented as they are, do not represent a complete portrait of Latin electronic music in 2023; they don't even represent an accurate portrait of the wider Latin diaspora.

Is that their fault? Of course not, and I don't mean to negate any of their work. The artistic expressions of those who left Latin America (and their descendants) can obviously still be valid in their own right. At the same time, privilege and proximity matter, especially when the electronic music industry is so heavily rooted in social interaction. While Latin artists living in Europe, the UK and the US—along with those who simply have the economic resources and legal ability to freely and easily travel to those places—undoubtedly face their own struggles, it's disingenuous to pretend that they don't have a massive leg up over their counterparts in Latin America.

It's not just a question of geography either. Electronic music, like all subcultures, is something that's governed by all kinds of informal rules, norms and ways of doing business, the vast majority of which haven't been written down. Those rules, which are largely native to Europe, the UK and the US, are something that most people in the industry (and even most dedicated fans) don't even think about, but they nonetheless color our collective expectations of how artists are supposed to produce, present and promote their work. Nobody is born knowing how to effectively word and format a promotional email. There's no industry handbook stating that audio files ought to be shared via Dropbox, WeTransfer or Google Drive. It's only in the past few years that Bandcamp has become the go-to sales platform for independent music. And yet, artists are generally expected to know and adapt their practice to all of these things.

Even for those who've spent their entire lives in Europe, the UK or the US, keeping up with those expectations—which are constantly changing—is a major challenge. For artists in Latin America, the difficulty level is even higher, as they have to face that same challenge while also navigating a language barrier and the fact that their own local music scenes most likely have a completely different way of doing things. It's no wonder that so few of them manage to crack the code, nor is it a surprise that the ones who do frequently come from relatively privileged backgrounds. The electronic music ranks are full of cosmopolitan "citizens of the world" that comfortably move across borders and can effortlessly exist in trendy cultural spaces all around the globe, but attaining that status is a lot harder when you come from a place where incomes are low, poverty is high and leaving the country is prohibitively expensive and/or legally difficult.

Parsing all of this is a complicated process, and unfortunately, "complicated" rarely translates in a music culture where merely posting "I did a thing" on social media tends to have a much bigger impact on someone's clout and influence than whether or not said "thing" has any real substance. Knowing that, key decision makers in the electronic music industry (e.g. festival bookers, journalists, editors, agents, labels, etc.), when faced with an obvious pressure to present a more diverse array of artists and sounds, have generally responded by taking the path of least resistance and promoting whatever is easiest.

In the case of Latin music, the widespread lack of understanding about what constitutes Latin culture and identity has made it particularly easy for the industry to do the bare minimum, as platforms can champion a bunch of white Latin artists—most of whom either live and/or grew up in the UK, the US or Europe—and claim that they're doing their part. Is this progress? Perhaps it is on some level, and to be clear, a white guy who grew up in the US, the UK or Europe can still be Latin and have unique perspectives to share. However, when the bulk of Latin representation in electronic music consists of that guy (and folks that share a similar level of privilege), it's absurd to act as though the current flurry of Latin hype represents some kind of towering achievement.

Simply put, electronic music—like most musical subcultures and industries—still has a long way to go when it comes to representation. With Latin music currently in the spotlight, it's already clear that those benefiting the most from the present wave of hype by and large aren't the ones located in Latin America.

Take the aforementioned raptor house: is it just a buzzword that tastemakers will use to sound cool and knowledgeable, or will there be a genuine effort to learn about the music's history and engage with those responsible for making it? Based on what we've seen so far, the former seems a lot more likely, and in the months ahead, it's a safe bet that we'll see a lot more DJs from Europe, the UK and the US being praised for playing DJ Babatr records than we'll see actual DJ Babatr DJ gigs outside of his native Venezuela.

Larger social, political and economic issues obviously come into play here, but it's nonetheless discouraging to think that the electronic music world still has such a strong tendency to conflate celebration with extraction. Latin music—and frankly, all music that comes from outside of the US, the UK and Europe—isn't meant to be a prop in some kind of clout-chasing diversity play, and when electronic music's biggest publications are bolstering their progressive bona fides with transparently shallow coverage, it's difficult to believe that any kind of substantive change has taken place. Although no one is expecting journalists—or anyone in electronic music—to become academic-level experts in Latin music and culture, there's plenty of room for improvement. (Hiring more Latin people, and particularly Latin people based in Latin America, would certainly be a good place to start.)

What's presently happening with Latin electronic music is exciting, but if it's going to be more than just another hyped trend that fades out in a year or two, a more thoughtful approach is necessary. That doesn't mean Nick León, TraTraTrax or anyone else who's popping at the moment still has to be the hottest thing in dance music five years from now; music is always changing, and certain styles will inevitably fall in and out of fashion. At the same time, it's no longer acceptable for the music industry to treat all of Latin culture—or any culture—as a trend, and the notion that Latin music, regardless of where it's being created, is only intermittently interesting and worthy of our attention is a perspective that needs to be tossed into the scrap heap of history.

The Crumbling Palaces of Electronic Music Media a.k.a. The press is in bad shape, so why does the industry routinely pretend otherwise?

January 31, 2023

—

Living in Barcelona, I see majestic old buildings every day. The city is full of them, and the local government mandates that their exteriors be maintained to a certain standard. This makes for quite the visual experience when one is strolling around town, but those of us who live here know that looks can be deceiving, and behind many of these beautiful facades are run-down spaces whose interiors are slowly falling to pieces.

In many ways, electronic music's most prominent publications have suffered the same fate. From the outside, they look like functioning media outlets, and continue to churn out glossy content that looks impressive to the casual viewer, but anyone who bothers to peek inside and take a closer look will quickly see not only a severely compromised framework, but people (most of them well intentioned, but also under resourced and poorly paid) scrambling to maintain the illusion of competence. It's a pantomime of journalism, and what's worse is that the wider electronic music industry, paralyzed by a need to constantly promote itself, continues to play along, happily reposting low-grade content and setting up media partnership agreements as the credibility of the entire enterprise slowly circles the drain.

This game has been going on for years, and while the pressure to keep up appearances is very real, it can't go on forever. If the electronic music world refuses to stop pretending, at some point these buildings are going to collapse.

———

Does anyone in electronic music actually like the press?

Oh sure, there are still a handful of individual journalists that discerning readers will champion and make a point to follow, and artists can still rack up likes when they land on the cover (or the digital cover) of a known publication, but how do people feel about the electronic music press in the aggregate? In 2023, is there even one media outlet that is both widely read and well respected, or even just not widely mocked?

As far as I can tell, the answer to that last question is "no."

Outlets like Resident Advisor, DJ Mag, Mixmag, Crack, FACT, XLR8R and numerous others all hold themselves up as bastions of discourse and information, but as institutions, they inspire very little faith from the wider electronic music community. Many of them appear to be struggling, and in the face of extremely difficult conditions for journalism of all shapes and sizes, these publications' collective credibility seems to be disintegrating almost as quickly as the quality of their content offerings.

Resident Advisor is perhaps too easy of a target, but given that it's arguably the closest thing to an electronic music bible, it's naturally going to face the most scrutiny. In recent years, the publication, which during the pandemic faced a torrent of public criticism concerning its editorial, economic and hiring practices, has gone to great lengths to overhaul both its staff and content, but even after all those changes, its future standing seems far from secure. The site was once buoyed by ticket sales, but one can only assume that the rise of dedicated ticket sellers like DICE has taken a major bite out of RA's business model, which already required a controversial £750,000 government grant to stay afloat during the pandemic.

Its editorial strategy seems similarly wobbly, as a pivot towards high-gloss fashion shoots, brand partnerships, advertorial features (e.g. long-form articles promoting Jägermeister's Save the Night initiative) and self-aggrandizement (e.g. the recent 2122 campaign celebrating the site's 21st anniversary) has alienated or turned off large swaths of its readership. A preponderance of well-meaning (but generally pretty shallow) political commentary hasn't helped either, and while that will undoubtedly be blamed on older readers' supposed small-mindedness and unwillingness to change with the times, there's also the fact that so much of that content simply isn't very well done. This is just one example, but it's honestly difficult to take RA seriously when its recent exploration of "dwindling working-class participation in the scene"[1] was published not only the same week as a fawning interview podcast with DJ and luxury lifestyle influencer Peggy Gou,[2] but also a listing for a full-time editorial position in the company's London office with a laughable annual salary of £25-30k.[3] Seeing stuff like that unfold does at times feel like watching a slow-motion car crash, and while it's likely prompted some folks to regularly hate-read the site, it's not likely to foster long-term audience growth, let alone genuine affection for the RA brand.

In fairness, Resident Advisor is far from the only flawed operation amongst the ranks of the electronic music press—more on that later—but what's perhaps more concerning is that despite the publication's many shortcomings, it continues to be treated as a vaunted institution by the industry at large. Why? Because it's a known quantity, and industry people don't know where else to devote their time and resources. After 20-plus years of existence, RA is a widely recognizable brand, and more importantly, it's a familiar place where artists and labels—themselves struggling to get noticed in an impossibly crowded music ecosystem—can hawk their wares. It doesn't matter whether or not the site is doing quality work; by simply managing to stay open, it's remained an industry reference point, particularly for PR and marketing reps, artist managers and everyone else whose continued employment relies upon banking "wins" (i.e. coverage) that they can show to whoever's signing their checks. (Not surprisingly, the question of whether that coverage is actually making a tangible impact is rarely considered within these circles.)

---

1. Lawson, Michael. "'It's definitely a harder grind': Is electronic music becoming inaccessible to the working classes?" *Resident Advisor*, January 10, 2023, https://ra.co/news/78312.

2. "EX.643 Peggy Gou." *Resident Advisor*, January 12, 2023, https://ra.co/exchange/643.

3. Resident Advisor. "International Content Writer." *Doors Open*, January 7, 2023, https://web.archive.org/web/20230112213810/https://www.doorsopen.co/job/4890/international-content-writer/.

The music industry is built upon countless behind-the-scenes ways of doing business, and those methodologies—which include promoting artists and new releases via press coverage, which of course must be cultivated through PR pitches and the sending of promos—often remain entrenched, even when they no longer make much sense. In 2023, does getting a news story, a review or even a feature in Resident Advisor, or any other publication, really do that much to move the cultural needle? Maybe in rare cases, but by and large all of this stuff is just content, digital ephemera that gets tossed online in hopes that social media algorithms will take notice.

While the official music press does still carry a certain prestige, that prestige is largely based on out-of-date notions of not only how the music industry works, but where the power lies. Ten or twenty years ago, certain electronic music publications had the power to set (or at least heavily influence) the cultural agenda for all of electronic music, but that's no longer the case. Music journalists these days are mostly just responding to what they see online, and that's because, like most other facets of modern culture, electronic music is now dominated by social media.

Unfortunately though, social media is a place where merely posting "I did a thing" tends to have a much bigger impact on someone's clout and influence than whether or not said "thing" has any real substance. It's absurd, but when very few of us are clicking the link in bio, the details rarely matter. If an artist lands on the cover of a magazine, is it important whether or not the accompanying story is well written? Not when most people—and even most fans—will never bother to read it. Oddly enough, the biggest benefit of a cover story these days is probably the fact that the featured artist can post a photo of the cover on their Instagram. It's sure to attract all kinds of likes—especially if the photos are striking and the publication is perceived as important—and that in turn will juice the algorithm, putting the post in front of more eyes and boosting the artist's visibility.

Is this depressing, particularly for those of us who make a living writing about music? Absolutely, but it also makes the electronic music industry's continuing support for and engagement with subpar media platforms all the more perplexing. What's driving this? Laziness? A lack of imagination? A lack of alternate options? Dewy-eyed sentimentality for the way things used to be? Whatever the motivation, we continue to see artists, labels, PR reps, booking agents, festivals and basically the entire industry apparatus—including music journalists themselves—engaging in what's ostensibly an elaborate game of pretend, putting visibly limping publications on a pedestal they no longer deserve.

As I said earlier, Resident Advisor tends to attract the harshest critics, but it's not like its competitors are doing much better. DJ Mag and Mixmag have both been around for decades, and both are global brands, at least in the sense that they've licensed their names to a variety of editorial teams in different regions and countries around the planet. (The finances around those licensing arrangements are opaque, but however much revenue they bring in, it wasn't enough to save Mixmag's print edition, which ceased a few years back.)

Editorially, both publications have admirably broadened their palate in recent years, but as long as DJ Mag insists on continuing its gag-inducing annual Top 100 DJs poll, it's unlikely to shake its reputation as a bastion of Ibiza hedonism, EDM bros, trance (the bad kind), tech house monotony and the more blatantly commercialized corners of electronic music. Mixmag is often dogged by the same associations, and further cheapens its credibility by regularly running drug-related "news" stories that read like something sourced from the Daily Mail. These trashy pieces undoubtedly generate clicks (one actual recent headline: "Pigeon Carrying Backpack Filled with Crystal Meth Detained at Canadian Prison"[4]), but they also perpetuate negative stereotypes about club culture, even when the stories themselves have little or nothing to do with electronic music.

---

4. Muk, Isaac. "Pigeon Carrying Backpack Filled with Crystal Meth Detained at Canadian Prison." *Mixmag*, January 13, 2023, https://mixmag.net/read/drug-smuggling-pigeon-backpack-crystal-meth-detained-canadian-prison-news. **239**

Who else is out there? Crack has some quality content, but aside from clearly lacking the staff and budget to keep up with its larger competitors, it's also busy chasing brand partnerships (via its in-house creative agency) to keep the doors open. Moreover, with folks like Yeah Yeah Yeahs, Carly Rae Jepsen and the cast of *Top Boy* all appearing on recent Crack covers, it's pretty clear that the magazine isn't purely focused on electronic music. XLR8R, a place where I was an editor for many years, was once a top publication, but its content offerings have dramatically receded over the years; the site's last long-form feature was published in 2019, and its brief attempt to become a go-to source for Web3 music information petered out last July. At this point, the site's editorial consists of little more than its paywall-gated mix series and a smattering of unbylined news stories. FACT has followed a similar route; once one of electronic music's most reliable (and forward-thinking) outlets, it bizarrely pivoted to video a few years ago and dropped virtually all written content, save for the words that accompany its weekly mix series.

Pitchfork routinely enlists some of electronic music's best writers, and when it does choose to focus on the genre, often publishes work that is both insightful and informative. At the same time, given its indie-rock history and ongoing prioritization of pop music—how many news stories about Drake does one publication need?—most dedicated electronic music fans will always look at the site with some level of suspicion. The same could be said for Dazed and The Face, two places which are more accurately described as fashion and youth culture publications than music outlets. They both cover electronic music from time to time, and will even occasionally commission some eye-catching photos to accompany that coverage, but there's no mistaking that their true priorities lie elsewhere.

Outlets like Inverted Audio, Ransom Note and Stamp the Wax don't have that problem, but while all three have always been scrappy underdogs with a clear love for electronic music, none of them appears to be thriving. Since July 2022, Stamp the Wax has rarely put up more than one or two posts per month, and while Ransom Note and Inverted Audio do still manage to publish articles more frequently, it's not promising that the former relies so heavily on artist-generated content (e.g. mixes, playlists) while the latter literally charges for the placement of track premieres.[5] (In their defense, that money is said to contribute to operating costs and the payment of writers.)

The Wire is perhaps electronic music's most beloved print publication (at least among the genre's more intellectual set), and there's no doubt that its pages continue to be filled with thoughtful writing. That said, its editorial orientation, which places a premium on more experimental sounds new and old, isn't really geared toward the contemporary dance music crowd, and the publication's reach is further limited by the fact that almost none of its content is posted for free online. There's nothing wrong with any of that of course—there's something to be said for zeroing in on a focused corner of culture and covering it better than anyone else—but it's delusional to think that the magazine's influence isn't limited, particularly with younger audiences for whom print media is practically a foreign concept. The Quietus does admirably work to bridge that gap, treading in similar editorial waters as The Wire while existing wholly online, but is yet another outlet that's clearly hamstrung by a lack of resources. (In fact, its editors explicitly mentioned that daunting financial reality when they launched subscriptions a few years back.)[6]

Attack is another fledgling outfit, but its heavy production focus means that it's more of a publication for people that want to make electronic music than it is a daily record of the culture. There was a time that Dummy carried some influence, but its editorial trailed off over the years, leading to a recent rebrand as DMY, an entity which now functions as both a media outlet and (probably much more profitable) artist services company. Test Pressing has cultivated a genuine cool factor—particularly amongst more digger-minded DJs—but its aims are modest, only publishing a handful of pieces each month, most of them reviews.

---

5. "FAQ." *Inverted Audio*, https://inverted-audio.com/about/faq/.

6. Things remain precarious at The Quietus, as the publication put out a fresh plea for additional subscribers in April 2023.

Over in Chicago, 5Mag continues to carry the torch for dance music's Midwestern originators, but does so with something of an irregular publishing schedule, its output almost surely constrained by limited resources.

In fact, "limited resources" is something that music media publications big and small would likely all cite as one of their biggest problems. Economically speaking, music journalism is in a tough place, and has been for years. Advertising revenue dried up during the shift from print to online media, and no reliable revenue streams have arisen to take its place. The present hope for salvation appears to be brand partnerships, but there's no guarantee that's going to work, and in the meantime, jobs have dwindled, freelance rates have stagnated and the economic reality of the craft now means that even the best electronic music journalists often need to take on other gigs in order to make ends meet. (That even includes Philip Sherburne, who despite being a contributing editor at Pitchfork and one of electronic music's most respected scribes, stated in a First Floor interview last year that he's "always had a matrix of different work because it's the only way to survive.")

In the face of such intense precarity, it's no wonder that the quality of the content on offer has also taken a nosedive. Layoffs and low pay have led to a massive brain drain over the years, with experienced journalists regularly walking out the door of their respective outlets and usually taking all sorts of institutional knowledge along with them. At many publications, things like line editing, fact checking and writing instruction (i.e. how to construct a narrative) have all but disappeared, and at some outlets, the entire premise of editorial feedback appears to be nonexistent. (As an experienced writer myself, it's frankly alarming how often I've submitted text and have subsequently seen it published with no changes whatsoever. I can assure you, my writing is not that good.)

Many of these problems aren't specific to electronic music media, or even the music press in general. Journalism as a field is in a state of crisis, and as of now, there are few promising solutions on the horizon. As much as I enjoy bashing out my newsletter every week and appreciate the support it's received, it's no replacement for a well-staffed, fully functioning media outlet. Niche concerns can be great, but healthy discourse—and healthy culture—require broader conversations. Right now, those conversations mostly seem to be happening on social media, and few people seem to be satisfied with the results. After all, as bad as the current state of electronic music media might be, it's got to be better than the chaos of Twitter, the vapid hyperreality of Instagram or whatever the hell is happening on TikTok, right?

Maybe so, but sticking to something solely because it's "better than the alternative" is a great way to stoke resentment and discontent, and it's hard to deny that the electronic music community's collective faith in media—including the media whose stated purpose is to document the genre and the culture around it—is more or less in the toilet. We've entered a bizarre zone where Boomkat and Bandcamp—two online stores which, despite the quality of their offerings, can't truly be regarded as objective sources of information—are arguably the most widely respected editorial platforms in electronic music.

That is not a sign of a healthy media ecosystem, and as long as the electronic music industry continues to ignore the fact that its dedicated press outlets are falling short in their duties, things are unlikely to improve. There's an obvious logic to this game of pretend—after all, artists, labels and festivals need to promote their product somewhere, right? A lot of people's jobs depend on the continued existence of the music press in its current state, but while continuing to devote time, resources and attention to these outlets may help to keep those people employed (often in unstable, low-paying positions), it doesn't necessarily benefit the music, or the quality of the conversations around it.

Furthermore, propping these places up only serves as a temporary fix; as long as press outlets are sitting on decrepit foundations, some of them are eventually going to collapse, no matter how much nostalgia-driven praise and prestige is funneled their way. That will be a bummer—again, particularly for those of us who work as professional music journalists—but it won't be the end of the world, or even the end of thoughtful discourse. It's not like people are going to stop talking about electronic music if Resident Advisor suddenly goes away.

Culture is a constant, and so are the conversations it inspires. When it comes to electronic music, it's far from clear what form those conversations will take in the years to come (or where exactly they'll be hosted), but perhaps the moment has arrived to stop pretending that the current system is working as intended. Rather than propping up crumbling palaces, maybe that energy can be applied to developing something better, or at least something that makes more sense for the present moment.

IV.

Applying a Historical Lens

Electronica's Last Gasp
a.k.a. Revisiting Paul Oakenfold's *Bunkka*.

April 5, 2022

—

My love of electronic music doesn't have a cool origin story. Although I can legitimately say that I went to raves in the '90s (eventually), my first exposure to the genre didn't happen at some illicit warehouse party. Like many teenagers during that era, I was introduced via the radio—alternative rock radio, to be exact. The Prodigy, Daft Punk, Fatboy Slim, Chemical Brothers... these were the first artists I heard, and they were presented to me as the leading figures in a "new" genre called "electronica."

It didn't take long for me to start digging deeper, but as the years have gone on, I've found myself increasingly fascinated by the "electronica" era, largely because it was a total music industry fabrication. (The genre's inherent irreality is why it's another word that I always put in scare quotes.) Moreover, it was a distinctly American phenomenon; this music was already massive in the UK and Europe, but in the US it needed to be "broken" into the marketplace, and an ahistorical narrative—one which depicted the genre as something from overseas—was used to do it. When people talk about Americans' struggle to properly grasp electronic music culture and its origins/history, "electronica" was arguably ground zero for when things started to go horribly wrong, and seeded countless misconceptions that persist to this day.

Even better, the whole thing was ultimately an abject failure. In purely commercial terms, "electronica" was a fleeting trend, and by the early 2000s, it was on its way out. As I explain in the following piece, I had something of a front row seat, so when the 20th anniversary of a truly terrible

album came around, I took the opportunity to look back and examine a truly bizarre chapter of electronic music history.

———

Back in 2002, I was working at a radio station called Live 105. It was San Francisco's alternative rock outlet, and every summer it staged a big concert called BFD. That year's lineup was a real hodgepodge; headlined by nu-metal acts P.O.D., Rob Zombie and Papa Roach, the bill also featured Cypress Hill, N.E.R.D. and The Strokes, not to mention alt-rock filler like The Vines and Hoobastank, breakout emo acts Jimmy Eat World and Dashboard Confessional, pop-punkers No Use for a Name, New Found Glory, Unwritten Law, Face to Face and Goldfinger, UK rock outfit Ash and Icelandic rap-rockers Quarashi. (Even looking through the lens of today's playlist-driven, "genres don't matter" climate, it seems bizarre that all of these acts were all in rotation at the same radio station, but 2002 was a very weird time for the "alternative" format.)

That wasn't all. The *Subsonic* stage, named after the station's Saturday night electronic music program, included trance DJs from the Bay Area rave scene (Mystrë, Dyloot, Tom Slik, Thomas Trouble), along with LA prog duo Deepsky, drum & bass stalwart Dieselboy and NYC hip-hop turntablists The X-Ecutioners. Headlining the stage that afternoon was superstar DJ Paul Oakenfold, whose debut solo album, *Bunkka*, was due to be released just a few weeks later.

Most people don't remember *Bunkka*, and for good reason—it wasn't very good. Although Oakenfold was already one of electronic music's most well-known figures—he'd previously nabbed the #1 spot in DJ Mag's Top 100 DJs list in both 1998 and 1999—the album was a clear attempt to cross over into the mainstream. Released in the US by Maverick Records—a Warner Bros. subsidiary co-founded by Madonna—the LP frequently veered away from the trance and progressive house sounds for which Oakenfold was primarily known, venturing into pop, hip-hop and trip-hop with a motley crew of all-star collaborators that included Ice Cube, Nelly Furtado, Jane's Addiction frontman Perry Farrell, Tricky and rapper Shifty Shellshock (of Crazy Town). Someone even convinced a 60-something-year-old Hunter S. Thompson to appear on the record.

Although *Bunkka* was greeted warmly by a few publications —funnily enough, a nascent Resident Advisor made a point to highlight the Tiësto remix of the song "Southern Sun" in its positive review[1]—the album was largely panned, with many of the harshest critiques coming from the mainstream outlets the record was seemingly designed to win over. Entertainment Weekly called Oakenfold "the Wal-Mart of DJs" while giving *Bunkka* a D grade,[2] while the AV Club noted that the LP was "bogged down by ambitious aims that translate blindness as blandness."[3]

The album wasn't a total flop; it spent two weeks at #1 on the Billboard Top Electronic Albums chart—a chart that had tellingly only debuted one year prior—and also reached #65 on the Billboard 200 and #25 on the UK Albums chart. *Bunkka* also produced two enduring singles: "Ready, Steady, Go," a swashbuckling rave-rock anthem that has since appeared in films like *The Bourne Identity* and *Collateral* (not to mention a litany of commercials), and "Starry Eyed Surprise," a soft-focus hip-pop number voiced by the aforementioned Shifty Shellshock.

Twenty years later, those two tracks undoubtedly continue to populate an untold number of bland playlists, but few people associate them with *Bunkka*, or even remember that *Bunkka* existed. Oakenfold never really became a household name in the US, but he's continued to do just fine for himself; critical acclaim has been largely out of reach, but he's spent the past two decades touring the globe, occasionally releasing music and generally enjoying his position as one of commercial electronic music's elder statesmen. Few would cite *Bunkka* as a career highlight,

1. O, Tom. "Paul Oakenfold – Bunkka." *Resident Advisor*, June 21, 2002, https://ra.co/reviews/406.

2. Hermes, Will. "Bunkka." *Entertainment Weekly*, June 21, 2002, https://ew.com/article/2002/06/21/bunkka/.

3. Battaglia, Andy. "Oakenfold: Bunkka." *The A.V. Club*, June 25, 2002, https://www.avclub.com/oakenfold-bunkka-1798197653.

but despite the album's status as a historical footnote, it's still something of a remarkable artifact, for one main reason: its release was arguably the last time that the mainstream music industry attempted to break "electronica" in the US.

Given the fact that genres like house, techno and electro were born in the US during the 1980s, it's ridiculous that the industry subsequently needed to repackage and "break" the music on American shores more than a decade later. It's been well documented how many of electronic music's originators found little institutional/industry support at home, prompting them to take their music across the Atlantic, where it found wider acceptance (and commercial success) in places like the UK and Europe. By the mid '90s, electronic music had been woven into Europe's pop fabric, and acts like The Prodigy, Fatboy Slim and Daft Punk were becoming legitimate stars.

Back in the US, rave and club culture had continued to exist, albeit on a more underground level that rarely intersected with commercial radio, MTV or the pop charts. Hip-hop and alternative rock dominated youth culture during the early '90s, and the average American listener considered electronic music to be something foreign, if they even considered it at all. (Not to belabor the point, but given the fact that so much of dance music was invented in the US, it's honestly tragic how little attention/respect the music's early innovators were given in their home country.)

As grunge faded in the years following Kurt Cobain's death, alternative rock went through something of an identity crisis, and responded by hoovering up one subculture after another. Genres like punk, ska, reggae, folk, swing, rockabilly, goth/industrial and emo all had "breakthrough" moments during the late '90s and early 2000s, and "electronica" (as it was branded) was part of that procession. Marketed to an angsty, largely white, largely suburban audience that had little familiarity with electronic music's history or existing culture, the genre was positioned as a sort of "alternative rock with beats," with people like The Prodigy's Keith Flint perfectly filling the role of the edgy frontman.

(That narrative often omitted the fact that another person, Liam Howlett, was the one who actually produced the majority of The Prodigy's songs.)

For a while, this strategy worked. In 1997, "electronica" was widely hailed as the American music industry's proverbial "next big thing," and during the next few years, acts like the aforementioned Daft Punk, Fatboy Slim and The Prodigy, plus artists like the Chemical Brothers, Underworld and The Crystal Method, all found some level of mainstream success in the US. Alternative rock radio stations around the country launched electronica-themed specialty shows, including KROQ Los Angeles' *Afterhours* (hosted by Jason Bentley, who later became the longtime host of KCRW's *Morning Becomes Eclectic*), K-Rock New York's *Solid State* (hosted by Liquid Todd) and Live 105 San Francisco's *Subsonic* (hosted by Aaron Axelsen). Although these shows were generally aired late on Friday or Saturday nights (i.e. time slots that US commercial radio doesn't prioritize), they often racked up huge audiences, and more importantly, served as an introduction to electronic music for audiences (again, mostly young, white and suburban) that likely wouldn't have engaged with the genre otherwise. (Full disclosure: I was the producer and occasional host of Live 105's *Subsonic* from 1999 to 2005.)

Not every "electronica" release was a success—the list of artists, many of them respected producers from the UK, whose albums failed to find mainstream traction in the US is incredibly long—but a foundation had been laid. During the late '90s, "electronica" was part of the cultural lexicon, an easy signifier of "cool" and "futuristic" which began to populate everything from film soundtracks to car commercials. (The soundtracks for films like 1999's *The Matrix* and 1998's *Blade* have become iconic, but big-budget movies like 1999's *Go* and 2000's *Groove* had stories that were literally based—albeit loosely—around rave culture.)

It was in that climate that Moby's 1999 album *Play* became a genuine cultural phenomenon, selling millions of copies while earning platinum certifications in more than 20 countries and eventually becoming one of the most licensed releases of all time. Although *Play* had little to do with rave culture—and the album's heavy reliance on archival recordings of Black spirituals and gospel songs is at the very least ethically dubious—it was a huge breakthrough for "electronica," which had never before achieved such widespread acceptance in the US. In retrospect, however, the record was likely the trend's commercial and cultural high-water mark. It's telling that the New York Times, which in 1997 had published an article examining the music's "next big thing" status,[4] in 1999 printed a piece by Jon Pareles pondering the genre's failure to connect in the US. Based on his observations at that year's CMJ Music Marathon, it included pessimistic lines like, "The auteurs of electronica tend to be short on star quality" and "Most electronica isn't made to sell albums."[5] (Side note: in a show of just how clueless most of the US music press was about electronic music, the 1997 article ignored the music's Black and American roots, emphasizing instead its ties to Europe.)

Accurate or not, Pareles' opinions were shared by many of the American music industry's decision makers, and once nu-metal outfits like Korn and Limp Bizkit became the hot new thing in alternative rock, "electronica" was largely kicked to the curb. By the time that *Bunkka* rolled around in 2002, the chances of any electronic music artist finding mainstream success in the US seemed small, even for a bona fide star like Oakenfold. (It probably wasn't a good sign that Eminem's smash hit "Without Me," which skewered Moby and famously included the line "nobody listens to techno," arrived in May 2002, one month prior to *Bunkka*'s release.)

That said, it's hard to fault Oakenfold—or the Maverick execs who signed and promoted him—for taking a stab at the US market. Regardless of what was happening with "electronica," he was still one of the biggest DJs in the world at that point. His 1998 mix CDs *Global Underground 007: New York* and *Tranceport* had both sold more than 100,000 copies (the latter record would later be

4. Strauss, Neil. "The Next Big Thing Or the Next Bust?" *The New York Times*, January 26, 1997, https://archive.nytimes.com/www.nytimes.com/library/music/012697dj-bust.html.

5. Pareles, Jon. "POP REVIEW; The Next Big Thing That Just Wasn't." *The New York Times*, September 22, 1999, https://www.nytimes.com/1999/09/22/arts/pop-review-the-next-big-thing-that-just-wasn-t.html.

included in Rolling Stone's 2012 list of "The 30 Greatest EDM Albums of All Time,"[6] and he'd also produced the soundtrack for the (terrible) 2001 film *Swordfish*. That same year, he was also one of the headline acts on Moby's traveling Area:One festival, which spent nearly a month touring across America.

Oakenfold clearly had an audience, but very little of *Bunkka* appeared to be directed at that audience's tastes. Like many of its "electronica" predecessors, the LP—which took its name from a room in Peter Gabriel's UK studio, where the album was recorded—found its creator trying his hand (and often failing) at new styles and sounds, usually with the help of star-studded collaborators. Acts like Basement Jaxx and the Chemical Brothers had previously followed a similar playbook, with varying degrees of success from one collaboration to the next, but they were at least building off an existing body of work. Oakenfold had had a hand in producing tracks before, but *Bunkka* was his first proper artist album, and it bears little resemblance to the trance and progressive house sound he was known for. Nobody expected him to deliver something true to the roots of dance music, but *Bunkka* was hardly even true to the (rather forgiving) norms of "electronica," and came across instead like a cynical attempt at pop success.

The album's press materials billed *Bunkka* as a return to Oakenfold's roots, and he was quoted as saying, "I grew up on pop music, I love guitar bands and I was very influenced and involved in hip-hop during the early days, so I wanted to build from those roots upwards rather than doing a contemporary dance record." Listening to the album now, however, the LP feels both disjointed and formulaic, its stylistic zig-zagging making it seem like the record's driving creative philosophy was "let's throw some shit at the wall and see what sticks."

"Zoo York" is an ill-advised, new-age-meets-trip-hop rework of Clint Mansell's "Lux Aeterna" (better known as the string-heavy theme from *Requiem for a Dream*), while "The Harder They Come" badly miscasts Nelly Furtado as a trip-hop chanteuse opposite a

6. Dolan, Jon and Matos, Michaelangelo. "The 30 Greatest EDM Albums of All Time." *Rolling Stone*, August 2, 2012, https://www.rollingstone.com/music/music-lists/the-30-greatest-edm-albums-of-all-time-160883/.

growling Tricky. "Nixon's Spirit" sounds like a *Pure Moods* castoff, and while the addition of a rambling spoken-word passage from Hunter S. Thompson makes for an intriguing WTF? moment, it doesn't add to the music's appeal. Ice Cube offers up some serviceable (albeit entirely forgettable) verses on "Get Em Up," but at no point is it clear what the hell he's doing on the album.

As a rousing big beat anthem, LP opener "Ready Steady Go" holds up admirably, although the song's blatantly *Matrix*-indebted video hammers home just how "of its time" the track was (and still is). Not surprisingly, *Bunkka* is often at its best when Oakenfold sticks to the dancefloor; he even makes Perry Farrell sound moderately compelling on breakbeat rave-rocker "Time of Your Life." Less successful is "Southern Sun," which essentially stitches some trance riffs to a melodramatic pop tune, but at least it's got a hook.

Speaking of hooks, "Starry Eyed Surprise" is full of them, which likely explains the track's enduring nostalgic appeal. It's also a fascinating historical artifact, a near-perfect encapsulation of the early-2000s rap-rock era. "Starry Eyed Surprise" might be Oakenfold's song, but in its garish video, he's relegated to a background role, intermittently smiling and bopping in the DJ booth while rapper Shifty Shellshock holds court and soaks up the spotlight. (The clip also features several instances of Oakenfold inexplicably scratching, which was an odd move for someone who was basically a trance DJ at that point.)

The idea of "DJ as appendage" didn't start with "Starry Eyed Surprise"—the nu-metal explosion had a lot to do with that, and the trend was arguably another example of something that was ported over (badly) from hip-hop—and it's admittedly awkward to feature a DJ anywhere in a music video, but it is nonetheless weird (and disappointing) to see that dynamic continued by Oakenfold, an artist whose entire career sprouted out of DJing.

It's impossible to know what kinds of pressures Oakenfold was facing as he was working on *Bunkka*, but it's certainly possible that industry people were in his ear about what the album needed to be. Even if he had total creative freedom, Oakenfold was already a veteran artist at that point, and surely noticed that the industry winds had shifted in relation to electronic music, especially in America; perhaps he adjusted his approach accordingly. Regardless of what happened, it's difficult to view *Bunkka* as anything but a failure. That's fine of course; most albums fail, and the chances of an even nominally "underground" artist breaking through with their major label debut are exceedingly poor. In that respect, Oakenfold isn't special, which is likely why *Bunkka* is (rightly) regarded as more of a footnote than an all-out embarrassment.

That said, the record also represents the end of a unique era, as it's hard to think of any other high-profile "electronica" albums that arrived in the years following *Bunkka*. Although the years between 1999 and 2002 saw a flurry of LPs from Daft Punk, the Chemical Brothers, Underworld, Fatboy Slim and Basement Jaxx, most of them underperformed in the US, and in the years that followed, "electronica" largely retreated from the American mainstream. (Two prominent exceptions would be Basement Jaxx's 2004 album *Kish Kash* and the Chemical Brothers 2005 LP *Push the Button*, which both featured pop/hip-hop-oriented collaborations and produced minor hits, but neither record made a huge cultural impact in America.)

Looking back, "electronica" was an odd cultural phenomenon. Arguably more of a marketing scheme than an actual genre, it was an ahistorical movement that ignored (some might say erased) the legacy of electronic music's originators, but also turned millions of people on to the power of the rave. That's a difficult thing to reckon with, which is why the death of "electronica" in the early 2000s (and the failure of albums like *Bunkka*) is nothing to be upset about.

Back at Live 105, "Ready Steady Go" dropped out of rotation pretty quickly after Oakenfold's performance at BFD, but *Subsonic*—the show that had featured his music and so many other electronica artists in the first place—soldiered on for several more years, outlasting most of its peers in the alt-rock realm. The program remained enormously popular, but as time passed, its content also grew further and further from Live 105's regular rotation, and the show was eventually canceled at the start of 2006.

As it happens though, the program was revived again a few years later. Why? Because a new electronic music boom had hit, only this time, it had a new name: EDM.

Techno and the Alternate Timeline
a.k.a. What happens when highly anticipated albums drop in the middle of a pandemic?

April 7, 2020
—

When I was putting together this book, I consciously made a decision to keep the pandemic content to a minimum. Of course there are still references to Covid sprinkled through these pages, but when I look back at my writings from 2020, particularly the ones questioning if/when venues would open again, considering what "safe" clubbing protocols might look like and parsing the dynamics of the so-called "plague rave" debate, they almost feel like dispatches from another universe. While there are plenty of lessons to be learned from the pandemic, they're probably best learned with the benefit of hindsight, and not via the various scribblings I put together during a time when everyone was stuck at home, concrete facts were hard to come by and speculation was rampant.

In this piece, however, I went down a different path. Published just a few weeks into lockdown, it zeroes in on a Minor Science LP that was dropping at the time (a record which, like most other 2020 releases, especially the ones oriented towards the dancefloor, wound up evaporating into the proverbial ether), but it's about more than a fouled-up album rollout. It's a contemplation of a profoundly strange moment in time, and the experience of a collective disruption that ultimately left us all pondering countless "what if?" scenarios.

———

A few weeks ago, I was asked to write something about what electronic music will look like after the Covid-19 pandemic is over. Although it sounded like an interesting sort of thought experiment, I ultimately wound up passing on the assignment, partly because I haven't been feeling terribly inspired to write while the world is teetering on the edge of collapse, but mainly because I was hesitant to write something that would essentially be a totally speculative piece.

One thing I've found interesting, however, is that while we've collectively hit the pause button on events and nightlife, the new releases keep on coming. Granted, the vast majority of new music we're hearing right now is from releases that were in the works long before the coronavirus hit—I suppose we can finally thank that global vinyl pressing backlog for something—but it's still bizarre to see the industry's promotional wheels keep on turning, especially when a lot of the music I'm checking out was specifically designed for use at events that have essentially (and hopefully only temporarily) become nonexistent.

Even amongst electronic music fans, I've seen a lot of talk in recent weeks about how lots of people have no appetite for dancefloor-oriented sounds. I haven't gone that far, but I certainly don't have much patience right now for anything that's overly abrasive. (My apologies to the noise acts sending me music these days.) Beyond that, I think most of us have found solace in older, more familiar music, a topic that Jeremy Larson recently tackled in an excellent article for Pitchfork.[1] I recommend reading the whole thing, but he digs into human brain chemistry and how we're naturally wired to reject sounds that are unfamiliar, and then manages to segue into an impassioned plea for listeners to avoid that impulse and continue exploring new music.

First Floor has always placed a big focus on new music, even before the newsletter started and it existed as a weekly radio program. As long as the new releases keep coming, I'll continue to write about them. At the same time, I've been thinking a lot about the weird fate of all the records that happen to be coming out in the middle of this pandemic. Just yesterday, I was specifically thinking about *Second Language*, the Minor Science album that dropped last Friday on Whities.

---

1. Larson, Jeremy. "Why Do We Even Listen to New Music?" *Pitchfork*, April 6, 2020, https://pitchfork.com/features/article/listen-to-music/.

I don't have a crystal ball, but I feel pretty confident in saying that 2020 was poised to be a big year for this Berlin-based British artist. *Second Language* reviews are still surfacing, but the album's sound—an intellectual, albeit danceable blend of broken techno, inventive bass music and IDM-style experimentation—is very "now," and even before the LP dropped, social media was full of accolades, often from the same folks who champion artists like Objekt, Beatrice Dillon and other critical darlings. For months, I've been under the impression that *Second Language* was going to elevate Minor Science to a new, more substantial tier of recognition, one with more press, more gigs and more fanboy fawning. (I'll leave it to you to decide whether that's what I'm doing now.)

Now that the record is out, however, I'm not so sure. In many ways, this pandemic feels like a weird alternate timeline, and what might have happened to Minor Science—or any artist—under "normal" conditions is a possibility that's effectively slipped away into the ether. For artists in this particular boat, especially the ones releasing their debut albums, this has to be incredibly frustrating, as this major document of their work is being greeted by an environment in which even hardcore music fans are sometimes struggling to maintain serious interest in new music. Fans aren't clamoring for insights into artists' processes; they want updates on when it'll be safe to go outside again. And while this situation undeniably sucks for the artists affected, there isn't even a whole lot of empathy out there, because folks can only feel so bad about a disrupted album rollout when thousands of people are dying every day.

Knowing this, some artists and labels are opting to postpone their releases until later in the year, although that route is also fraught with risk. Rescheduling a release date is tricky when nobody knows how long this crisis is going to last, and whenever it does end, the market will almost surely be flooded with a glut of new releases. If the Minor Science album had been pushed back to, say, October, would it make a bigger impact? Would the music still sound fresh? Releasing the record now may seem like a bad idea while everyone is worried about the coronavirus, but with the global economy largely shut down and people home from work, audiences also have a lot more free time in which they could (theoretically) check out new music. So maybe staying with the originally scheduled release date was the right move? I have no idea, and there really are no correct answers here.

I should probably clarify that my thoughts here do go beyond the new Minor Science album. That LP just happened to come out during the past week, and felt like a good example of this "what might have been" mental sojourn. Looking ahead, DJ Python and Laurel Halo have albums out next week, and in May, new full-lengths from Kelly Lee Owens, Peaking Lights and Kaitlyn Aurelia Smith are all on the calendar. What will happen to these records? Will they become unexpected quarantine classics? Will they be released and ignored? Or maybe they'll just be quickly forgotten? Again, I'm not really sure. None of us are. Whatever happens though, it'll certainly be different than what these artists were hoping for only a couple of months ago. We're all stuck in this alternate timeline, and at least for now, all we can do is wait and see what happens.

Did Basement Jaxx Invent Hyperpop?
a.k.a. A look at the UK duo's 2001 album *Rooty*
and how it influenced today's musical landscape.

August 31, 2021
—

Hyperpop is not something most readers would expect to find in First Floor, but even though I'm not someone who's particularly inclined to listen to 100 gecs and other artists of their ilk, there's no denying that the genre—which is arguably more of an aesthetic and creative approach than it is a coherent sonic template—has upended the musical landscape in recent years. Pop music on the whole is getting faster and more chaotic, reflecting a culture in which streaming and social media have not only flattened traditional genre boundaries, but encouraged listeners to metaphorically gorge themselves on anything and everything in sight.

The following isn't really an article about hyperpop. (For those interested in a deeper dive, I assure you that proper think pieces on the genre are not hard to find elsewhere.) Basement Jaxx is the primary focus, and specifically their 2001 *Rooty* LP. It was a weird and brazenly garish album when it came out, and more than 20 years later, it's still an off-the-wall collection of tunes, albeit one whose everything-but-the-kitchen-sink aesthetic now seems oddly contemporary. Thinking that the record quite possibly deserved a more prominent place in the canon, I took a fresh look.

———

Over the past month or so, I've found myself thinking a lot about Basement Jaxx, and specifically their 2001 album *Rooty*—a rambunctious record that, incidentally, I didn't even like all that much when it first came out.

Twenty years later, I've warmed to the album somewhat. It's still not something I'd cite as a personal favorite—as far as I'm concerned, the London duo of Felix Buxton and Simon Ratcliffe have never topped the brilliance of their 1997 single "Fly Life"—but as I've been thinking about *Rooty* and its legacy, my own preferences have largely taken a backseat. What's far more interesting is the fact that I've increasingly been seeing tracks like "Romeo" and "Where's Your Head At" pop up in DJ sets and playlists from artists who were probably in grade school when those songs first dropped. Why now? How exactly did *Rooty* become a source of multiple Gen Z anthems?

Admittedly, my pondering of *Rooty* was further fueled by a recent article that music journalist Ben Cardew wrote about the album for DJ Mag's *Solid Gold* series.[1] In many ways, it's a thorough dissection of the LP, its genesis and how the music was initially received 20 years ago, but what really got my mental gears turning were lines like these:

> *Rooty pulls together individual strands of London music that typically wouldn't mix, particularly in the pre-broadband internet era when musical boundaries were more zealously guarded. No one would bat an eyelid at a punk house jam or R&B garage shuffler in 2021; back then, these kinds of mixtures were more unusual, which makes* Rooty *a very prophetic album — a 5G release in the era of dial-up.*

Saying that an album was "ahead of its time" is a well-worn cliché, but *Rooty*—a brash, colorful, genre-busting effort that shamelessly engaged with pop music and largely ignored notions of what was "cool" in electronic music at the time—is something that arguably arrived decades too early. The subheading of Cardew's piece describes the LP as "a paean to the adaptable power of house music," and while that's certainly not inaccurate, perhaps it doesn't go far enough. As an album stuffed with big swings, *Rooty* cries out for audacious hyperbole, and to my ears, it sounds like

---

1. Cardew, Ben. "How Basement Jaxx's 'Rooty' conquered pop in the name of UK house music." *DJ Mag*, July 20, 2021, https://djmag.com/longreads/solid-gold-how-basement-jaxx-s-rooty-conquered-pop-name-uk-house-music.

an obvious ancestor of today's hyperpop boom.

For what it's worth, I don't particularly like hyperpop, but the shadow cast by artists like SOPHIE, 100 gecs, Charli XCX, A.G. Cook and the wider PC Music collective has flipped music—both mainstream and underground—on its head in recent years. Dispensing with genre orthodoxy (and, in many cases, gender orthodoxy), their neon-streaked, overcaffeinated brew is seemingly everywhere, an insane sonic tapestry that's as inspired by dayglo Eurotrance and head-splitting gabber as it is by nu-metal thrash, zonked-out mumble rap and glittering teen pop. And that's just a partial list of influences; R&B, trap, reggaeton, drum & bass, pop-punk, emo (especially the screamy stuff), synth-pop, blog house—it's all fodder for today's hyperpop mayhem.

That diversity makes tracing hyperpop's family tree a rather daunting task, but while songs like Aqua's "Barbie Girl" are considered foundational and the influence of artists like Limp Bizkit, Justice, Young Thug and Britney Spears is frequently mentioned, Basement Jaxx rarely seem to enter the conversation. Back in 2014, when the duo were promoting their most recent full-length, *Junto*, the word "hyperpop" did appear once in an interview with PopMatters[2]—although its usage seems coincidental and was likely unrelated to the then-emerging genre—and given the pair's limited output since then, few subsequent opportunities have arisen for journalists (or the artists themselves) to further explore the connection.

Back in 2001, however, Basement Jaxx were the subject of many conversations, and *Rooty* raised more than a few eyebrows. Famed music scribe Robert Christgau gave the record an A-, but his five-line review also squeezed in a crude joke about cyborgs and fellatio before delivering this bit of backhanded praise: "no catchier collection of jingles has come to my attention since Steve Miller made his mint off jet airliners."[3] Writing for SPIN, Simon Reynolds cleverly referred to songs like "I Want U," "Get Me Off" and "Where's Your Head At" as "headbanger house," but

2. Sawdey, Evan. "Power to the People: An Interview with Basement Jaxx." *PopMatters*, October 29, 2014, https://www.popmatters.com/187474-power-to-the-people-an-interview-with-basement-jaxx-2495597170.html.

3. Christgau, Robert. "Consumer Guide: Throw Your Hands in the Air." *The Village Voice*, January 29, 2002, http://www.robertchristgau.com/xg/cg/cgv202-02.php.

while he celebrated Basement Jaxx and "the way they go from cartoon disco to sick drug-noise," he also opined that "there's a side to [them] that's a bit too ditzy-ditty and quirky-verging-on-twee" before comparing the duo to Paul McCartney's Wings.[4] The Guardian's Maddy Costa followed a similar path, slipping the following line into an otherwise rave review: "The one thing 'Romeo' isn't is cool. It's the kind of song you can imagine being a huge hit at teenage discos, holiday camps, all the places real clubbers wouldn't be seen dead."[5]

In 2021, this sort of snobbery is largely frowned upon in music journalism, but 20 years ago—long before the great poptimism debates took place—sneering condescension was rather commonplace, especially within "indie" and "underground" music circles. *Rooty* was loud, brash and gaudy, and while the music was primarily rooted in various strains of house and UK garage, Basement Jaxx had also folded in elements of funk, R&B, hip-hop, pop and hard rock, not to mention a whole lot of notes cribbed from Prince. For those allergic to anything that offered even a whiff of mainstream pop—and yes, I was absolutely part of that crowd at the time—the LP crossed lines that weren't supposed to be crossed, and was therefore derided as an unserious effort or, even worse, a blatant attempt at crossover success.

Pitchfork published a merciless (and overly self-confident) *Rooty* review, tagging the album with a 3.8 while asserting, "Basement Jaxx have taken kitsch a few steps too far" and slamming "Romeo" for its "mindless lyrics... predictable, shallow melodies, bland beats and clichéd basslines."[6] Even for those who haven't drunk the poptimist Kool-Aid, it's pretty cringey stuff, and highlights just how white, straight and uptight the narrative around dance music could be back then.

(Admittedly, my perspective here is very American, as *Rooty* was a legitimate pop smash in the UK, where it reached #5 on the album charts and spawned several hit singles, two of which landed in the Top 10. In the US, the LP did hit #5 on the Dance/

4. Reynolds, Simon. "Basement Jaxx - Rooty." *SPIN*, August 2001, p. 127.

5. Costa, Maddy. "The real daft punks." *The Guardian*, June 22, 2001.

6. "Rooty - Basement Jaxx." *Pitchfork*, September 18, 2001, https://pitchfork.com/reviews/albums/571-rooty/.

Electronic Albums chart, but only reached #149 on the Billboard 200. As such, its success in America has been more of a slow burn, with tracks like "Do Your Thing," "Romeo" and especially "Where's Your Head At" gradually seeping into the national consciousness via endless placements in movies, television shows, video games and commercials. "Where's Your Head At" has also become a staple at sporting events, particularly those of the "extreme sports" variety.)

In his review of *Rooty* for Blender, Michaelangelo Matos wrote, "The near-metal swagger of 'Where's Your Head At' is a smarter (and no less fun) half-sibling of 'Who Let the Dogs Out?'"[7] Matos, who liked the album, meant it as a compliment, but back then, a line like that surely solicited groans from a sizable portion of the tastemaker set. Nowadays, however, it reads like a blueprint for hyperpop. In retrospect, even the song's official video feels like a portal into the future, as it foreshadows today's deepfakes by digitally grafting Buxton and Ratcliffe's faces onto some rowdy lab monkeys. Basement Jaxx had clearly tapped into something on *Rooty*, and as the album's legacy has swelled, a sort of re-evaluation has taken place. (In a particularly telling example, Pitchfork publicly changed its tune, showering the LP with praise and lauding its "manic" vibe while slotting the LP at #33 on its list of "The 200 Best Albums of the 2000s."[8])

Irreverence is at the heart of *Rooty*'s appeal, and while its devil-may-care attitude surely helped lay the spiritual groundwork for today's musical troublemakers, Basement Jaxx did care about more than just mischief. As NME noted in its review, the LP also made the case for a brighter, more inclusive musical landscape:

> *Basement Jaxx's second album presents an insanely optimistic vision of their hometown [of Brixton], where a bewildering range of dance styles are mashed together into a seamless and invigorating new music. It may be no more plausible a version of reality than the sallow mono-culturalism of Little*

---

7. Matos, Michaelangelo. "Basement Jaxx - Rooty." *Blender*, June - July 2001, https://web. archive.org/web/20040803043959/http://www.blender.com/guide/index.html.

8. "The 200 Best Albums of the 2000s." *Pitchfork*, October 2, 2009, https://pitchfork.com/ features/lists-and-guides/7710-the-top-200-albums-of-the-2000s-20-1/?page=9. **265**

Englander Britpop, but it's a damn sight more idealistic and entertaining, for sure.[9]

As observations go, that one wound up being pretty insightful, though it failed to recognize one key point about the artists coming down the pipeline: for many of them, "reality" would no longer be a primary concern. Listening to today's hyperpop offerings—and their manic relatives across the musical spectrum—it's striking just how unreal the music often seems to be. In a time when even basic concepts like "truth" and "facts" are seemingly up for debate, perhaps it's not surprising that young artists are frequently more interested in the fantastic, whether they're splicing together seemingly incongruous sounds or crafting elaborate avatars for themselves in the metaverse.

There are few rules in the hyperpop sphere, a place where once-foundational DIY ideas like "keeping it real" and "selling out," if they have any currency at all, are rarely interpreted as rallying cries to maintain an artificial divide between the mainstream and the underground. In that sense, Basement Jaxx were seemingly way ahead of the curve with *Rooty*; when it came to pop music, they had no fear, whether they were borrowing beatmaking ideas from Timbaland ("S.F.M.") or flipping a track from synth-pop pioneer Gary Numan into a would-be jock jam ("Where's Your Head At"). They even lined up Janet Jackson to contribute vocals to "Get Me Off," though Buxton and Ratcliffe say she wound up withdrawing from the collaboration after realizing that she'd mistaken them for loungey downtempo outfit Zero 7.[10]

That may have bruised their egos, but it didn't faze their creative efforts, and in the years that followed *Rooty*, the duo's pop dalliances continued, as *NSYNC heartthrob JC Chasez guested on "Plug It In," a song from their 2003 album *Kish Kash*. That LP also included collaborations with Dizzee Rascal, Siouxsie Sioux and Meshell Ndegeocello, while later releases have featured the likes of Kelis, Mykki Blanco, Yoko Oko, Santigold,

9. Mulvey, John. "Basement Jaxx : Rooty." *NME*, June 23, 2001, https://www.nme.com/reviews/reviews-nme-5270-329752.

10. "The pop idol's pop idols." *The Scotsman*, November 16, 2003, https://www.scotsman.com/whats-on/arts-and-entertainment/the-pop-idols-pop-idols-2461991.

Lightspeed Champion (a.k.a. Dev Hynes a.k.a. Blood Orange), Amp Fiddler, Yo! Majesty and many others. To some, that list of all-stars might seem like a stylistically confused mess, but is it all that different from the Frankenstein-ed rosters often found on today's pop albums? Putting seemingly random artists together in the studio—or simply splicing them together with the help of recording software—and hoping for musical magic has become standard operating procedure across the industry, but Basement Jaxx were doing it 20 years ago, long before algorithms and SEO created an incentive to do so.

Rooty was famously named after a club night Basement Jaxx had been doing in Brixton, and when talking about that party, the duo said, "It's not geared to one specific vibe. Musically, we made it so that it wasn't just for cokeheads who wanted pounding beats all night. That gave us musical freedom."[11] That same philosophy carried over into the album, and whether or not Basement Jaxx intended it, their idea of "musical freedom" has since taken root, to a point where it's now become a foundational value for an entire generation of artists. The LP's boundary-breaking spirit didn't stop at music either; although Basement Jaxx themselves aren't queer, they openly played with notions of gender on *Rooty*, occasionally tweaking their own vocals to sound like those of a wailing diva—or a lust-filled robot.

So did Basement Jaxx invent hyperpop? Probably not, and claiming that they did would require ignoring (or at least minimizing) the contributions of many other artists (past and present), not to mention the many social, cultural and technological changes that have shaped music during the past two decades. (The rise of streaming, for instance, is an obvious contributing factor.) Culture doesn't develop in a straight line, and a lot of ingredients—many of which predate *Rooty*—went into the hyperpop recipe. Nevertheless, the album does appear to be one of the first instances where those ingredients were gleefully—and intentionally—mashed together.

That intention matters, and goes a long way toward explaining *Rooty*'s enduring influence. Listening to the album now, the music on the whole still sounds incredibly contemporary. (Ironically, the LP's stale patches largely reside in the songs that most closely hew to standard house formulas.) Basement Jaxx broke new creative ground, and while they did achieve a certain level of commercial success with *Rooty*, the album's continued relevance can't be chalked up to nostalgia alone. The LP helped establish a template, one in which misfits could thrive, genre barriers went out the window and "exuberant fun" was a lot more important than "detached cool." That approach isn't for everyone, but like it or not, a lot more of today's club kids (and pop producers) were profoundly impacted by "Romeo" and "Where's Your Head At" than "The Bells," "Spastik" or whatever other seminal '90s techno anthem you can think of.

Knowing that, the next time that someone breaks down the roots of hyperpop, Basement Jaxx at least warrant a mention, no? If the likes of Slipknot, Backstreet Boys and even SpongeBob SquarePants can all get their hyperpop credentials, then surely the creators of *Rooty* deserve a seat at the table.

Skrillex Is Green Day, and This Is Dance Music's *American Idiot* Moment
a.k.a. Why I passed on reviewing the new Skrillex album.

February 21, 2023

—

The obvious irony of this piece is that despite being inspired by my decision not to review the latest album from Skrillex, I wound up writing something much longer and more in-depth about an artist who I'd basically spent the previous decade-plus actively ignoring in my work. So perhaps the joke was on me, but while I'm not a Skrillex fan—and most likely never will be   it would be silly for me to deny the outsized influence he's had on dance music. In many ways, the story of Skrillex is the story of modern dance music, and I suppose this essay was my attempt to not just reckon with that, but make peace with the culture as it stands now.

Admittedly it's a bit weird that the process involved a parallel analysis of Green Day's career trajectory, but A) it makes sense once you dive into the piece, and B) anyone who thinks that the rise of EDM is the first time an "underground" subculture has been absorbed into the mainstream hasn't been paying attention.

———

Last week a publication I sometimes write for contacted me, asking if I'd be up for reviewing the new Skrillex album, *Quest for Fire*.[1] (It hadn't yet been announced that a second new Skrillex LP, *Don't Get Too Close*, would be released literally one day after the first one dropped.)

I declined the offer.

---

1. For anyone who's curious, the publication in question was Pitchfork.

As someone who's been involved in dance and electronic music since the late '90s, I'm supposed to hate Skrillex. When he first broke big in the early 2010s, I was working as an editor at XLR8R, where we collectively decided to ignore his work. It didn't matter how popular he was; as far as we were concerned, the guy was a joke and an interloper, a goofy-looking mall emo refugee who'd somehow become the face of the equally contemptible EDM genre. That genre was filling arenas—and raking in oodles of profit in the process—but amongst self-respecting electronic music fans, it wasn't something to be taken seriously. A bastion of braindead bros and glowstick-carrying fangirls, EDM wasn't seen as an organic cultural movement; it was a perversion that swapped out decades of DIY-driven history for gaudy spectacle, corporate excess and a seemingly endless parade of mind-numbing drops.

This attitude wasn't just some fringe position either. When Skrillex won his first Grammy in 2012 and gave a nervous acceptance speech shouting out labels like Dub Police and the "Croydon dub guys," it wasn't hailed as a transcendent moment for dance music. It was regarded as just another signal of how profoundly disconnected the awards (and by extension, the mainstream music industry) were from the genre's roots and authentic fanbase. Even as EDM kept growing, reaching a point where its biggest stars could play 50-date tours across the US—something that was previously unheard of for dance music acts—it remained an object of derision, and not just amongst embittered old heads, self-assured tastemakers and rock dudes who reflexively hated any music without guitars. By the time *Saturday Night Live* spoofed the genre in 2014, pretty much anyone who thought of themselves as having a modicum of good taste felt comfortable shitting on EDM.

That contempt lingered throughout the 2010s, even as EDM began to fizzle. I spent much of the decade's latter half working with Red Bull Music Academy, and can vividly remember an argument that broke out on Slack one day when someone merely suggested that we should do something with Skrillex. To me, the idea felt like a betrayal, and I penned a multi-paragraph screed outlining not only why this was a Very Bad Idea, but how Skrillex—and the cultural moment he'd ushered in—represented the complete opposite of the artistic values and musical history that RBMA had been working to celebrate and preserve for more than a decade. (In retrospect, Slack probably wasn't the best venue for that little diatribe, and my words were met with multiple eye rolls—and at least one "Old Man Yells at Cloud" GIF—by my younger colleagues.)

RBMA has been closed for more than three years now, and in the end, we never did anything with Skrillex. (Oddly enough, he did walk in unannounced to say hello one day while Red Bull Radio was doing an extended pop-up in Los Angeles in 2016. Nothing came of it, but he was friendly, genuinely curious about what we were doing and, true to his reputation, did appear to be exceedingly nice.) As the 2010s wore on, he took a step back from dance music, but also quietly stayed busy, working with many of pop and hip-hop's biggest names—Justin Bieber, Ty Dolla $ign, Kendrick Lamar, Travis Scott, Mariah Carey, The Weeknd, Jennifer Lopez and FKA twigs are just some of folks he's collaborated with—and gradually becoming ensconced in the upper echelons of the music industry's hit-making machinery. It's hard to imagine that he's worried much about his standing in electronic music circles in recent years, and though he's never really won over the folks who railed against him during the early 2010s, many of them have by now aged out of the scene/industry anyways. (Grumbling on Facebook doesn't really count as being truly active in the genre.)

Perhaps that's why during the run-up to *Quest for Fire*, Skrillex has been treated as a returning hero, his every move documented not just in the mainstream music press, but also in the electronic music outlets that once turned their nose up at his work. Many of those moves have happened alongside his buddies Four Tet and Fred again.., and last Friday, the three squeezed into a converted school bus and DJed for throngs of fans in Times Square. That performance was broadcast by The Lot Radio, a world-renowned online radio hub which, despite being home to many of NYC's critically celebrated and nominally "underground" DJs (not to mention whatever fashionable left-of-center acts happen to be passing through town), was seemingly thrilled to hop aboard the Skrillex train. The following night, the trio went even bigger, playing a sold-out show (which was billed as a "pop-up rave") at Madison Square Garden.

It may seem odd, but this is what dance music is now. The genie is out of the bottle, the borders between the underground and the mainstream have largely been eliminated, and regardless of the music's humble roots in places like Detroit, Chicago and (in the case of dubstep) Croydon, it now belongs to the masses. Pop culture doesn't care about things like local scenes, DIY values and exactly who came up with a particular sound in the first place; it's a ravenous beast, and one that's determined to drink up everyone's milkshake. What's happening now isn't the first time that it's come for dance music, but while '90s "electronica," 2000s Eurodance and 2010s EDM were all met by major pushback, this time around, it seems that the resistance has finally been vanquished.

More than a decade after he first appeared, Skrillex is now both seemingly everywhere and more beloved than ever before, to the point where even dance music's biggest snobs have to admit that "Rumble" is a pretty phenomenal tune. It no longer matters much whether the critiques hurled at Skrillex over the years were right or wrong; he's transcended them, building a body of work that's so large and consequential that much of the dance music spectrum (not to mention a good chunk of the pop sphere) has been sucked into his gravitational orbit.

Watching this latest round of Skrillex hype unfold, I've repeatedly found myself thinking of an unlikely parallel: Green Day, and specifically the East Bay punk band's landmark 2004 album *American Idiot*. It's often hailed as their finest hour, and though its contents didn't actually sound all that punk—for the uninitiated, the politically charged record was touted as a rock opera and eventually spawned a Broadway show—there's no question that the album catapulted the group to a newfound level of respect and stardom that exceeded the heights of their initial break into the mainstream.

That break happened 10 years earlier, when the group's 1994 full-length *Dookie* became a multi-platinum smash, introduced millions of young people to punk rock and forever altered the trajectory of the genre. Although punk had started decades prior, and had a long and storied history as a vital (and for many people, genuinely life-changing) subculture, *Dookie*, perhaps more than any other punk LP, proved that not even the most fervent "DIY or die" orthodoxy could shield the genre from the relentless suction of the pop mainstream. Nirvana might have opened the floodgates, but Green Day, with all due respect to acts like the Sex Pistols, the Ramones and The Clash, were punk rock's first pop superstars.

Fueled by Green Day's success—and that of the countless bands that followed in their wake—punk music, and more importantly, its signature aesthetics (e.g. safety pins, leather jackets, tattered clothes, dyed hair, youthful angst and an anti-establishment disposition), were no longer exclusive to the genre's diehard fans, who had previously operated within an extended network of largely self-sustaining local communities. Seemingly overnight, adopting a punk persona required little more than turning on alternative radio (or MTV) and taking a trip to the mall, and while this development didn't necessarily go down well with the genre's preexisting fanbase, no amount of lecturing could stop (or even slow down) the tide of recent converts. Punk had a deep, complex history, but it was a newer and unquestionably more shallow conception of the genre—one that basically began with Green Day—that got burned into the wider culture's collective psyche.

That initial burst of mainstream punk excitement didn't last long, and as the '90s wore on, the genre gave way—at least within the pop and alternative rock spheres—to successive waves of ska, swing, goth, nu-metal, emo and numerous other subcultures-turned-microtrends. Throughout it all, Green Day remained the world's biggest punk band, but even they fell victim to the whims of the hype cycle; after *Dookie*, the band's next three albums (1995's *Insomniac*, 1997's *Nimrod* and 2000's *Warning*) were met with declining record sales and increasingly little fanfare. Although the punk aesthetics they'd help to popularize had never left the pop sphere—even today, those aesthetics continue to be referenced by everyone from rappers to boy bands—Green Day themselves did retreat from the limelight in the post-*Warning* years leading up to *American Idiot*, and were then welcomed back as veritable rock royalty once the LP—their first #1 album in the US—dropped in 2004.

Does any of this sound familiar? Swap Green Day for Skrillex, *Dookie* for *Scary Monsters and Nice Sprites* and *Quest for Fire* for *American Idiot*, and these two stories start to look awfully similar. Just as Green Day's success flew in the face of punk tradition, Skrillex and the EDM boom upended dance music orthodoxy, and while that pissed off a lot of people in the process, it also took the genre to new commercial heights while ushering legions of young listeners into the rave tent for the very first time. For those newbies, what came before didn't really matter, and as their adoration turned Skrillex into a kind of demigod, it was their ideas about what constituted dance music that seeped into the mainstream. *SNL* certainly never made any skits about Jeff Mills and Richie Hawtin, and even now, when dance music and DJ culture are depicted in movies, TV shows or pretty much anywhere else outside the club, it's a lot more likely to look like a Steve Aoki concert than a night at Bossa Nova Civic Club.

(On a more serious level, even the fact that the term EDM, which was roundly rejected by pretty much everyone in dance music's preexisting fanbase, not only persevered, but is still in circulation today, says a lot about which side came out victorious in the genre's internal power struggle.)

Is *Quest for Fire* a great dance music album? Having not listened to it, I can't say for sure, but looking over the tracklist, it very much looks like the average major label pop record, one whose abbreviated track times and litany of guest appearances have been optimized for a music landscape in which streaming is the predominant method of listener consumption. That doesn't mean it's bad, but it does mean the LP was created for a paradigm in which dance music's traditional priorities have largely been sidelined.

Skrillex's work is on some level rooted in club culture, but it's also been made with arenas and festival stages in mind—places where DJs jumping on tables and whipping up massive crowds into a mosh pit-style frenzy is not just encouraged, but expected. Dance music has historically frowned on this kind of blatant "DJ as rock star" behavior—and overwrought grandiosity in general —but following a year in which even the genre's supposedly "underground" corners embraced both star worship and the caning of commercial pop tunes like never before, it makes sense that present-day Skrillex has ascended to towering new heights. EDM may have lit the spark more than a decade ago, but with Skrillex and pals leading the way, it sure feels like dance music as a genre has now entered its *American Idiot* phase, becoming larger than ever before despite bearing only a passing resemblance to its former self.

American Idiot was a punk album in name only, but its messaging was perfect for the moment, taking aim at a post-9/11 United States that was mired in multiple wars and rife with disillusionment. Green Day gave a voice to that disillusionment, and music fans, having lived through several years of rock music being dominated by the jockish inanity of nu-metal outfits like Limp Bizkit, were elated to welcome the trio back to the fray, even if the youthful punk edge had been sanded off their tunes.

Quest for Fire has also shown up at an opportune moment. Young music fans have not only weathered a pandemic and multiple lockdowns, but a seemingly endless string of political, economic and environmental crises. Hypothesizing about exactly when and how the world is going to end—and possibly making a meme about it—has become a regular part of their daily discourse. With their anxieties through the roof, many people are simply looking to let off some steam, and Skrillex—a familiar face who many youngsters never disliked in the first place—has re-emerged at just the right time to help make that happen. It doesn't matter what *Quest for Fire* sounds like, or what it's relationship is to the history of dance music; it's Skrillex himself that people are excited about, and in what feels like a deadly serious time, his mere presence promises an onslaught of the joyous bangers and visceral release that pent-up ravers so desperately crave.

It's just a coincidence, but *American Idiot* really is a perfect descriptor for what's happening in dance music right now. The EDM model that Skrillex helped build and still represents—and specifically its crass commercialization and concertization of the club experience—is based upon an inherently American misinterpretation of dance music culture. Moreover, it's also heavily reliant on big, brash and often objectively dumb tunes. Although dance music's stated preoccupation with "intelligence" has always been overblown—nobody ever described Fatboy Slim and his Big Beach Boutique parties as bastions of refinement and sophistication—we're now living in a time where DJs are proudly playing remixes of "Cotton Eye Joe" at Panorama Bar. It's fair to say that the bar has been lowered.

A new generation has made its way into dance music, and while their presence has already caused quite a bit of friction, they were always destined to reshape the culture in accordance with their own worldview. When EDM first exploded, most members of contemporary nightlife's dominant cohort (i.e. young adults under 30) were literally children and teenagers. Of course they love Skrillex! They have no emotional attachment to the way things used to be, and having been reared in a streaming-centric, largely genre-agnostic musical ecosystem, they make no major distinction between what he's doing and what prior generations would describe as more "authentic" dance music.

Again, this is just what dance music is now, and as a music journalist, it is interesting to watch it all unfold, at least on an academic or sociological level. As a fan, however, I can't say that it sounds like a particularly good time. I suppose there's something exciting about artists like Skrillex, Fred again.. and Four Tet being showered with adulation while playing weird-ish Chloe Robinson, Nikki Nair and Overmono records. But when those records are being played with a bunch of bargain-bin wobblers, and the parties are happening at sold-out arenas where the party literally ends at midnight, is that really a win for dance music and DJ culture? If this is where things are headed—and with festivals multiplying as clubs everywhere struggle to keep the lights on, it's not such a far-fetched idea—then I honestly can't say that dance music is something that I'll continue to follow with much passion.

When *American Idiot* dropped back in 2004, I didn't pay it much attention either. I'd liked Green Day well enough as a teenager, but having spent the post-*Dookie* years diving into independent creative communities that operated outside of (and frequently stood in active opposition to) the cultural mainstream, I forged a specific set of ideas about what punk was and why it was important to me. *American Idiot* had little to do with those ideas (and wasn't meant to), and I feel much the same way about Skrillex and how he relates to my conception of dance music.

Regardless of whether or not the LP bangs—and to be fair, it probably does—it's a blatantly commercial product that's been designed for mass appeal, and since that's not what I'm interested in (especially when it comes to music), I'm probably not the right person to review it. What exactly would be the point? Writing some version of "I don't really like this or what it represents, but it's not for me anyways" isn't particularly useful to anyone, and the alternate path—penning some mean-spirited takedown and trashing his music based upon an artistic and ethical rubric to which he likely doesn't even subscribe—would do nothing but stroke the egos of people for whom the album wasn't made in the first place.

I'm not a Skrillex apologist. EDM sucked, and frankly still sucks, and while Skrillex will forever be tied to that awfulness, it's also true that at this stage of his career, he's become an established part of the musical landscape. Lots of people flat-out love the guy, and while popularity alone should never be used as a measure of artistic success, it does seem that dance music's harshest critics myself included have largely decided to direct their ire elsewhere. Ten-plus years is too long to hold onto a grudge anyways (especially a musical one), and while a few embittered holdouts might think that dance music discourse has gone soft, it's worth noting that even the punks eventually grew tired of calling Green Day sellouts.

Afterword

As I write this, the second weekend of Coachella 2023 is currently underway in the Southern California desert. Talk of the festival always seems to dominate the music world this time of year, and in recent days, the conversation has been focused on Frank Ocean, who abruptly canceled his second weekend performance after the first was marred by delays, last-minute changes and what his representatives have said was a serious leg injury. To fill the gap, Coachella rushed to add another headlining act to the bill, and quickly settled on the trio of Four Tet, Fred again.. and Skrillex.

When I saw the news, I laughed out loud.

It wasn't a mocking laugh. Validation is what I felt. Less than two months after I'd penned that "Skrillex Is Green Day" essay, he and his two besties were tapped for a top slot at Coachella, arguably the most important music festival in the world. Of course they were—these guys are basically pop stars now, and the booking made perfect sense for everyone involved.

As mentioned many times in this book, dance music has crossed over into pop culture, and even if the current fascination with Skrillex and his impromptu EDM boy band dies down, Pandora's Box has been opened. DJs, clubs, raves... this stuff all belongs to the masses now, and as time goes on, it's only going to get further and further away from its roots and "underground" past.

Longtime fans of the genre already know this. Dance music's tilt toward the mainstream started long before Covid hit, but the culture's pandemic-induced pause was a proper break in the timeline, one that delineated clear before and after eras. Call it a vibe shift, or chalk it up to generational change, but things just feel different now, both on and off the dancefloor, and many people in dance music (i.e. the ones reared in the "before" times) are despondent.

The long-awaited return of IRL dance music in 2022 was expected to be a celebratory moment, but thinking about the discourse during the past year, the prevailing mood has at times been downright funereal. Granted, there's been a lot to worry about. Inflation. Lingering Covid worries. Touring difficulties. Struggling media outlets. The growing presence of brands. Declining music sales. Exploitative streaming platforms. The pervasive influence of social media. The list of problems seems endless, and to top it all off, the genre's old guard has another issue to contend with: all these new kids have found their way into the scene, and they're weirdly insistent on playing pop music and other garish trash that flies in the face of dance music's "underground" traditions.

That's a lot for anyone to process, and dance music's elder generation, convinced that something has been lost, has effectively been in mourning. Traces of that can surely be detected in the pages of this book, but I'm not the only one whose words have been infected by a certain gloomy sensibility. Media coverage of dance music's aforementioned structural shortcomings has become commonplace, and even articles about the music itself frequently reflect a level of worry about the current state of the genre. I recently came across the March 2023 edition of Jaša Bužinel's (generally quite good) *Hyperspecific* column for The Quietus. The piece is ostensibly about the latest Surgeon album, but his thoughts pretty quickly digress into hand-wringing about the dance music's generational divide, pondering "what a twentysomething, immersed in the currently trendy fast-paced industrial techno sound and brand-sponsored warehouse raves, would have to say" about the UK veteran's latest record.[1]

It's not just the press either. Social media, rife with debates about rising BPMs and opening DJ etiquette, has become a place of near-constant moral panic, and many of these topics have leaked into offline conversations as well. In recent months, I've had countless exchanges with friends and colleagues that descended into impromptu grief sessions, in which dance music lifers—many of them successful artists and industry figures—openly lament all the ways the culture and industry has gone awry. Even as

1. Bužinel, Jaša. "Hyperspecific: Dance Music For March." *The Quietus*, March 21, 2023, https://thequietus.com/articles/32743-surgeon-doctor-jeep-luxe-air-max-97.

these people continue to benefit from dance music (and, more specifically, its economic growth), they acknowledge that things have gotten rather silly. The Zoomers have seized control of the genre, and it doesn't seem that much can be done about it.

And yet, people keep dancing.

No matter how bummed dance music's professional and commenter class may be, clubs are open, festivals have resumed (and only seem to be growing in number) and even the illegal party circuit appears to be up and running. People are raving again, possibly in larger numbers than ever, and they're having a great time.

Just a few weeks ago, Mixmag published a feature on the return of Los Angeles' rave underground.[2] Written by veteran music journalist Vivian Host (who's also been DJing under the name Star Eyes since the '90s) and artist Bianca Oblivion, who together throw a party called Warp Mode, the piece is bursting with optimism, portraying a scene that's not only thriving, but taking place largely off the grid. Staggeringly comprehensive, the article mentions seemingly every promoter crew in the greater Los Angeles area, and specifically cites the contributions of the city's newest rave generation. Many of these recent arrivals literally got started in the middle of lockdown, but they're now throwing parties and DJing all over Southern California, contributing to an intensely local scene that's not only young, but significantly more diverse than its pre-pandemic predecessor.

I don't want to put too much stock into a single article, but this piece—and more specifically, its obvious enthusiasm—felt like a wake-up call, highlighting an obvious gap between how dance music is predominantly being talked about and how it's being experienced on the ground. The music and raves described in this piece may not sound particularly enticing to me and those of my generational cohort (some actually seem like the exact opposite of what I'm looking for in a night out), but they're happening all the same, and appear to be massive. The story isn't even a new one; off-the-grid warehouse parties have been happening in LA

2. Host, Vivian and Oblivion, Bianca. "Wild Wild West: After the Pandemic, LA's Rave Underground Bounces Back Stronger Than Ever." *Mixmag*, March 23, 2023, https://mixmag.net/feature/los-angeles-la-rave-undergruond-diy-dance-music-scene-post-pandemic-club-music.

for decades, but what's changed from previous eras of dance music is that the generation driving the culture currently has very little role in documenting it.

The olds have yet to relinquish control of the narrative, and even if they did, it's not clear exactly who would step in to take their place. The dance music press has done a terrible job bringing new voices into the fold, and is perhaps even worse when it comes to retaining the select few that show actual promise. And in a fractured content landscape, it's not even clear that traditional media outlets are where younger generations would go to read about and consider dance music culture. If nobody is reading—or if they're only scanning the photos and headlines that pop up on their social media feeds—it's hard to argue that it matters who's writing dance music's latest batch of stories, or whether said stories are any good.

In the meantime though, dance music marches on. It's happening in warehouses, it's happening at Coachella, and it's going to keep happening in the years to come. (Young people wanting to congregate and dance to loud music is about as close to a cultural constant as I can imagine.) The genre's place in the wider culture is sure to continue changing—most likely in ways that will further upset its existing fan base—but dance music has always been impermanent, and the anguish around its most recent metamorphosis is primarily driven by sentimentality, not logic.

I'm certainly guilty of the former from time to time, but I do my best to be guided by the latter.

Acknowledgements

I'm pretty sure that Todd Burns was the first person I knew that had a newsletter. We'd been working together for years at Red Bull Music Academy (and had initially met years before that, when he was the editor of Resident Advisor), but in early 2019 he started Crambe Repetita, a daily mailout that included a few recommendations. It was a modest endeavor, but it nonetheless planted a seed in my head, and got me thinking about the possibilities of the newsletter format.[1]

That thinking quickly became a lot more serious once we found out that RBMA was coming to an end, and as I grappled with the notion of what to do next, I received some much-needed encouragement from Colin Nagy, who co-authors the essential Why Is This Interesting? newsletter, and my old friend Aja Badame, who insisted that I start one of my own. (Despite the fact that Aja wisely escaped from the electronic music industry years ago, she still reads—and even claims to enjoy—my writing on the topic, which is a sign of true friendship.)

So many people have helped and supported me during the past four years, but if I focus specifically on this book, I have to first give thanks to Martyn, who overcame his initial shock when I asked him to write the foreword and delivered a text that really cuts to the heart of what First Floor is all about. On a more practical level, I also owe a huge thanks to Chal Ravens (another former RBMA colleague), who kindly volunteered to swoop in at the last minute and provide some much-needed copy editing assistance, (She's also an amazing writer, easily one of electronic music's best, so do yourself a favor and track down her stuff.)

Joe Gilmore designed the book's sharp cover (an impressive feat considering the vague instructions I provided), and the saintly Soumeya Bendimerad Roberts took time out from her job as a successful literary agent to help me decipher and sort out the contract with Velocity Press. That reminds me—it was Colin Steven from Velocity Press who came up with the idea

---

1. Todd still does Crambe Repetita, but he also now runs the Music Journalism Insider newsletter, which is both an incredible resource and anything but modest. **283**

of compiling the newsletter into a book in the first place, so he deserves an obvious thank you for that, but he was also extremely patient with my repeated requests for deadline extensions and many inquiries about printing, production, promotion and distribution. Key advice also came from Matt Anniss, Gabriel Szatan, Ben Cardew and Ed Gillett; all are excellent writers, and they graciously shared insights they'd picked up in the process of putting together their own books.

Beyond that, I owe a huge debt of gratitude to everyone who's read, shared, supported or subscribed to First Floor during the past few years. As I said in the introduction, I had no grand ambitions when I started the newsletter, so watching it grow into something that thousands of people read, discuss, reference and seem genuinely excited about has been such a rewarding experience. Never before in my life have I received so much direct feedback about my work, and it means so much to me every time I get a message from someone saying they liked an essay I wrote or a particular piece of music I recommended.

Not surprisingly, many of those notes have come from friends and colleagues in the music world, and I while I'm surely going to forget some people, folks like Ethan Holben, Avalon Emerson, Mat Dryhurst, Philip Sherburne, Cat Zhang, Brian Foote, Vivian Host, Richie Hawtin, Zak Khutoretsky, Matthew Schnipper, Sam Valenti, Tom Lea, Jacob Sperber, Igor Escudero, Unai Lazcano, Alan Brinsmead, Zora Jones, Emilie Friedlander, Meri Bonastre, Avril Ceballos, Forest Juziuk, Aimée Portioli, Anthony Naples, Charles McCloud Duff, Elijah, Andrew Thompson, Sam Barker, Ray Philp, Mor Elian, Alex Tsiridis, Oriol Riverola, Penelope Trappes, Patrick Holland, Gerd Janson, Jeremy Guindo, Thomas Ragsdale, Yumi Mannarelli, Jiovanni Nadal, Carter Adams, Julian Brimmers, John Howes, Silvia Jiménez Alvarez, James Bangura, Reece Cox, Marea Stamper, Cherie Hu, David Turner, Tim Sweeney, Albert Salinas, Dean Grenier, Chandler Shortlidge, Sarah Mackenzie, Brendan Neal, Damien Roach, Franc Sayol, Adam Shore, Justin Kay, Marke Bieschke, Seb Diamantis, Brian

Shimkovitz, Pau Cristòful, Nick León, Jonathan Trujillo, Daniel Gomez, Jessica Gentile, Fallon MacWilliams, Daniel Martin McCormick, Ben Thomson, Grant Dull, Bert de Rooij, Regina Pozo, Oswaldo Terrones, Joseph Kamaru, Chanel Kadir, Ben Turner, Steve Braiden, Tom Reid, Nathan Micay, Melissa Maristuen, Juns Castella, Ignasi Sadurní, Daniel Fisher, Jonathan Galkin, Stephen Hindman, Salvatore Carlino, Liam Butler, Jack Jutson, Callan Clendenin, Phil Aubin-Dionne, Jason Voltaire, Maël Péneau, Najaaraq Vestbirk, Leon Smart, Gilbert Cohen, Paul Woolford, Arthur Cayzer, Jamie Roberts, Ron Morelli, Tess Roby, Bianca Bracho, Declan McGlynn, Will Pritchard, Peter Kirn, Katie Gately, Angus Finlayson, Maral Mahmoudi, Cara Daley, Phil Bloomfield, Jaša Bužinel and Patricia Wolf have all been consistently and vocally supportive.

I've been incredibly lucky to work in the music industry for more than two decades, and have come across so many amazing people in the process, many of whom lent a hand and gave me opportunities I wouldn't have had otherwise. Several RBMA people have already been mentioned above, but I have to thank Torsten Schmidt, Mani Ameri, Yannick Elverfeld, Niklas Jansen and everyone else I was lucky enough to come across in the course of that truly special project. Going further back in time, I also have an undying love for the XLR8R crew, especially folks like Tim Saputo, Ken Taylor, Glenn Jackson, Andrew Smith, Patric Fallon, Kerry McLaughlin, Brianna Pope, Sally Mundy and Mark Bartling.

Over the years I've had the pleasure of DJing at and throwing more parties than I could possibly remember, but I will forever count the nights I spent doing both Icee Hot (with Will Fewell, Ryan Merry, Bryant Rutledge and honorary member Claire Cichy) and Tormenta Tropical (with Gavin Burnett) as some of the best times of my life. I also have a major soft spot for Popscene—the first party that ever made me a resident DJ—and fondly remember all the time I spent alongside Aaron Axelsen, Jeremy Goldstein, Omar Perez, Miles Anzaldo and Miriam Anderson.

Speaking of Aaron Axelsen, he was also the first person who put me on on the radio, and his decision to pluck a 19-year-old kid off the Live 105 request lines and make him the producer of his weekly specialty shows—a decision that was likely rooted, at least initially, in the fact that I just happened to be sitting near his office at the time—inadvertently put me on a path toward becoming a music industry professional. He wasn't the only Live 105 person who made an impact though; Spud hired me in the first place, Ben Gill was always incredibly generous with his time and knowledge, Jason Chudy was the other young guy getting his start in radio, Jenn Leibhart was a dear friend (and way cooler than me) and DJs like Mike Nelson, Rick Stuart and Renee Richardson all showed me the ropes when I had no real idea how anything worked.

Speaking of learning, so much of my education, both musical and personal, took place at KALX 90.7 FM, the official radio station of the University of California, Berkeley. Starting out as a volunteer and later becoming the operations manager, I spent the better part of a decade there. It's the place where I first had a radio show of my own, but more importantly, it's where I found my first real taste of a working music community, meeting incredible people like Sandra Wasson, Mo Herms, Mona Deghan, Stephanie Chang, Caroline Partamian, Suzanne La, Esme Shaller, Pantea Javidan, Lily Chou, Jillian Okter and frankly hundreds of others who profoundly affected my life. I haven't been there in years, but on some level, KALX will always be home.

Outside of the music world, I'd like to thank my siblings Tyne Kennedy and Luke Brambir. Neither one has ever really understood what my job entails, but they've always been supportive all the same.

And finally, the biggest thanks of all goes to my incredible wife Dania Shihab, a beautiful, intelligent and immensely talented human being who I'm lucky enough to share my life with. She's hilarious, has impeccable taste and literally saves lives (part-time), but she also accepts me for who I am, even as she (gently) urges me to lighten up a bit—a push that I very much need. Together we've traveled around the world, eaten many delicious things and bought ceramics in an inordinate number of places, but even when we're at home sitting on the couch, I've never been happier to spend time with someone. Hands down the biggest supporter of me doing this book (and First Floor in general), she's my best friend, my teammate and my closest family, and I love her so much.

ABOUT THE AUTHOR

Shawn Reynaldo is a Barcelona-based writer and editor who specializes in electronic music. A Bay Area native who first found his way into the rave scene during the late '90s, he's spent decades immersed in independent music culture, logging countless hours running labels, throwing parties and hosting radio shows. However, it's his work as a music journalist that's made him one of electronic music's most prominent voices.

Author of the First Floor newsletter, Shawn was formerly an editor at Red Bull Music Academy and XLR8R, and has also contributed to such publications as Pitchfork, NPR, SPIN, Resident Advisor, DJ Mag, Bandcamp Daily and Beatportal.